For Marcia,
not only for her
expertise, but also for her
kindness while staying with
the manuscript from its early
days until its fin... ...m
for publication.
           Sincerely,
             James

THE DYNAMICS OF THE IMAGERY IN THE THEATER OF FEDERICO GARCÍA LORCA

James T. Kiosses

University Press of America,® Inc.
Lanham • New York • Oxford

Copyright © 1999 by
University Press of America,® Inc.
4720 Boston Way
Lanham, Maryland 20706

12 Hid's Copse Rd.
Cumnor Hill, Oxford OX2 9JJ

All rights reserved
Printed in the United States of America
British Library Cataloging in Publication Information Available

Library of Congress Cataloging-in-Publication Data

Kiosses, James T.
The dynamics of the imagery in the theater of Federico Garcia Lorca
/ James T. Kiosses.
p. cm.
Includes bibliographical references.
1. García Lorca, Federico, 1898-1936—Dramatic works. 2. García Lorca, Federico, 1898-1936—Symbolism. 3. García Lorca, Federico, 1898-1936—Technique. I. Title.
PQ6613.A763Z7345 1999 862'.62—dc21 99—25406 CIP

ISBN 0-7618-1409-4 (cloth: alk. ppr.)

♾™ The paper used in this publication meets the minimum requirements of American National Standard for Information Sciences—Permanence of Paper for Printed Library Materials, ANSI Z39.48—1984

For Mom and Dad, with love

Permission Acknowledgments

The author wishes to thank Herederos de Federico García Lorca, c/o William Peter Kosmas, for permission to reprint from the works of Federico García Lorca. Spanish language works by Federico García Lorca from *Obras completas* (Aguilar, 1966 edition) © 1996 Herederos de Federico García Lorca. All rights reserved. For information regarding rights and permissions for works by Federico García Lorca, please contact William Peter Kosmas, Esq., 8 Franklin Square, London W14 9UU, England.

Grateful acknowledgment is made to the following for permission to reprint material:

Alianza Editorial, S.A.: excerpts from *Soledades de Góngora*, ed. Dámaso Alonso, © Revista de Occidente, S.A., Madrid, 1927; © Alianza Editorial, S.A., Madrid 1982

The Belknap Press of Harvard University Press: excerpt from "La Belle Dame sans Merci: A Ballad" by John Keats, from *Complete Poems: John Keats*, ed. Jack Stillinger, ©1978, 1982 by the President and Fellows of Harvard College, reprinted by permission of The Belknap Press of Harvard University Press

Ediciones Cátedra, S.A.: excerpts from Lope de Vega, *El caballero de Olmedo*, ed. Francisco Rico, Madrid, Cátedra, 1985, 6ª ed. by © Ediciones Cátedra, S.A., 1985

Éditions Gallimard: excerpts from "Orphée," "La Jeune Parque," and "Le Cimetière marin" by Paul Valéry in *Oeuvres*, tome 1, by Paul Valéry; ed. Jean Hytier, © 1957Éditions Gallimard

Editorial Castalia: "En la muerte de tres hijas del Duque de Feria" by Luis de Góngora in *Sonetos completos* by Luis de Góngora, ed. Biruté Ciplijauskaité, Clásicos Castalia, n° 1, © Editorial Castalia, 1969. Also, excerpts from Eduardo Marquina's *La ermita, la fuente y el río* in *En Flandes se ha puesto el sol/La ermita, la fuente y el río* by Eduardo Marquina, ed. Beatriz Hernanz Angulo, Homenajes, Clásicos Madrileños n° 13, © Editorial Castalia, 1996

The Dynamics of the Imagery in the Theater of Federico Garcia Lorca

Editorial Planeta, S.A.: excerpts from *La vida es sueño: drama y auto sacramental* by Pedro Calderón de la Barca, ed. José María Valverde, © 1981 Editorial Planeta, S.A.
Espasa-Calpe, S.A.: excerpts from "Ite, missa est," "Divina Psiquis," "Nocturno," and "Yo soy aquel . . ." by Rubén Darío in *Antología/Rubén Darío*, ed. Carmen Ruiz Barrionuevo, © 1992 Espasa-Calpe, S.A. Also excerpts from "El año lírico" and "Autumnal" by Rubén Darío in *Azul . . ./ Cantos de vida y esperanza* by Rubén Darío, ed. Álvaro Salvador, © 1992 Espasa-Calpe, S.A. Also, excerpts from *Poesías completas* by Antonio Machado, 3rd ed., 1977, © 1975 Espasa-Calpe, S.A.
Herederos de Antonio Machado, % Fd°. José Rollán Riesco: excerpts from "Hacia un ocaso radiante . . ." (*from Soledades {1899-1907}*) and from "La tierra de Alvargonzález," in *Poesías completas* by Antonio Machado, © 1940 Herederos de Antonio Machado
Herederos de Juan Ramón Jiménez, % Dª Carmen Hernández-Pinzón Moreno: excerpt from "Tenebrae" by Juan Ramón Jiménez in *Melancolía* in *Segunda antolojía poética (1898-1918)* by Juan Ramón Jiménez, © 1959 Herederos de Juan Ramón Jiménez
Herederos de don Ramón Menéndez Pidal and Fundación Menéndez Pidal: excerpts from "Canción de una gentil dama y un rústico pastor," "Por el val de las Estacas . . ." Sexto romance del Cid, "Rosaflorida," "Romance de don Tristán," and "Ya se salen de Castilla . . .," Historia de los siete infantes de Lara in *Flor nueva de romances que recogió de la tradición antigua y moderna R. Menéndez Pidal* (1928), © Herederos de don Ramón Menéndez Pidal
Maurice Maeterlinck estate, % Maître André Schmidt: excerpts from *Pelléas et Mélisande* by Maurice Maeterlinck, Copyright © 1950 by Maurice Maeterlinck estate
Simon & Schuster: excerpts from *The Land of Heart's Desire* and *The Shadowy Waters* by W.B. Yeats, reprinted with the permission of Simon & Schuster from *The Collected Plays of W.B. Yeats*, Revised Edition, Copyright 1934, 1952 by Macmillan Publishing Company; copyrights renewed © 1962 by Bertha Georgie Yeats, and 1980 by Anne Yeats
Tamesis Books and Boydell & Brewer Ltd.: excerpt from *Federico García Lorca y las vanguardias: hacia el teatro* by Antonio F. Cao, © 1984 Tamesis Books
University of California Press: excerpt from "Dice Mía" by Rubén Darío in *Antología poética/Rubén Darío*, ed. Arturo Torres Rioseco, © 1949 by University of California Press. Also excerpts from "L'après midi d'un faune," "Autre Éventail" and "Hérodiade" by Stéphane Mallarmé in *Selected Poems by Stéphane Mallarmé*, Bilingual edition, ed./trans. C.F. MacIntyre © 1957, 1986 C.F. MacIntyre

Contents

Introduction

Chapter 1: A Trajectory in the Development of
 Lorquian Imagery in the Theater 1
  I. Affinities with the Past
    A. The Symbolist Theater of Maeterlinck
       and Yeats 2
    B. Symbolist Poetry 4
    C. Góngora 7
    D. The Traditional Spanish Ballad 10
    E. Golden Age Theater 12
       1. Lope de Vega 12
       2. Calderón 14
  II. Lorca Within and Beyond Affinities
     with the Past 17
    A. Lorca, Maeterlinck and Yeats 17
    B. Lorca and Symbolist Poetry 20
    C. Lorca and Góngora 24
    D. Lorca and the Traditional Spanish Ballad 27
    E. Lorca and Lope de Vega 29
    F. Lorca and Calderón 31

Chapter 2: Lorquian Image Criticism 40

Chapter 3: *El maleficio de la mariposa* 51

Chapter 4: *Mariana Pineda* 80

Chapter 5: *Amor de don Perlimplín con Belisa en su jardín* 110

Chapter 6: *Bodas de sangre* 127

Chapter 7: *Doña Rosita la soltera* 159

Chapter 8: *La casa de Bernarda Alba* 184

Conclusion 204

Bibliography 207

Index 219

Acknowledgments

In view of the fact that this book evolved from my doctoral dissertation, I wish to acknowledge with sincere gratitude Professor Philip W. Silver for his invaluable observations and instructive guidance throughout the development of the dissertation; Professor Dian Fox for the benefit of her insight, the time and scrutiny she gave to the text and her ever-present encouragement; Professor Félix Martínez-Bonati for reading the text and for his sincerity and understanding in directing a student through a graduate program; and to Professors Gonzalo Sobejano, Marcia L. Welles and Alfred J. MacAdam for reading and commenting on the manuscript. I am also grateful to Marcia Gilbert for her dependable expertise in the technical preparation of the manuscript. Finally, special thanks go to a loving family that always supported every endeavor leading ultimately to the completion of this book.

Introduction

Imagery in the theater of Federico García Lorca is most often examined with respect to its symbolic and thematic content. In our study, we will view Lorca's imagery as following a trajectory that begins with the symbolist qualities of the images in the earliest plays and then moves towards a more dynamic involvement of imagery in the presentation of drama. *La casa de Bernarda Alba* is the culmination of this development of Lorquian poetic drama, for in this play, poetic images not only convey meaning, reveal thoughts and heighten emotional content, but also constitute a subtextual narrative reflecting the sequential movement of the action and dialogue. Throughout his career, Lorca develops the use of imagery that serves drama. By employing elements of the traditional Spanish *romance* and techniques used by Góngora and Golden Age playwrights (especially Lope de Vega and Calderón), Lorca develops a presentation of poetic images that help shape dialogue, anticipate action, underscore important information and provide momentum which impels the dialogue forward.

We, therefore, go beyond much Lorquian imagery criticism by demonstrating that the imagery in Lorca's theater is dynamic rather than static. We assert that Lorca developed poetic drama in which images are placed in specific dramatic contexts to which they contribute symbols or thematic content and interact in such a way that they depict stages in the development of the human relationships in the drama. In fact, the imagery narrates at the metaphorical level what transpires at the dramatic level.

The plays that will serve as textual examples are *El maleficio de la mariposa*, Lorca's first play; *Mariana Pineda*, the playwright's second play and first theatrical success; *Amor de don Perlimplín con Belisa en su jardín* and *Bodas de sangre*, representatives of the middle years; and finally *Doña Rosita la soltera* and *La casa de Bernarda Alba*, both completed in the final two years of Lorca's life. We will examine these plays from the point of view of a reader of the texts, not as a spectator might see

The Dynamics of the Imagery in the Theater of Federico Garcia Lorca

them in performance. The plays were chosen because they 1) span the course of the career of Lorca as a dramatist who develops a dynamic use of imagery and 2) constitute a body of dramatic texts that are thematically unified and exemplary in the use of poetry to express drama. These works dramatize an individual's desire to escape a reality that represses the expression of his or her inner spirit—a desire that is so strong that it results in death (except for Doña Rosita who does, however, suffer a metaphorical death).

From *El maleficio de la mariposa* to *La casa de Bernarda Alba*, imagination emerges as a very important aspect of the human psyche and shapes the form of escape that Lorca's protagonists attempt, almost always with tragic consequences. The protagonist of *El maleficio de la mariposa* is a poet who strives to capture his ideal of love and beauty but discovers that it can exist for him only in his imagination. Mariana Pineda gradually recedes into the vision she has of herself as the personification of liberty, and Don Perlimplín uses imagination to reveal for Belisa the essence of a soul. In *Bodas de sangre*, Leonardo sweeps La Novia into a world of love that becomes enveloped in unreality. Doña Rosita holds onto an illusion of love that avoids the realities of the passage of time; and in *La casa de Bernarda Alba*, the youngest daughter feels her confinement most acutely because her clandestine meetings with Pepe el Romano have led her to envision herself in a world outside the walls that imprison her. In the earliest plays, Lorca's images primarily underscore thematic material related to imagination and a character's desire to escape confinement. Poetry in these plays also heightens our sense of the emotional content of dialogue. In the later plays, Lorca expands the dramatic possibilities of images by setting them in dramatic contexts. As imagination takes hold of an individual looking for escape from a repressive environment, imagery reflects the changing relationships between this character and the others engaged in the drama.

In his analysis of Milton's "L'Allegro" and "Il Penseroso", G. Wilson Knight makes an observation that one can apply directly to dynamic imagery such as Lorca developed. Knight maintains that these poems are static and that their images are pictorially still and therefore lack a dynamic, evolving energy. In reference to both poems, Knight observes that action and total design do not coalesce. Movement and solidity, although separately stressed, do not shape an architectural unity.[1] Knight, however, does see "organic cohesion" in *The Tempest* where Shakespeare manipulates a process of poetic actualization through tempest-music opposition.[2]

The Dynamics of the Imagery in the Theater of Federico Garcia Lorca

According to Knight, "All Shakespeare's tempests of passion are also a passionate music," and he sums up the poetic explicitness of this idea by quoting Alonso's lines from Act III, Scene 3: "O, it is monstruous, monstruous! Methought the billows spoke and told me of it; / The winds did sing it to me and the thunder, / That deep and dreadful organ-pipe, pronounced / The name of Prosper." Knight concludes that that poetry in *The Tempest* is a player in a drama of extended imagery.[3]

Reuben Brower also examines the dynamics of the metaphorical design of *The Tempest*, but whereas Knight views the entire play as a metaphor in which loss, revival and restoration are represented by the tempest-music opposition, Brower stresses the harmony of the metaphorical design, with the key metaphor being "sea-change." Brower speaks of Shakespeare's use of a "super-design of metaphor" through which ongoing dialogue relates with other dialogues.[4] For example, Brower traces cloud imagery through the play, finding it related to "the gradual dramatic movement from tempest and punishment to fair weather and reconciliation;" from Trinculo's "black cloud" recalling for us the original tempest, through the "curl'd clouds" on which Ariel rides and the clouds that Caliban thought "would open and show riches;" and then on to Prospero's "cloud-capp'd towers" speech in which clouds become a symbol for the "unsubstantial splendor of the world" (107-108). Brower, in other words, does for *The Tempest* what we propose to do for selected plays by Lorca: to demonstrate that imagery and action are united. Brower observes that Shakespeare has not placed a significant image in a static position but rather has transformed it into a "character" whose role at the metaphorical level runs parallel to the events surrounding the characters in the drama. According to Brower, "the cloud sequence, as an arc of metaphor, is in perfect relation to the gradual dramatic movement from tempest and punishment to fair weather and reconciliation, the images having meanings more and more remote from any actual storm" (108). With respect to "arcs of metaphor," Brower identifies six principal continuities in *The Tempest* (among which are sleep-and-dream, sea-tempest and music-and-noise) (97), and he relates them to the controlling metaphor of metamorphosis that coincides with changing human feelings and relationships transpiring in the action and dialogue of the play.

Although Knight and Brower both take as their starting point a thematic approach to *The Tempest*, Brower sees in the Shakespearean drama imagery that reflects, moves with and fleshes out the dramatic action of the play—a process that one can also observe developing in Lorca's poetic

*The Dynamics of the Imagery in the Theater
of Federico Garcia Lorca*

dramas. For example, as early as *El maleficio de la mariposa*, there is a suggestion of dynamism in some images. In this play, the star image gradually stops serving as the icon of a real star and assumes an important role in the metaphorical design of the play. The star image adjusts its "movements" to the basic narrative line of the unfolding drama. Initially the image prefigures the death of the protagonist and his illusions. Subsequently it reflects Curianito's love and his elusive ideal and finally becomes associated with the butterfly herself. The star image can therefore be considered one of the main continuities relating to the controlling metaphor; i.e., an unsuccessful escape into the imagination.

A similar manipulation of the dynamics of key images, but developed with greater complexity, characterizes Lorca's later poetic dramas, including his final "realistic" play, *La casa de Bernarda Alba*. To cite an example from that play: images of heat permeate the drama by radiating outward from the central metaphor depicting Bernarda's house as a living hell. The overbearing heat of the summer and the daughters' desire to seek fresh air form part of the network of images associated with the seething emotional frustration and increasing sexual tension as the drama unfolds. Thus, when Angustias says at the beginning of Act II "Pronto voy a salir de este infierno" (1472),[5] the image commands special attention.

As Brower demonstrated with *The Tempest* and as we will observe in the plays of Lorca, what happens to the images as they appear in the metaphorical design determines the degree to which drama and metaphor are united. Brower maintains that Shakespeare's total metaphor is related to the development of the unfolding drama, with specific metaphors adapting themselves to new dramatic situations and anticipating events that follow. For Brower, recurring images are associated with felt qualities set in particular dramatic contexts (116, 120). These procedures that provide imagery with a capacity to mark various stages in the changing emotions and relationships are also present in Lorca's theater, beginning with several early examples in *El maleficio de la mariposa* that set the course for the fusion of poetry and drama in the later plays. If the early plays do not develop fully into what we call Lorquian poetic or lyric drama, they do at least plant and nurture some of the salient features of Lorca's use of poetry in the theater.

By drawing on resources from Góngora, the theater of the Golden Age, popular songs and the traditional Spanish ballads, Lorca manages to separate himself from the primarily Symbolist and Modernista nature of his early dramatic imagery and make poetry expressive of drama. That is

*The Dynamics of the Imagery in the Theater
of Federico Garcia Lorca*

to say, by refining techniques drawn from the past, Lorca, in *La casa de Bernarda Alba*, brings the fusion of poetry and drama to full maturity.

Considering Lorca's use of brief images whose cumulative effect fleshes out a mood or makes feelings "visible," we recall techniques employed in Symbolist poetry and Symbolist theater, with Verlaine, Maeterlinck and Yeats serving as prime examples. In *Mariana Pineda*, for example, when various images are linked, they convey Mariana's inner emotional state which is an important aspect of the drama. Through their suggestive potential, images such as "Dijo que en tus ojos / había un constante desfile de pájaros" (790)[6] and "La plaza, al par que la tarde, / vibraba fuerte, violenta" (794) are directed towards making Mariana's agitated condition more palpable. They are images that suggest rather than state an idea explicitly—a characteristic one observes in Maeterlinck's *Pelléas et Mélisande* and Yeats's *The Shadowy Waters*. Further, Yeats's ability to project a sense of being lifted out of ordinary life, and Maeterlinck's ability to create the atmosphere of a dream[7] can be compared to Lorca's treatment of the inner thoughts of the protagonists of *El maleficio de la mariposa*, *Mariana Pineda*, *Perlimplín* and *Doña Rosita*.

Bearing in mind the affinity between Modernismo and Symbolism, we also note that Lorca's early plays yield characteristics found in Modernista theater. Miguel García-Posada has indicated that Lorca's first two plays are "modernista" and that his use of poetry as a primary ingredient of the dialogue shows an affinity for Modernista drama. García-Posada cites especially the rural world depicted in the plays of Eduardo Marquina as indispensable to a study of Lorca's theater.[8] Also in the context of Modernismo, we would include Martínez Sierra as an important forerunner of poetic theater as evidenced in Lorca's earliest plays.

Lorca's theater moves beyond Symbolist and Modernista theater when it begins to yield imagery placed in dramatic contexts; imagery that is so structured that its components adapt themselves to the evolving human relationships. Maeterlinck's theater is static. It is a drama of inwardness with powerful images that draw ordinary people into mystical experiences;[9] whereas Lorca uses powerful images to explore the attraction that imagination and mystery have in individuals grappling with conflicts that are essentially human.

Although Lorca's accomplishment of setting images in dramatic contents is very similar to what Brower articulates in his analysis of Shakespearean imagery in *The Tempest*, his poetic drama has an individual style. This is the result of the direction taken by the trajectory of Lorca's use of

*The Dynamics of the Imagery in the Theater
of Federico Garcia Lorca*

imagery. In his earliest plays, Lorca begins with Symbolist techniques. He then goes beyond Symbolism, however, by drawing on the past to further his development of poetic drama. He reaches back into classical and traditional Spanish literature—as far back as the early ballads—and finds there, to varying degrees, methods for structuring images and symbols that would help him move the metaphorical language in the direction of uniting poetry and drama.

Three important landmarks in Lorca's career—*Romancero gitano* (begun in 1924 and completed in 1927), "La imagen poética de don Luis de Góngora" (a paper delivered in 1927) and the playwright's work with La Barraca in presenting classical Spanish drama (initiated in 1932)[10]—are evidence of periods in which Lorca directed his attention to works of the past. As we follow the development of Lorca's theater, we can observe specific techniques drawn from earlier Spanish literature. Although there are no clear demarcations indicating when Lorca implemented these techniques, we can see an accelerated refinement in their use.

Closely allied to the suggestive nature of Lorca's images, especially in the early plays, is Góngora's metaphorical process. Lorca's expressions of esteem for Góngora, particularly in "La imagen poética de don Luis de Góngora," show the highest regard for this Golden Age poet. Dámaso Alonso has written that "todo el arte de Góngora puede reducirse a un constante intento de eludir la representación directa de la realidad sustituyéndola por otra que indirectamente la evoque, pero ya nítida, realzada, con especial intensidad estética. Esto se verifica centralmente en la metáfora."[11] Alonso also speaks of a "hiperrealidad" in Góngora; a superreality that is actually an illusion.[12] Carlos A. Disandro says that Góngora has endeavored to describe an interior path that is both a link to and a revelation of the external world;[13] and W. Pabst asserts that the majority of Góngora's metaphors essentially transmit the poet's *impression* of an object rather than its real nature.[14] Together with the poetic techniques used by the Symbolists to make abstract feelings and perceptions "visible," Góngora's metaphorical process in which language has the power to create an inner reality helps us examine Lorca's use of imagery especially in the early plays. Here Lorca evokes the feelings and sentiments of characters, giving the reader a sense that inward thoughts are "observable." Lorca, however, wants to take the "visibility" of thoughts beyond poetic images by incorporating them into the actions of characters. The distorted mechanisms of speech in the figures of Góngora

*The Dynamics of the Imagery in the Theater
of Federico Garcia Lorca*

that create in the mind's eye such images as winged flowers and stationary butterflies[15] also appear in Lorquian dialogues. But Lorca dramatizes the images. La Mariposa, a butterfly unable to take wing, *is*, in effect, a winged flower; and the role she plays in the evolving drama becomes closely associated with this image of her in the metaphorical language of the text.

As one follows the development of Lorca's ability to invest imagery with more dynamic potential within the dramatic structure, it becomes apparent that the playwright also drew significantly on the poetic techniques common to the traditional Spanish ballad. *Romancero gitano*, begun in 1924, is prime evidence of Lorca's indebtedness to the traditional Spanish ballad. This was also the period of *Mariana Pineda* (completed in 1925), a play that, according to J.B. Trend, demonstrated Lorca's mastery in the use of the ballad.[16] For a playwright who expresses drama through poetry, the ballads offer outstanding examples of narrating dramatic events poetically. Because of the compression of its language, a ballad can lead one's imagination to fill in details that a more fleshed-out narrative would supply. In other words, a ballad can create "saltos ecuestres" in the imagination (a term Lorca uses to describe the power of metaphor). A ballad thus acquires a narrative rhythm that can be useful to a lyric poet as he attempts to fashion poetic drama rather than dramatic poetry.

In addition to its ability to narrate through poetry, a ballad has other characteristics which we see in Lorca's methods for infusing metaphorical language with dynamism. Repetitions and alliterations that provide narrative poetry with a sense of ebb and flow were adapted to movement inherent in interaction among characters in a drama. Even sudden outbursts by characters in Lorca's dramas are reminiscent of those uttered by the narrator in a ballad who comments on events. As early as *El maleficio de la mariposa*, one can find evidence of ballad techniques such as those mentioned above. As Lorca's theater develops, there is evidence of not only the rhythm of narrative poetry transmitted orally by *juglares*, but also what E.M. Wilson says occurs in ballads: persons unaffected by the tragedy tell those concerned the truth they do not know.[17]

In developing techniques for placing imagery in dramatic contexts without destroying the narrative flow of events as they unfold, Lorca also shows an affinity for the theater of Lope de Vega and Calderón. Therefore, we will include specific passages from plays by these two Golden Age playwrights, relating them to Lorca's poetic techniques. In light of the fact that Lorca devoted a great deal of time to the university players in the

*The Dynamics of the Imagery in the Theater
of Federico Garcia Lorca*

organization known as "La Barraca," participating in almost every aspect of the presentation of classical plays from the Golden Age, the extent of the playwright's immersion in traditional Spanish theater is beyond question.

Lope de Vega was greatly attracted to popular Spanish poetry, and he frequently incorporated traditional songs and *romances* into his plays.[18] Lope also had the extraordinary ability to place a popular song or the words of a song of his own creation in the very center of the dramatic action, a prime example being the refrain that Alonso hears in Act III of *El caballero de Olmedo*.[19] Lorca, like Lope, also draws on traditional songs, as evidenced in the *romances* of *Mariana Pineda*, the cradle song of *Bodas de sangre* and the song of the harvesters in *La casa de Bernarda Alba*. Lorca, however, reaches back into the past for popular songs and ballads for a different purpose; i.e., to give images a setting in which they can blend with the dramatic conflict at a given point in a play. By commenting on and foreshadowing events, Alonso's refrain heightens the moment yet is, in effect, a self-contained song that momentarily arrests the development of the dramatic line. For Lorca, songs form part of the sequential development of the action and continue the line of associations already established in the imagistic subtext. This is what happens when the image of the horse in the *nana* in *Bodas de sangre* follows Leonardo as he moves through the action of the play. Similarly, the land and sea images in the ballads of *Mariana Pineda* correspond to Mariana's gradual submersion into legend as she becomes more involved in a struggle for liberty. Also, in *La casa de Bernarda Alba*, the passing chorus of reapers singing as they go to work despite the heat, is heard at a moment in the drama when the frustration in Bernarda's daughters is intense.

Bruce W. Wardropper has written that "poetic drama" in the twentieth century is less related to the preceding theater of ideas than to the theater of the Golden Age.[20] The fact that poetry is such an important ingredient of the Spanish classical theater is, according to Wardropper, often subordinated to an analysis of dramatic structure when dealing with the plays of the Golden Age (3). Angel Valbuena Prat remarks that a dominant characteristic of Lope's and Calderon's theater is the fusion of poetry and drama.[21] Thus, because of its close alliance with poetry, the Golden Age theater could be a valuable model for a poet like Lorca who turns to drama.

Calderón, like Góngora, employed images in order to make an idea representable, and his plays are often extended metaphors.[22] This fusion of

The Dynamics of the Imagery in the Theater of Federico Garcia Lorca

drama and poetry, accomplished by a dramatist in the Golden Age, is also present in the theater of García Lorca, but with a very significant difference. In his religious plays, Calderón's images are cosmic in nature and placed in contexts that make them instruments for illustrating religious concepts with deep social and philosophical implications. Darkness, for example, symbolizes sin; light, divine grace. Lorca, however, roots his imagery in human and personal contexts.

In Calderón's *comedia La vida es sueño*, Segismundo assumes a larger-than-life profile as a symbol of man's awakening from a life of the senses to that of the spirit.[23] He plays out his drama on earth with the stars hovering overhead as reminders of man's insignificant role in the drama of the cosmos. In contrast with this point of view, for Lorca's characters, among whom are Curianito, Perlimplín, Mariana Pineda, Doña Rosita and Adela, the stars, the flowers, heaven and the surrounding landscape offer images that they internalize and which we perceive as expressions of their personal feeling and anguish.

Although Lorca does employ archetypal symbols such as light, blood and water, he embeds them in contexts that develop a sense of the inner feeling of a human character confronted by human problems in a human setting. In *Bodas de sangre*, for example, the word "sangre" is infused with archetypal meaning, but it is invested with the ability to assume multiple connotations (family relationships, wounds, life, death, passion) that permit it to participate in the expression of various aspects of the dramatic conflict.

Lorca himself dismissed the idea that he belonged to any particular literary school.[24] But in order to recreate the dynamics and the spirit of Lorca's imagery in the theater, we find that reference to past sources as diverse as Symbolist poetry and the traditional Spanish ballad is very important. The spirit of those works, as well as the nature of their poetry, helps us see the development of the dynamics of Lorca's images as they interact to express drama. We will indicate what many critics have already stated; namely, that Lorca's images contain specific symbolic value that is crucial to the cohesiveness of the thematic content of a given play. However, we maintain that what charges Lorquian imagery with dramatic content producing a natural fusion of poetry and drama is the dynamics of the imagery; the manner in which the playwright impels the images in the direction of the action.

With respect to such a fusion in *Bodas de sangre*, Robert Barnes cites C.W.M. Johnson's reference to Marcel Proust's *A la recherche du temps*

The Dynamics of the Imagery in the Theater of Federico Garcia Lorca

perdu as a matrix of images that subtly relate to each other, develop, and in general reflect the behavior of the principal characters.[25] Not only do Lorca's images behave like the main characters, but they also use their power to make visible for us qualities that are felt—what Frank Kermode describes as things that are known but cannot be discursively analyzed, forming a "continuous whole" that is accessible to intuition.[26] Thus, the poet-playwright uses imagery to penetrate the core of such characters as Mariana Pineda, Adela, Curianito, Perlimplín, Doña Rosita and María Josefa; and in so doing, he helps us perceive changing human feelings and relationships which the characters experience. While drawing on the capacity of poetry to concretize meaning, Lorca also shapes dialogue with images that move in the same direction as the thoughts and actions of the characters. This process is especially evident in Lorca's later dramas, but its development can be traced back to his very first play. Despite the fact that *El maleficio de la mariposa* is essentially symbolist in nature, to follow the course of the stars and their imagistic association with flowers is to follow the course of Curianito, the protagonist, who moves from exultation in the power of the imagination through disillusionment to eventual death. In other words, there is cohesion between metaphorical language and action.

Before examining selected plays in detail, we will include a summary and comment on significant studies that have already treated the subject of imagery in Lorca's theater. Thus we will establish points of reference which, in effect, will become points of departure for exploring several plays with respect to the way Lorca creates a symbiotic relationship between images and dramatic contexts dealing with human relationships.

Numerous critical studies of Lorca's imagery in the theater have, indeed, exhibited an awareness of the dramatic possibilities of the metaphorical language. Some critics, like Calvin Cannon in his analysis of the imagery of Lorca's *Yerma*, have focused on patterns of imagery to convey and confirm the essential tension of a drama.[27] Other critics have isolated specific images in terms of their symbolic value with respect to the theme of a play.[28] While reference will be made to those who "hear" the message contained in selected images at various points in Lorca's plays, we will demonstrate that almost all these critics tend to trace *symbolic* imagery through a given play rather than focusing on the *dramatic* potential of an image at a given point in the drama. Although many studies do, to varying degrees, relate the imagery of selected plays to their thematic and dramatic content, they do not open up scenes in order to penetrate the method

*The Dynamics of the Imagery in the Theater
of Federico Garcia Lorca*

whereby Lorca employs imagery to sustain the pulse of the dramatic movement. We, therefore, shift the emphasis from thematic and symbolic imagery to the dynamic expansion of imagery and metaphor as they interact with the unfolding drama.

Notes

1. *Poets of Action* (London: Methuen and Co., 1967), p. 23.
2. *The Shakespearian Tempest*, 3rd Edition. (London: Methuen and Co., 1960), p. 247.
Two examples of this process cited by Knight are 1) Prospero's speech describing the treachery of his brother ("To cry to the sea that roar'd to us, to sigh / To the winds whose pity, sighing back again, / Did us by loving wrong")—a speech that echoes the Shakespearean theme of the tempest that is interwoven with music possessing the power to diminish the grief and fury of the waters (Ferdinand: "This music crept by me upon the waters, / Allaying both their fury and my passion, / With its sweet air") and 2) the sweet music accompanying the Act III banquet, softly restored after being first interrupted by thunder and lightning when some of those present are accused of being sinners. Thus there is a cohesive design in which tempest is associated with grief and treachery and music with love, union and reunion. (248-252)
3. *The Shakespearian Tempest*, pp. 256-257.
4. *The Fields of Light* (New York: Oxford Univ. Press, 1962), pp.95-96.
5. All page numbers within parentheses that refer to *La casa de Bernarda Alba* are from the following text: Federico García Lorca, *La casa de Bernarda Alba*, in *Obras completas*, ed. Arturo del Hoyo, 12th ed. (Madrid: Aguilar, 1966), pp.1439-1532.
6. All page numbers within parentheses that refer to *Mariana Pineda* are from the following text: Federico García Lorca, *Mariana Pineda*, in *Obras completas*, ed. Arturo del Hoyo, 12th ed. (Madrid: Aguilar, 1966), pp.781-891.
7. Katherine Worth, *The Irish Drama of Europe from Yeats to Beckett* (Atlantic Heights, N.J.: Humanities Press, 1978), pp.21, 22.
8. "Introduction" to *Teatro*, I, by Frederico Garcia Lorca (Madrid: Akal Editor, 1980), pp.17, 18.
9. Worth, p.72.
10. Arturo del Hoyo, in "notas" for *Obras completas* de Federico García Lorca, 12th ed. (Madrid: Aguilar, 1966), pp.1903-1906.
11. Góngora y el "Polifemo", 6th ed. (Madrid: Editorial Gredos, 1974), I, 173.
12. *Cuatro poetas españoles* (Madrid: Editorial Gredos, 1962), p.60.
13. *Tres poetas españoles* (La Plata, Argentina: Ediciones Hosteria Volante, 1967), p.99.
14. *La creación gongorina en los poemas "Polifemo" y "Soledades"*, trans. Nicolás Marín (Madrid: Imprenta Aguirre, 1966), P.97.

*The Dynamics of the Imagery in the Theater
of Federico Garcia Lorca*

15. Rudolf Schevill, *The Dramatic Art of Lope de Vega* (Berekley: Univ. of California Press, 1918; Revised, 1964, by Russell and Russell, New York), p.49.
16. *Lorca and the Spanish Poetic Tradition* (New York: Russell and Russell, 1971), p.21.
17. "Tragic Themes in Spanish Ballads" in his *Spanish and English Literature of the 16th and 17th Centuries* (Cambridge: Cambridge Univ. Press, 1980), p.229.
18. J.B. Trend, *Lorca and the Spanish Poetic Tradition* (New York: Russell and Russell, 1971), pp.167-168,
19. Angel Valbuena Prat, *Historia de la literatura española*, 8th ed. (Barcelona: Editorial Gustavo Gili, 1968), II, p.368.
20. "Poetry and Drama in Calderón's *El médico de su honra*," *Romanic Review*, 49 (1958), p.3.
21. *Historia*, p.531.
22. Wardropper, pp.4-5;9.
23. E.M. Wilson, "On *La vida es sueño*," in *Critical Essays on the Theater of Calderón*, ed. Bruce W. Wardropper (New York: New York Univ. Press, 1965), p.78.
24. "Galería, Federico García Lorca" in Entrevistas y declaraciones in *Obras completas*, p.1771.
While discussing his keen interest in drama, Lorca said: "Yo tengo un gran archivo en los recuerdos de mi niñez de oír hablar a la gente. Es la memoria poética y a ella me atengo. Por lo demás, los credos, las escuelas estéticas, no me preocupan. No tengo ningún interés en ser antiguo o moderno, sino ser yo, natural." (1771).
25. "The Fusion of Poetry and Drama in *Blood Wedding*," *Modern Drama*, 2, No. 4 (1960), p.401.
26. *Romantic Image* (New York: Vintage Books, Alfred A. Knopf and Random House, 1957), p.129.
27. García-Posada (69-70) "hears" the narrative line of the dramatic action in the images of *Bodas de sangre*, especially as they appear in the three choruses of the final act. Sumner M. Greenfield observes that the unrelenting heat in *La casa de Bernarda Alba* runs parallel to the sexual heat of the daughters ("Poetry and Stagecraft in *La casa de Bernarda Alba*," *Hispania*, 38, No. 4 [1955], p.459); and André Belamich states that the same play has "une logique organique, essentiellement intérieure," especially with respect to heat (*Lorca* [Paris: Éditions Gallimard, 1962]), pp.127-128.
28. The heat-thirst imagery of *La casa de Bernarda Alba* is an important thrust of González del Valle's critical comments (*La tragedia en el teatro de Unamuno, Valle-Inclán y García Lorca* [New York: Eliseo Torres and Sons, 1975], p.164). Reed Anderson underscores the repeated allusions to blood in *Bodas de sangre*, with its multiple meanings (families, violence, life-force, loss of virginity, erotic passion) constituting the symbolic nucleus of the play (*Federico García Lorca* [London: The Macmillan Press, 1984], p.100); and María Teresa Babín points to the signs of impending tragedy in *Mariana Pineda*, giving special attention to the images of death associated with the flag Mariana is embroidering (*Estudios lorquianos*, 1st ed. [Barcelona: Colección Mente y Palabra, 1976], p.318).

Chapter 1
A Trajectory in the Development of Lorquian Imagery in the Theater

Lorca's earliest plays are symbolist in nature. They have the spirit of the Symbolist theater of Maeterlinck and Yeats and show an affinity for Symbolist poetry as well as the works of Modernista authors. However, Lorca goes beyond Symbolism. Although Symbolist elements are discernible in later plays, we observe that Lorca develops a trajectory that takes imagery beyond a static presentation to one of dynamic involvement with drama. By refining techniques used earlier by the *juglares* of the traditional Spanish *romance* as well as techniques employed by Góngora and dramatists of the Golden Age (especially Lope de Vega and Calderón), Lorca develops a style of presenting images in dramatic contexts without interrupting the flow of a drama. From *El maleficio de la mariposa* to *La casa de Bernarda Alba*, Lorca moves away from theater with a predominantly symbolist character towards complete poetic drama.

Although Lorca's earliest plays can be placed in the realm of Symbolist theater, it is difficult to present clear lines of demarcation pertaining to the "beginning" of Lorca's affinity with Calderón, for example. Nevertheless, it is evident that in the later plays Lorca refines techniques used by classical writers and the *juglares* to such a degree that they finally coalesce to produce what we may call Lorquian poetic drama, an outstanding example of which occurs in the following passage from Lorca's final play. In Act II, Bernarda Alba shouts at her daughters: "¡Qué escándalo es éste en mi casa y en el silencio del peso del calor!" (1492). In these words, we perceive more than overbearing outrage, because throughout the preceding dialogue the playwright has been expanding the metaphorical content of such words as "silencio" and "calor." Bernarda's words not only refer to the circumstances of that specific dramatic moment (an argument taking place in the heat and silence of the afternoon) but also carry a subtext pertaining to imagery continuities embedded in the text up to this point. The first word Bernarda utters demands silence; and her daughters, enveloped in the "heat" of sexual tensions, yearn for release from their confinement. In the line delivered by Bernarda which we cited from Act II, one "hears" previous images associated with heat, refreshment, confinement, release, silence and outburst—images accumulating in the text as the tension increases. Similarly, when the harvesters sing "Abrir puertas y ventanas / las que vivís en el pueblo" (1487), one "hears" a subtextual allusion to the closed doors of Bernarda's house. Thus, key images (in this case, "heat" and "silence") carry multiple values that radiate outward from the immediate dramatic context and help our mind's eye perceive the shape of the developing conflict. In this way, *La casa de Bernarda Alba* demonstrates that Lorca's imagery in the theater finally reaches the point of expressing human drama.

Let us now turn our attention to writers from the past whose works contain elements with which Lorca's imagery bears an affinity. Here we will outline the nature of the affinity and indicate points of contact between Lorca and those authors. Then, through works chosen from various stages in the playwright's career, we will preview how we see Lorca within and beyond these affinities with the past.

I. Affinities with the Past

A. The Symbolist Theater of Maeterlinck and Yeats

The cumulative use of images to evoke feelings or ideas—one of the techniques that Lorca employs to move imagery along with the dramatic current of a play—is strongly reminiscent of the Symbolist theater of Maurice Maeterlinck. Lorca was familiar with this writer's works[1] and, like Martínez Sierra, he read Maeterlinck and was fond of the Belgian playwright's poetic dramas.[2] The attraction of Maeterlinck for a dramatist whose earliest plays exhibit characteristics of Symbolism appears natural considering the fact that in *Pelléas et Mélisande*, the Symbolists saw the theater of the future.[3] As C.M. Bowra has written, Symbolism was especially in eidence in Maeterlinck's dramatic works in which characters are symbols of the poet's dreams rather than indivudalized personalities.[4] Similarly, one can say that the butterfly in *El maleficio de la mariposa* is a symbol of the poet's dreams of love and beauty and that in *Mariana Pineda*, Mariana symbolizes the concept of liberty that has filtered through her mind after finding its inspiration in her love for Pedro.

One immediate contact with the theater of Maeterlinck can be strongly inferred from Lorca's theatrical association with Gregorio Martínez Sierra who, as Patricia W. O'Connor points out, staged and directed *El maleficio de la mariposa* in addition to works by such playwrights as Shakespeare, Ibsen and Marquina. Martínez Sierra was especially fond of the imagery of Maeterlinck, and in collaboration with his wife María, translated a five volume edition of the dramatist's complete works.[5] When O'Connor states that the melancholic young men in the plays of the Martínez Sierras bring to mind Goethe's Werther, she further observes that the Martínez Sierras show the influence of Maeterlinck in their use of imagery in poetry to express the inner life (97). Referring specifically to Martínez Sierra's *Teatro de ensueño*, John Garrett Underhill calls the short plays of this Spanish Modernista "symbolic, mystical dialogues with pronounced Maeterlinckian tendencies."[6]

The Symbolist theater of Maeterlinck is an important point of refraction through which we observe Lorca's earliest attempts to fuse poetry and theater. Because Maeterlinck figures prominently as the starting place for Yeats,[7] we will also include references to the Irish dramatist in order to sharpen the focus of Lorca's use of imagery as he began to write for the theater. Further, since Lorca's imagery in his plays is firmly rooted in contexts pertaining to human relationships, Lorca's quest for true poetic drama can be compared to Yeats's. Joseph Chiari writes that Yeats (like Maeterlinck) retains mystery and music for poetry but is aware that the only way to approach the ideal is through human emotions grounded in the phenomenal world.[8] For Yeats, words are capable of giving substance to something beyond the senses if they have a "mysterious life" like that of a flower or a woman.[9] This is also the spirit that Lorca conveys when he states that a poet should know that an apple in the course of its life is as mysterious as the rise and fall of the tides.[10]

Kermode in *Romantic Image* elaborates upon Yeats's idea of giving body to something that moves beyond the senses. According to Kermode, no static image will do for Yeats; the image is movement "with a kind of stillness."[11] For Lorca, also, an image has both stillness and movement; one supplied by thematic content and the other by interaction with other images as they relate to specific moments in the drama. Yeats, furthermore, had to find a theatrical means of standing *outside* the dreaming mind in addition to representing what is in a character's mind while he is dreaming. Therefore, Yeats sought images other than those of characters steeped in their own reflections. He employed techniques such as the dance for putting birds onstage as well as childish motifs and nursery rhymes to represent the basic drives of the unconscious.[12] In this context, we recall especially the lullaby in Act I of *Bodas de sangre*.

B. Symbolist Poetry

In tracing the development of the role of images in Lorca's theater, the resemblance of the earliest plays to Symbolist theater (with Maeterlinck and Yeats as prime examples) leads one to place those works in the context of the Symbolist movement in literature in the second half of the nineteenth century, especially as manifested by the French poets. In exemplary verses by these writers, we can see certain characteristics of Lorquian imagery, particularly in the early stages of its development.

Before exploring Lorca's affinity with the Symbolists, one should bear in mind that Modernismo also contributed to the early stages of the development of Lorquian poetic drama. Lorca himself paid tribute to the liberating possibilities of the imagery of Rubén Darío, Modernismo's standard bearer.[13] In the context of Lorca and Modernismo, the theater of Marquina is important. Both F. Lázaro Carreter and García-Posada point out Lorca's debt to Marquina. The former labels *Mariana Pineda* a modernista drama, saying that Lorca, in his literary adolescence, felt the influence of the sonorous and episodic dramas of Marquina. According to Lázaro Carreter, Lorca, especially under the early influence of Marquina, produced in *Mariana Pineda* a modernista drama, both thematically and structurally. The major characteristics of Modernista theater that Lázaro Carreter applies to *Mariana Pineda* are: 1) plot material taken from the past, 2) the continuous use of verse, 3) poetic adornment for its own sake, and 4) lyrical and descriptive "arias" that are "extradramáticas" because they interrupt the movement of the narrative line of the plot. Finally, in his overview of Lorca's theater, Lázaro Carreter observes that from *Mariana Pineda* to the final tragedies (except *La casa de Bernarda Alba*), these "arias" do appear. (*El maleficio de la mariposa* is also excluded from this direct line pertaining to technique because, in the critic's view, it was merely a search for a definite personal literary style.)[14] García-Posada calls Lorca's first two plays "modernista" and indicates the importance that selected images from Marquina's *La ermita, la fuente y el río* have for Lorca's theater. "Son imágenes," states García-Posada, "que expresan toda esa temática de amor y erotismo desenfrenados, y en este sentido establecen una cierta relación con las de los textos lorquianos."[15]

Curianito, Mariana Pineda and Perlimplín are among Lorca's characters who are attracted by the inner world shaped by the imagination. In Symbolism, Lorca finds one means of helping these characters form an inner voice of poetic images through which they strive to express (and hence make visible) what they "see" in their mind that sets them apart from the less imaginative characters that surround them. In *From Baudelaire to Surrealism*, Marcel Raymond traces opposing views of the manner in which man perceives the world; i.e., the rational view wherein only the real is considered knowable as opposed to the view that encourages the spirit to break the chains tying it to what it perceives as merely external. The Symbolists and the Surrealists, according to Raymond, tipped the scales in favor of the inner world, with Baudelaire, Mallarmé and Rimbaud advocating poetry as an instrument of knowledge.[16] Baudelaire's "forest" of symbols urged man to see them as a means for bringing to life a dream-like state where he can find correspondence with nature.[17] The Symbolist, like Mallarmé, for example, is drawn towards an elusive reality; towards an inner "knowledge" beyond the objective world. This is accomplished by words forming part of the whole line of a poem continuously in movement without arrested images—words that suggest rather than describe and that move like musical notes through cumulative effects rather than through logical, rational developments.[18] Edward Engelberg cites Verlaine's "precise nuance" to describe a controlled composition that creates the effect of vagueness but actually shapes a correspondence between man and nature through the exact arrangements of words, blending effects such as synesthesia, and the mixing of metaphors and converging symbols.[19] Authors like Verlaine and Maeterlinck revolted against confining words to a depiction of the external world and turned to symbols that could make the soul of things visible.[20]

In light of the foregoing observations, one can understand why Symbolism would strike a resonant chord in a writer of poetic drama such as García Lorca; for he was also engaged in making "visible" the inner sensibility of characters through images that reach progressively towards an elusive reality. Carlos Ramos-Gil has indicated that Lorca reflects what modern poetry, beginning with Baudelaire and Rimbaud, projects: i.e., something scarcely capable of being expressed in words, using them as a "trampolín" that catapults one towards a reality that is discerned or divined; a reality beyond the realm of observable phenomena. For Lorca, poetry sets its course towards the ineffable.[21]

6 The Dynamics of the Imagery in the Theater
of Federico Garcia Lorca

Lorca's fascination with the *duende* and the dark regions of the soul is evidence of the poet's interest in man's inner world, the power of the imagination and the expression of invisible reality;[22] a fact that also encourages the idea that he was receptive to the spirit of Symbolism. For Lorca, the *duende* approaches places where shapes are in a realm beyond their visible expressions.[23] But again we note that although his first plays have characteristics of Symbolist poetry and Symbolist theater, Lorca proceeds to integrate images (including those frequently used by the Symbolists) into a textual scenario that, in effect, represents the course of the human relationships of the characters as they move through the drama. The following statement made by Lorca in a lecture after the appearance of both *El maleficio de la mariposa* and *Mariana Pineda* supports the fact that he drew on but looked beyond symbolist techniques as a means for structuring his dynamic imagery: "La imaginación poética viaja y transforma las cosas, les da un sentido más puro y define relaciones que no se sospechaban; pero siempre, siempre opera sobre hechos de la realidad más neta y precisa."[24] This view of the relationship between art and the real world contrasts with that of "symbolisme," defined by Joseph Chiari as a belief in a world of ideal beauty that can be realized through art.[25]

Lorca came in contact with French Symbolism especially when he lived in the Residencia de Estudiantes in Madrid. His friend Jorge Guillén had translated Valéry's *Charmes* into Spanish, and the French poet himself lectured in the Residencia.[26] Rafael Ferreres, in a book entitled *Verlaine y los modernistas españoles*, cites Verlaine as a key figure linking the French Symbolists and Spanish poets of the late nineteenth and early twentieth century. A brief observation by Ferreres will suggest opportunities Lorca had to become acquainted with French Symbolism. In 1893, Rubén Darío mentioned Verlaine in a publication called "Los Raros," and Juan Ramón Jiménez said that he and Antonio and Manuel Machado read Verlaine before Darío and had lent the Nicaraguan poet books by Verlaine. Marquina, one of the first translators of Verlaine in Spain, had rendered the French poet's "Art poétique" into Spanish. This poem was also translated into prose by Manuel Machado. The book by Verlaine most preferred by the Modernistas was *Fêtes Galantes*, and "L'Heure du berger," "Il pleure dans mon coeur," and "Mon rêve familier" were among the poems of Verlaine that they knew best. Further, Verlaine was one of the French writers read by Benavente; and Jiménez had translated three of Verlaine's poems ("L'Heure du berger," "Claire de Lune" and "Mandoline") that appeared in 1903 in the publication "Helios."[27]

Symbolist poetry was thus available to Lorca in his formative years as a playwright.

C. Góngora

Lorca called Góngora the father of modern lyric poetry and considered him to be a master in the use of metaphor. According to Lorca, Góngora invented for Spanish a new way to seek and shape images, believing that the everlasting life of a poem depends on the quality of its imagery. Further, Lorca asserted that an image of Góngora's can create a myth, expanding in such a way that it takes us to different levels of reality.[28]

Among Lorca's comments attesting to the highest esteem in which he held Góngora, the following contain a significant expression of Lorca's views on poetry, a vital ingredient of his theater:

> La originalidad de don Luis de Góngora, aparte de la puramente gramatical, está en su método de *cazar* las imágenes, que estudió utilizando sus dramáticos antagónicos por medio de un salto ecuestre que da el mito . . .[29] Góngora tuvo un problema en su vida poética y lo resolvió. Hasta entonces, la empresa se tenía por irrealizable. Y es: hacer un gran poema lírico para oponerlo a los grandes poemas épicos que se cuentan por docenas. Pero ¿cómo mantener una tensión lírica pura durante largos escuadrones de versos? . . . Góngora elige entonces su narración y se cubre de metáforas.[30]

Bearing in mind the symbolist quality of Lorca's earliest plays, one notes that the Symbolists were also attracted to Góngora. Since his arrival in Madrid in 1919, Lorca and poets of his generation were drawn to Góngora who reached them after having passed through Mallarmé and Valéry.[31] Indeed, it was the symbolist lyric poets who began to re-evaluate Góngora.[32] Dámaso Alonso refers to a connection between Góngora and the Symbolists, although he minimizes the extent of the attention they gave the Spanish poet. However, through the Symbolists, Rubén Darío learned to admire Góngora, and through Darío, Góngora permeated the more vibrant elements of the Spanish literary world at the beginning of this century.[33]

An important link between Góngora and the dynamics of Lorca's imagery in the theater emerges when we combine Lorca's views concerning the nature of metaphor and imagination with his detailed analysis of the metaphorical processes in the poetry of Góngora. For Lorca, imagination provides the ability to discover and gives life to fragments of the reality through which one moves, thereby giving birth to metaphor.[34] Lorca maintained that a poetic image has its own planes and orbits. For a metaphor to have life, Lorca asserted that it must have two components: "forma y radio de acción." Thus is metaphor invested with the power to unite two "antagonistic" worlds by means of "un salto ecuestre que da la imaginación" (62, 68, 69). Lorca, like Góngora, provides metaphors with "radios de acción" and thereby acquires a vehicle for liberating static metaphorical language so that it may move in the direction of specific dramatic contexts. By referring to metaphor in terms such as "da vida clara," "una traslación de sentido," "órbitas," "radio de acción" and "un salto ecuestre," Lorca, as poet-dramatist, leads us to conclude that he considered *movement* one of the most important characteristics of poetic imagery.

One of the passages that Lorca quotes to demonstrate Góngora's ability to give imagery life and movement comes from the "Soledad segunda" when the sweetest but least distinct syllable of a youth's love song is absorbed in an echo:

Eco—vestida una cavada roca—
solicitó curiosa y guardó avara
la más dulce—si no la menos clara—
sílaba, siendo en tanto
la vista de las chozas fin del canto.[35]

In citing these lines, Lorca underscores the importance he places on life and movement as components of imagery.

Through Góngora's metaphorical process, an object tends to lose its individuality and is "entered in a metaphorical category."[36] When Góngora calls the limbs of a girl "snow," she is not *like* snow; she *is* snow.[37] This process has significant implications for a poet writing for the theater, for it forms a basis for the natural or unforced appearances of objects and manifestations of nature as they assume metaphorical value through imagery. Thus, an element of imagery becomes capable of acting in the subtext as if it were playing a role in a drama reflecting the interaction among the characters. If, for example, a star is a symbol of ideal love, its course (shining brightly, falling to earth etc.) may be employed as a metaphorical manifestation of the fortunes of a protagonist in love.

Images that radiate outward from a center in what Lorca called a "radio de acción" can indeed be those that a playwright might select to express a change in human relationships and to flesh out the dramatic core of a play. This is the type of imagery that Amado Alonso refers to as image—symbols that radiate poetic allusions[38] and which Philip Wheelwright outlines as semantic movement or the outreaching and combining that is the metaphoric process.[39]

In addition to the process of expanding images, Lorca incorporates in his poetic dramas another technique employed by Góngora: the fusion or fluid combination of images. Raymond points out in *From Baudelaire to Surrealism* that this process of taking familiar objects and sensations and placing them in contexts with which they are not usually associated; of interlocking images in such a way that things "escape from themselves" and "glide from one form to another," was used by the Symbolists and Surrealists. Raymond traces a tradition of "lyrical transfiguration" that includes Baudelaire, Rimbaud and Mallarmé as well as Maeterlinck, with the latter searching for verbal associations combining the spiritual and the physical; and it is in this tradition that Raymond also places Góngora.[40] Both Raymond and Eunice Joiner Gates point out that the identification of one image with another in unusual associations is a characteristic of Góngora, with Raymond indicating the fundamental kinship of all things in Góngora (287) and Gates stating that one of the significant features of Góngora's style is that of associating elements that seem to be very different and unrelated to each other.[41] The fusion of images also figures prominently in Dámaso Alonso's analysis of Góngora's ability to take two different concepts pertaining to real matter and convert them into a single image. For example, clear water ("cristales") as a generic concept becomes associated with a beautiful woman so that finally only one aesthetic concept, one image, emerges.[42]

Ramos-Gil has observed that Lorca also blends images. According to Ramos-Gil, "emblemas," or symbols petrified because of their constant use, are united with newly created symbols; and he cites this example from *Yerma*: Water becomes associated with clothing ("para que el agua cante / por tu camisa"), and then the article of clothing evokes the image of a ship ("Es tu camisa / nave de plata y viento / por las orillas").[43] It is this "verbal magic," this use of a word-symbol of multiple resonances"—a characteristic of Góngora's poetry—that provides Lorca as dramatist with another method of moving one image towards another so that both images may flow with the current of the developing human drama. Thus, the playwright avoids stasis which results if imagery interrupts or impedes the dramatic movement of a play. As Dámaso Alonso has stressed, Góngora greatly depended on the senses in "Soledades."[44] In this regard, Góngora provides a model for Lorca, especially with respect to the sense of sight. Indeed, Lorca's statement that all images evolve in the milieu of the visual was made in the context of examining the imagery of Góngora.[45]

As we have already indicated in the context of Lorca's symbolist beginnings in the theater, there is in Lorquian imagery a flight from reality in the sense that images are directed towards making visible that which does not have physical substance or is not physically present. In Góngora, there is also a flight from reality, described by Ramos-Gil as "la metáfora como un escotillón mágico para evadir de lo real y crear, dignificándola, otra nueva realidad 'intencional,' que no reside en las cosas ni en el poeta, sino que simplemente se reverbera en el choque asociativo y sugeridor de las imágenes."[46] Lorca, however, begins to put this flight from reality to dramatic use as a means of removing layers of conventional reality in order to approach another reality to which characters aspire through their imagination, dreams and desires.

Lorca's affinity with Góngora may be summarized in the words of García-Posada writing in his interpretation of Lorca's *Poeta en Nueva York*: "Todo lo expuesto hasta ahora—y lo que aún diremos—sobre la metáfora neoyorquina, se ajusta perfectamente a la teoría del poeta. Y ello sin perjuicio de que, como veremos más adelante, Góngora no fuese el model estético de la poesía neoyorquina. Pero Lorca le fue fiel en la estilística de la metáfora."[47]

D. *The Traditional Spanish Ballad*

During the course of developing an individual style of poetic drama that makes imagination and inner feelings more palpable or "visible," Lorca moves away from (but does not abandon) Symbolist and Modernista theater as exemplified by playwrights such as Maeterlinck, Yeats, Marquina and Martínez Sierra. He goes beyond the relatively static poetic techniques of layered imagery as practiced by the Symbolist poets and Góngora, in order to develop further the sense of animation that he ascribes to images and metaphors in "La imagen poética de don Luis de Góngora." Since Lorca's plays are poetic dramas, it is no surprise to discover that certain of his *dramatic* poetic techniques are already present in the traditional Spanish ballad, of which he was an early master.

To place Lorca's interest in the ballad in historical perspective, one notes that *Romancero gitano*, of 1928, was in progress between 1924 and 1927; significant dates when we bear in mind that *Doña Rosita la soltera* was first conceived in 1924, *Mariana Pineda* completed in 1925, and

Amor de don Perlimplín con Belisa en su jardín projected in 1928. Specifically referring to *Perlimplín*, Francis Fergusson has indicated that for Lorca's theater poetry, balladry holds a more promising clue to drama than does the "symboliste" lyric. To support this position, Fergusson emphasizes the movement of the play as a whole, especially with the poetic effect in the transition from one scene to another, as well as the ceremonious quality of the scenes which preserve an "oft-told feeling."[48]

Movement, a characteristic of the ballad that Fergusson applies to the structure of the scenes in *Perlimplín*, is a key word in describing Lorca's use of imagery in the theater. The energy that sets Lorquian imagery in motion and directs it towards the narrative line of a drama owes much to Lorca's devotion to the traditional Spanish ballad. In one of his recital-lectures, Lorca stated that his preoccupation with the *romance* began in 1919, instilling in him a desire to fuse the narrative *romance* with the lyric.[49]

The fact that Lorca's poetry draws on the heritage of the ballad tradition has been noted by many critics.[50] In this context, one also notes that Juan Ramón Jiménez frequently drew inspiration from popular Spanish ballads.[51] Lorca himself has left us a rich legacy of his own *romances*, demonstrating his affinity with the ballad. But this does not mean that Lorca's imagery is derived from the ballads. On the contrary, Lorca's metaphorical imagination in general is outside the tradition established by the early Spanish ballads;[52] for these are decidedly narrative in their form and intent.[53] As E.M. Wilson has observed, ballads rarely contain similes and are seldom metaphorical.[54] Nevertheless, the ballads did provide Lorca with elements of a style in which poetic techniques were able to sustain and enhance the flow of the dramatic line. The traditional ballads were replete with repetitions, and the simplicity of their rhetorical resources gave the scenes within them an innate liveliness and strong emotion.[55] The stylistic axis of the traditional *romance* consisted of varied repetitions and antithesis, thereby permitting them to transmit an impression of dramatic energy.[56] Parallel construction, alliterations, anaphoras, analogies and near repetition in word order are a few of the repetitive devices employed by the *juglar* to focus action or the emotion and at the same time imbue the narrative with a rhythmic flow. Further, the dynamic quality of a ballad was enhanced by the abrupt presentation of an action, fleet and fragmentary descriptions and use of dialogue.[57] Particularly significant in the context of Lorca as a poet-playwright is William Entwistle's remark that ballads assume some of the qualities of drama. This is the result of omitting much narrative in order to leave the dialogue in the forefront, in addition to the use of dramatic devices such as: 1) paring away details so that the scene may be actualized, 2) lyrical outbursts, and 3) prophecy, followed by events confirming the prophecy.[58]

Another characteristic of the ballad, especially significant for imagery in the theater, is its effect on the imagination of the reader (or listener). Fragmented scenes and images or the suddenness with which a scene closes without explicit dramatization can result in stimulating the imagination of the reader or listener. Menéndez Pidal describes this characteristic of the ballad as follows: "La fantasía conduce una situación dramática hasta un punto culminante, y allí, en la cima, aletea hacia una lejanía ignota, sin descender por la pendiente del desenlace."[59] In this context, the conclusion of Act I of *Bodas de sangre* will serve as a notable example.

Although the foregoing summary of significant characteristics of the ballad may not appear to address directly the topic of imagery, it suggests one frame a playwright can use to present images, especially those of a brief, suggestive nature. If, for example, images are to break away from the patterns in which they are repeated, they must find ways not only to link themselves to other images and still retain their symbolic base, but also enter the mainstream of the dialogue without impeding the movement of the action of the drama. Ballads, with their ability to be dramatic as well as poetic, contribute to Lorca's structuring of images in such a way that the fragmentary nature of the images gathers momentum and sweeps them along in the same direction as the dramatic events. Thus, the flow of the dialogue is neither impeded nor obliterated by metaphorical language.

E. Golden Age Theater

1. Lope de Vega

As imagination or single-minded determination moves the protagonists of Lorca's later plays away from the world that surrounds them, isolating them and leading them into tragic circumstances, the imagery that expresses this movement reflects the dramatic events. This occurs because the playwright has developed a means for fusing poetry and drama in a process whose trajectory begins within the framework of techniques prevalent in Symbolism and Góngora, passes through characteristics of the traditional Spanish ballad and finally includes elements in techniques present in the theater of the Golden Age. The incorporation of popular traditional songs and ballads in the dialogue of a play, images taken from everyday life and natural surroundings, metaphorical language used to explicate fundamental beliefs, and universal themes such as honor and death are features of Lorca's theater that are also present in works by the great Golden Age playwrights Lope de Vega and Calderón. Concerning the dynamic nature of Lorca's imagery, these features make important contributions to the "imagistic dramas" that parallel the action and provide material that is important not only to the immediate narrative line but to the establishment of focal points of expanded imagery as well.

García-Posada cites Lorca's great admiration and knowledge of the theater of the Golden Age and especially singles out Lope as a major influence on Lorca's theater.[60] Lorca himself referred to the eminent greatness of Spanish classical theater, and he extolled Lope for his prodigious facility in creating a monumental oeuvre of exceptional beauty, flexibility and harmoniousness.[61] Like Lope, Lorca was a lyric poet with a dramatic instinct and a desire to communicate with the people,[62] a fact that does much to explain the use of traditional songs and ballads in the theater of these two dramatists. Lope absorbed the ballad technique. Old *coplas* or *glosas* of popular traditional *estribos* frequently appeared in his plays.[63] A notable example is Alonso's farewell in *El caballero de Olmedo*, singled out by Wilson as an outstanding example of the appearance of the *glosa* of an old *copla* ("Puesto ya el pie en el estribo") that Cervantes had already cited and that had been printed in *Flor de romances, y glosas, canciones y villancicos*.[64]

The function of the "copla lopesca" and the language of dramatic poetry (with special attention given to symbolically rich rustic language) are two significant features of the Golden Age drama that left an imprint on the theater of Lorca.[65] From Lope, Lorca learned the strategic placement of the popular song and used it both as a "plastic and orchestral illustration" and as a means for creating a dramatic climate.[66]

Lorca's interest in popular songs is further borne out by the fact that he collected Spanish *nanas* and incorporated elements of these lullabies into several of his plays. The *nana* of the second scene of Act I of *Bodas de sangre* is an outstanding example of how Lorca extended the dramatic possibilities of popular songs beyond their use as an effective means of summarization or of foreshadowing. Through imagery, Lorca further taps a song's potential for fleshing out feelings, relationships or actions of the characters in the drama. Thus, within the *nana* of *Bodas de sangre*, one sees Leonardo drinking from the dark river of passion that will destroy him.

Lorca said the following about the dramatization of a song: "Yo considero que escenificar la canción . . . es una labor de más trascendencia que la que puede inferirse de su tono. La canción escenificada tiene sus personajes; que hablan con música, su coro, que juega el mismo papel que la tragedia griega. Por tanto, es dentro de un marco reducido, sobre todo tiempo, un espectáculo breve, pero completo, lleno de sugerencias y de belleza."[67] These assertions could also be applied to the imagistic dramatization that takes place in songs that contribute to the shape of the texts of his plays, for the strategically placed song is one means whereby Lorca provides images with a way to interact like characters in a play as they follow their course in expressing the changing human relationships in the drama. Thus, when the daughters of Bernarda Alba hear references to open doors in the song of the harvesters, in effect they are listening to portions of their own drama at a time when the "closed doors" of Bernarda's house have placed a severe strain on the emotional relationships among the women who live within.

As García-Posada points out,[68] Lorca learned a great deal about the use of popular songs in the theater from Lope de Vega, and he frequently included them in his plays (the nuptial song in *Bodas de sangre*, the *romances* in *Mariana Pineda*, the song of the harvesters in *La casa de Bernarda Alba*). What Lorca did, however, was to use songs to provide images with a milieu for advancing the metaphorical continuities through which they carry out their association with the dramatic context of the play. Thus, in the use of songs, Lorca has found another means of fusing the lyrical atmosphere of a play with the conflict so that, as Brower stated, "we cannot feel the peculiar quality of what is taking place or grasp its meaning apart from the metaphorical language through which it is being expressed."[69]

2. Calderón

Given the central position of images and metaphor in Lorca's works,[70] his keen interest in the metaphorical process especially as exemplified by Góngora, and his great respect for the classical plays of the Golden Age, our study of the dynamics of Lorquian imagery leads us to Calderón as the playwright after Lope who helps us see the techniques Lorca uses to provide imagery with a sense of movement.

Lorca called Calderón's *comedia La vida es sueño* the apex of Spanish catholic theater;[71] and La Barraca, the traveling theatrical company so closely associated with Lorca, frequently presented Calderón's *auto sacramental* also entitled *La vida es sueño*.[72] This is the work that García-Posada singles out when writing about Lorca's concept of the theater as "espectáculo total." García-Posada points out significantly that La Barraca's first season included Calderón's *auto sacramental*, a perfect example of total theater.[73] In writing about the theme of honor in Lorca's plays, Gwynne Edwards also links Lorca and Calderón by stating that Lorca was especially influenced by the honor plays of Calderón, with *The House of Bernarda Alba* particularly influenced by *The Surgeon of His Honor*.[74] Edwin Honig also connects these two playwrights through the theme of honor and adds that Lorca, like Calderón, portrays life symbolically, with death as its prominent feature.[75] Although the foregoing references concern thematics rather than imagery, they help underscore the fact that Lorca, a poet-dramatist, was drawn to Calderón, a dramatist whose works exhibit metaphorical language as one of their major characteristics.

Wardropper remarks that we so often discuss the Spanish *comedia* in terms of plot and character that in the process we neglect the poetic core of what should be called dramatic poetry rather than drama.[76] In Wardropper's view, the main techniques of the Golden Age dramatists were adapted from techniques essentially related to poetry—techniques such as the use of an idea as a poetic theme and the use of images and metaphors. That is to say, plays of the Golden Age often contained "pilot metaphors," with poetry underpinning plot and character (343-349). In this regard, Wardropper's analysis of Calderón's *El médico de su honra* is especially illuminating. For Wardopper, this entire play is an extended metaphor incorporating into dramatic action the traditional metaphor of love as illness (4-7).

Lorca's admiration for the metaphorical process employed by Góngora also helps to explain an affinity with Calderón. In comparing Calderón and Góngora, Eunice Joiner Gates refers to Calderón as the most Gongoristic of the Golden Age dramatists, very much influenced by the "Soledades" in phraseology and the use of images and metaphors;[77] and in an essay titled "The Four Elements in the Imagery of Calderón," Wilson concludes that Calderón probably derived his metaphorical process from studying the works of Góngora in which the same method adheres but to a less "academic" degree.[78]

The method to which Wilson refers may be summarized as follows: The basic elements—fire, air, earth and water—are central to Calderón's metaphorical structure. They have a fixed order, and their equilibrium is essential to the differences between order and chaos in the world. For each element there are three categories: 1) the element itself, 2) a creature, such as a horse or a bird, associated with each element, and 3) a special characteristic of the creature or element (34-43). Calderón's imagery, therefore, is framed in cosmic terms with, as Wilson points out, such visual exchanges between the spheres as flowers viewed as stars on earth and stars as flowers in heaven. Lorca also engaged words in "visual exchanges" ("nardos de espuma," "pétalos encendidos," "flor que vuela"); and he, like Calderón, used archetypal symbols such as light, blood and water. In Lorca's imagery, however, these symbols are constantly in touch with drama at a human level. Calderón's *autos* and religious plays are dominated by meaning in cosmic terms in a drama with fundamental social and cultural implications. Especially in the *autos* where the Eucharist is made "theatrically visual," Calderón makes the spiritual visible through the senses. Fate is identified with God's will, and people and actions assume archetypal dimensions. Calderón's characters serve as examples of cosmic powers that control Man rather than as figures engaged in a human drama.[79] In the *autos sacramentales*, God is reflected in all creation, and there is a marriage between man's body and soul, with the latter aspiring towards the rewards of heaven, sustaining itself with spiritual food of the Eucharist. Flowers often represent the shortness of human life, cypresses symbolize death and dew stands for the tears of dawn.[80] For Lorca, however, images associated with natural phenomena are primarily used to evoke various aspects of human emotions, thoughts and actions.

It is especially in the expansion of metaphor and its incorporation into dramatic action that one sees Calderonian drama reflected in the works of Lorca. As Wilson has observed, Calderón was a poet serving theater. His poetry cannot be separated from the dramatic context in which it appears, for it is firmly set in and sustained by the entire work.[81]

Wilson's observation could be applied to Lorca; for he, like Calderón, places metaphorical language in dramatic contexts. However, Wilson's analysis of Calderón also holds a clue to the difference between the two playwrights with respect to the use of metaphor. Calderón, as Wilson states, "generalizes" or "comments" on human conduct. Imagery, especially in the *autos sacramentales*, often reflects a cosmic struggle with forces such as faith, evil and love vying for control over Man. Lorca, on the other hand, brings archetypal symbols close to a localized human drama. For Lorca, the theater is a place for displaying human society and illuminating the human heart through living examples.[82]

II. Lorca Within and Beyond Affinities with the Past

A. Lorca, Maeterlinck and Yeats

There are striking similarities in thematic content and imagery between *El maleficio de la mariposa, Mariana Pineda* and works by Maeterlinck. The capture of the bird in Maeterlinck's *The Blue Bird*, symbolizing possession of the secret of the universe, has its parallel in *El maleficio de la mariposa* in Curianito's desire to capture the essence of love and beauty represented by the butterfly. (Here one also recalls Alcino's search for "la reina Sol" in Martínez Sierra's *Pastoral.*) The tension between light and darkness in both *The Blue Bird* and *Pelléas et Mélisande* also has its counterpart in *El maleficio de la mariposa* and *Mariana Pineda*. The harmony between the natural world and the inner feelings of the main characters in *Pelléas et Mélisande* is also present early in Lorca's theater, as exemplified by Nigromántica's intuitive perceptions expressed through words pertaining to natural phenomena ("Vengo de soñar que yo era una flor / hundida en la hierba;" "y sentí caer / en mi corazón / un anochecer" [671, 672]) and by Mariana Pineda's identification with Granada ("Ya no verán tus ojos las naranjas de luz / que pondrá en los tejados de Granada la tarde" [890]).

Maeterlinck's early plays are based on symbols, ritual and gestures; and everything, including the lighting and the scenery, flows into one central image.[83] His technique of employing silence, pauses and evasions that help create a mysterious and mesmerizing world that one would think belonged to another dimension, is one of his most notable contributions to the modern theater.[84] In the context of this "other dimension," the imagery of *Mariana Pineda* becomes a force that eventually removes Mariana from reality and places her in the world of abstraction that has been taking shape in her imagination. Further, one senses in this play an atmosphere that has its own life, with images such as "Si toda la tarde fuera como un gran pájaro" making visible an abstraction such as time.[85] Through an accumulation of images, a brooding atmosphere in *Mariana Pineda* "comments" on the ill-fated relationship between Mariana and Pedro. For example, Lorca expands the previously cited "tarde-pájaro" image with this foreboding exclamation: "¡Cuántas / duras flechas lanzaría / para cerrarle las alas!" (795). Such a moment in a series of connected images echoes the process whereby Maeterlinck surrounds Pelléas and Mélisande with an atmosphere that speaks of their love with words which only they can hear and understand.

These similarities, however, do not imply that Lorca's plays constitute Symbolist theater exactly as conceived by Maeterlinck. Whereas Maeterlinck sacrificed dramatic action and characterization to poetic symbolism,[86] Lorca brings Mariana Pineda to life as a character with a sense of purpose and the strength to see it through. While Mélisande simply exists in a dream-like world that sweeps her along with it, Mariana takes unequivocal steps towards her escape into the symbol she imagines herself to be.

For specific examples of the similarities and differences in the purpose of imagery for Maeterlinck and Lorca, one can turn to the treatment each playwright gives images associated with light and darkness. In both *Pelléas et Mélisande* and *Mariana Pineda*, darkness hangs heavily over the principal characters, suggesting a stifling atmosphere and impending doom. For Lorca, the presence or absence of darkness is more directly tied to the dramatic moment in the narrative line of unfolding events; whereas for Maeterlinck, darkness and light, however momentary, serve to reveal the unspoken feelings of characters who appear to move *through* rather than act *in* a haunting and almost haunted landscape.

Lorca does not employ archetypal symbols such as stars, forests, the sun and the moon in the near-allegorical manner in which Maeterlinck integrates them into his plays, nor do Lorca's symbols have the supernatural, extrasensory quality that takes them outside human experience. Even in the symbolist poetry that opens the final act of *Bodas de sangre*, the unreality of the appearance of death and the moon is related to the actual flight of the lovers in their desperate search for escape into their love-darkness. During the almost surreal dialogue, one does not lose sight of the unfolding human drama as the light-darkness imagery becomes more intense. In Maeterlinck's *The Blue Bird*, Light for Tyltyl and Mytyl in their quest for the Blue Bird is Reason and Wisdom that sides with Man, leading the children through realms of Memory and Happiness. In *El maleficio de la mariposa*, light and darkness are used to reflect the elusive and illusory course of Curianito's imagination in his unsuccessful attempt to escape; but the action remains rooted in the world in which he lives. Even the use of repetitions, common to both playwrights, often serves different purposes. For Maeterlinck, the recurrence of words, images and silences creates a dreamy atmosphere, whereas for Lorca, the technique of repetition frequently reinforces waves of images already set in motion, in a manner more akin to the function of repetition with respect to the narrative flow of a traditional Spanish ballad.

What both playwrights do reflect, however, is a propensity for creating characters who perceive the world through the senses and participate in a network of imagistic associations between man and nature. This is done in such a way that even fragments of scenes contain an imagistic structure that heightens or illuminates the feelings, thoughts and actions of the characters. For Maeterlinck, the effect of this process is predominantly evocative; for Lorca, primarily dramatic. The accumulation of symbolic images in *Pelléas et Mélisande* creates a correspondence between nature and human emotions so that one feels the presence of unspoken thoughts. In Act III, Scene 4, Yniold looks at Pelléas and Mélisande through a window and repeatedly tells Golaud that they are doing nothing but looking at the light. Because the playwright has gradually associated light with freedom from the oppressive air that surrounds Pelléas and Mélisande, we sense that in their silence, they are communicating their love for each other. To a certain extent, this symbiotic relationship between nature and human emotions is also present in *Mariana Pineda*, especially in the scene when Mariana muses on the night that descends on Granada. Nevertheless, in Lorca's play, the light-dark imagery is less marked by symbolic connotations and more directly tied to the dramatic sequence of events. By establishing through imagery a palpable correspondence between emotions and the perceptible natural world, Lorca employs a technique favored by Maeterlinck and the Symbolists. But Lorca uses this technique to move images to support the information transmitted in the dialogue. In *Mariana Pineda*, the image of twilight giving way to night is embedded in the dramatic context of Mariana's moving from apprehension to extreme agitation because of the conspiracy in which she is involved.

In addition to Maeterlinck, the spirit of Yeats's symbolist theater is present especially in Lorca's earliest play. By comparing and contrasting Yeats's *The Shadowy Waters* with Lorca's *El maleficio de la mariposa*, one can gain insight into the role of imagery in structuring key metaphors, particularly in Lorca's representation of human relationships. In Yeats's drama, the promise of the mysterious birds to bring Forgael to a strange love is not unlike the hopes that Curianito has placed on La Mariposa. Forgael himself resembles not only La Mariposa (for he has awakened Dectora to love through the spell cast by the magic strings of his harp) but also Curianito, because both can "see" the mystery that beckons through images in their mind. Further, both plays contain images of darkness and light that propel the thoughts of their protagonists towards the idea of escape from the abyss of reality into the starry light of imagination. Indeed, this power that the imagination has over the mind is present, to varying degrees, in Lorca's later plays, as evidenced in the imagery of passages involving such personages as Mariana Pineda, Perlimplín, Doña Rosita, La Novia, Leonardo and Adela.

With respect to the images used by Yeats to "concretize" contemplative thought and as further evidence of the affinity of Lorca's theater with that of Yeats, we observe that the mind's retina retains Lorquian images such as La Mariposa's dance movements as she prepares to leave Curianito, the content of the children's songs and games in *Mariana Pineda*, the horse that dominates the lullaby in *Bodas de sangre* and the fragmented images of the ditties sung by María Josefa in *La casa de Bernarda Alba*—all poetic elements that not only engage the imagination but also meet the demands of specific dramatic instances.

B. Lorca and Symbolist Poetry

Lorca's images, like those of the Symbolists, move towards what Chiari calls an elusive reality.[87] An outstanding example of this is the silver thread that gives direction to the flight of the butterfly in *El maleficio de la mariposa*. But unlike the imagistic process employed by the Symbolists, and most important for the development of Lorca's theater beyond Symbolism, Lorquian imagery also moves in the direction of a narrative line. That is, the mind gathers images which accomplish functions such as foreshadowing events, confirming what has occurred and impelling the dramatic action forward. In this sense, Lorca differs from the Symbolists who rejected narrative techniques in their endeavor to make visible inner states of thinking or feeling. As we have already indicated, Lorca embraced techniques of the ballad which, unlike the "symboliste" lyric, suggests a story or a situation and finds its inspiration in what is dramatic rather than in the feeling of an isolated poet.[88]

As early as *Mariana Pineda*, Lorca places most of his characters in real settings and human situations which supply imagery that moves with the imagination yet is rooted in the drama of human relationships. The *romance* that Mariana Pineda's children recite contains images that further define Mariana's plight. The metaphorical language of flowers in *Doña Rosita* evolves naturally from dramatic contexts where flowers are either present or are the topic of conversation; and the rural setting of *Bodas de sangre* provides images that reinforce La Madre's obsession with deadly instruments. Even the light of the moon in the symbolist scenes of the final act of *Bodas de sangre* appears and disappears in the context of Leonardo and La Novia seeking a darkness to shelter their love.

Turning briefly to Lorca within the orbit of the heritage of Symbolist theater—specifically within the realm of Modernista theater—a comparison with Marquina shows how Lorca refines techniques used by his predecessors. Like Lázaro Carreter and García-Posada, we see in Lorca's earliest plays affinities with Marquina in the use of "arias" and in similarities of selected images. The difference between Marquina and Lorca can be seen in the manner in which they control the appearance of key images. In Marquina's *La ermita, la fuente y el río*, the key images are relatively static. The song-poetry elements stand out by framing specific ideas represented in the action of the characters (a process that also occurs in *Mariana Pineda* in the *romance* that frames the drama), and they become "congealed" at several points in the play as Deseada is torn between her spiritual and worldly instincts. However, in *Mariana Pineda* and *Doña Rosita*, to choose two plays that have specific *romance* elements as frames, Lorca is developing a method of blending poetry and drama in such a way that the metaphorical language cannot be separated from the events and emotions it expresses. Unlike Marquina, Lorca brings to the theater what Concha Zardoya calls poetry that flows naturally and constantly from both the characters and their environment, creating an emotional power that is also dramatically forceful.[89] In other words, Lorca's theater reaches beyond Modernism and Symbolism for a style of modern poetic drama uniquely his own.

Despite the aforementioned difference between Lorca and the tradition of Symbolism, Lorca's use of images to evoke the presence of thoughts and feelings, especially in the early stages of his development as a playwright, place him within the orbit of Symbolism. Even in *La casa de Bernarda Alba*, which is late Lorca, there is a layered structure of images that establishes the presence of such forces as silence and heat as important "characters" in the drama. But Lorca combines this manner of presenting images with techniques that impel the imagery into a course parallel to that of the evolving relationships among the characters. For example, the heat of summer that "rises from the ground" not only underscores the heated tension in Bernarda's house but also becomes progressively associated with the intensification of the frustration of Bernarda's daughters as Bernarda's house becomes converted into a living hell. The layers of meaning that Lorca has assigned to heat (the heat of summer that produces thirst and a desire for fresh air; the heat of Hell; sexual "heat") have laid the foundation on which the dynamics of the image will build an edifice that houses the dramatic content of the play. Writing about such layers of meaning in Blake's "The Sick Rose," Howard Young touches on aspects of the process just described, relating it to Spanish literature:

> By compressing layers of meaning into symbols and trusting to their unfolding in the mind of the reader, this poem clearly anticipates a great body of work in the nineteenth century. Jiménez, who would have first come across it as an epigraph in *The Land of Heart's Desire*, was in a fine position in the twenties to appreciate its effect and technique.[90]

For the Symbolists, every word is a symbol used to evoke reality beyond the senses. According to Mallarmé, poetry should not inform but evoke and suggest; it should not name things but create an atmosphere.[91] This is precisely what occurs in Lorca's earliest attempts in the theater when, for example, Doña Curiana brings Scene 1 of *El maleficio de la mariposa* to a close by saying "Yo voy a barrer / mi puerta con brisa del amanecer," or when La Mariposa describes a mysterious realm above that awaits her, or when Mariana Pineda meditates upon the approaching night in Scene 5 of Act I in the play that bears her name. Although the presence of Symbolism is clear in Lorca's early works, one should still bear in mind that his poetic theater will extend beyond Symbolist theater as exemplified by *Pelléas et Mélisande*. Referring to *Mariana Pineda*, Lorca describes himself as an author who brings to the theater a natural and constant flow of poetry emanating not only from the characters but also from the environment surrounding them.[92] Lorca emphasizes the fact that he is more interested in the drama of the people who inhabit the landscape than in the landscape itself.[93]

Paradoxically, the static nature of Symbolist imagery holds a clue for the development of the dynamic nature of Lorca's imagery. When the layers of images are removed, they reveal changing relationships among the characters as well as help make visible an elusive reality. What Lorca brought to the allusive imagery emanating from a vocabulary favored by Symbolist and Modernista writers was a sense of the dramatic possibilities of lyrical images as they accumulate to help the mind's eye make ideas, thoughts and emotions "visible." The images of rain in *Mariana Pineda* not only create an atmosphere but also reveal and reflect Mariana's behavior as her involvement in the conspiracy deepens. Lorca, in the tradition of Symbolism, uses words such as "shadows," "dawn," "dusk," "flowers," "water" and "moon" to aim directly at the senses in order to reach the inner sensibility of the one who receives the image. But in *Mariana Pineda*, in poetic phrases such as ". . . ese gris fino y glacial / que viene de la Alhambra" and "El aire helado / que clava agujas sobre los pulmones"—phrases that describe a cold, rainy night—one "hears" allusions to the fatal struggle in which Pedrosa and Mariana are engaged. Similarly in *El maleficio de la mariposa*, images such as "estrella caída de un ciprés soñoliento," "viene del alba," "una flor errante," and "volaré por el hilo de plata" accumulate not only to help one imagine the nature of La Mariposa but also to communicate the ominous and mysterious movements of this creature who has cast an evil spell on the protagonist. In fact, La Mariposa and her movements are visible in the imagery.

In Verlaine's "Art poétique," an image in which music takes flight holds a clue to Lorca's process of taking a static image and prodding it into motion:

> De la musique encore et toujours!
> Que ton vers soit la chose envolée
> Qu'on sent qui fuit d'une âme en allée
> Vers d'autres cieux à d'autres amours.[94]

In *El maleficio de la mariposa*, Lorca takes an evocative flight image very similar to Verlaine's static "une âme en allée vers d'autres cieux à d'autres amours," and he begins to dramatize it in the form of a butterfly:

> Mariposa: Volaré por el hilo de plata.
>   Mis hijos me esperan,
>   allá, en los campos lejanos. (708)[95]

The image of a butterfly in flight expands into a metaphor for a poet's search for ideal love and beauty, and the flight imagery that evokes the presence and expresses the thoughts of La Mariposa also becomes closely associated with Curianito's "reaching for the moon." The result is that the poetry outlines the frustration the protagonist experiences in his unsuccessful attempt to hold onto the butterfly who represents what he wants to possess.

The process whereby Lorca accumulates images to establish the presence of an abstraction is very similar to what occurs in a poem such as Valéry's "Le Cimetière marin," in which images of devouring evoke destruction and death.[96] Even in later plays this process is at work, as for example in *Bodas de sangre* when death makes its presence felt in images of knives, farm implements, axes and arid land. However, Lorca goes beyond the thematic design that one observes in Valéry's meditations on life and death in the seaside cemetery. The images of death that hover over *Bodas de sangre* are set in dramatic contexts. Even the casual mention of harvesters or a young man badly maimed in an accident involving a machine reverberates with thoughts of foreboding a character has when the utterance is made.

The fact that the dynamics of Lorca's images give them a dramatic life and move them away from being static figures appearing intermittently throughout a composition does not diminish the importance of this playwright's Symbolist and Modernista beginnings. On the contrary, these movements gave the dramatist poetic models of imagery embedded in the dialogue of a drama—a significant step towards setting them in dramatic contexts.

C. Lorca and Góngora

As Lorca proceeds towards plays that give more life and movement to imagery within the total context of a drama, the extension of metaphor plays an increasingly important role in the total imagistic structure of the drama. The metaphor of the "rosa mutabile" that dominates *Doña Rosita* and the outer-inner, revealed-concealed, love-death counterpoints through which we follow Perlimplín's imagination as it takes him to his death are evidence of movement towards a complete integration of poetry and drama.

Lorca, especially in his early plays, reflects Góngora's ability to make Nature come alive in such a way that imagery clothes the narrative whose outline is still visible. In the following fragment of *El maleficio de la mariposa*, the dramatic reality (that is, the reality of the sequential action by the characters as they interact with each other) is present in the images that "narrate" the events of the drama. Doña Curiana admonishes Nigromántica to abandon her dream-like thoughts and return to reality, which Nigromántica, according to the stage direction, manages to do. In addition to being informed of the change in Nigromántica's behavior through a stage direction ("Volviendo a la realidad en una brusca transición"), the reader perceives the change through metaphorical language that 1) retains thematically important imagery associated with dew ("rocío") and 2) moves in the direction taken by the dramatic reality in subsequent scenes. Nigromántica speaks:

El prado está silencioso.
Ya parte el rocío a su cielo ignorado (675)

In this passage, Nigromántica observes and comments on the physical surroundings first in concrete terms ("El prado está silencioso") that confirm the reality of the moment; and then she uses a phrase ("Ya parte el rocío a su cielo ignorado") which introduces an elusive idea that impels the passage forward on the strength of the dew-love imagery already aimed in the direction of the culminating action of the play (i.e., La Mariposa's return to her "cielo ignorado"). Although Lorca has clothed the narrative line of the drama in imagery that is somewhat elusive, he has still kept the reader mindful of its presence. This is the process that Lorca praised in Góngora when he stated that one of Góngora's great achievements was to create the great lyric poem ("Soledades") not by cutting the thread of narration but by transforming it into imagery. In Lorca's words:

> Góngora elige entonces su narración y se cubre de metáforas. Ya es difícil encontrarla. Está transformada. La narración es como un esqueleto del poema envuelto en la carne magnífica de las imágenes. Todos los momentos tienen idéntica intensidad y valor plástico, y la anécdota no tiene ninguna importancia pero da con su hilo invisible unidad al poema.[97]

Although this observation addresses poetry rather than theater and minimizes the role of narrative in Góngora's poetry, it nevertheless alludes to an idea that is very important with respect to the dynamics of the imagery in Lorca's poetic dramas: i.e., the extensive use of metaphor without destroying the cohesiveness of the basic dramatic line.

Although the process of the expanding image that Lorca described in Góngora as the "doubling" and "tripling" of images is essentially static in Góngora's poetry, it provides Lorca as playwright with a starting point for giving an image dramatic direction. Step by step, an image that has been set in motion leads to larger dramatic contexts. For example, the lines delivered by El Tío in the opening moments of *Doña Rosita* contain fundamental components of the imagery associated with flowers that tell Rosita's story:

> ¿Y mis semillas? . . . Pues no están. . . . Es necesario que cuidéis las flores.
> . . . Ayer me encontré las semillas de dalias pisoteadas por el suelo" (1351-1352).[98]

In passages such as this, one "hears" the name "Rosita" while following the course taken by the imagery.

In addition to the expanding image, Lorca employs Góngora's technique of blending images. But as a poet writing for the theater, Lorca goes beyond establishing an autonomous pattern of poetic images inserted at various points in a drama. What is ostensibly autonomous within a developing poetic context is actually one element of a metaphorical continuity contributing to the imagistic narration of a character's struggle to escape an oppressive reality. This is the context in which we would place images in *Bodas de sangre* that are associated with each other although they appear to be unrelated (among which are "slicing a young man's body," "dagger in the eyes," and "thorn in the heart"—images which Barnes calls a dynamic foreshadowing of violence[99]).

Imagery in Lorca's plays, as in the poetry of Góngora, relies very much on the senses. Color, for example, abounds in the dialogue of *El maleficio de la mariposa*, and *Mariana Pineda* contains many phrases also heavily dependent on the senses, especially sight. As Ramos-Gil states in comparing the imagery of Góngora and Lorca: "Como Góngora, Lorca es un poeta más de los sentidos que de la inteligencia." He adds:

> . . . el método sería parecido, mas a Lorca no le interesa sobremanera poner de relieve el lado bello; escoge imágenes de sueño en las que el detalle, no importa cuál, vence al conjunto, pasando a primer plano, con menoscabo de lo esencial. De esa manera la imagen lorquiana, como la gongorina en parte, nunca está completa, o lo está sólo en cuanto evoca secundarios en el lector.[100]

Images that are deeply rooted in the senses and radiate outward from a central point comprise a fundamental characteristic of the poetic language that Lorca brings to the theater. In this regard, one might say that when Lara Pozuelo observes (in *El adjetivo en la lírica de Federico García Lorca*) that the color green of Lorca's "Romance sonámbulo" infuses the entire poem with dramatic urgency and that the elements of Nature participate in crystalizing the tragedy,[101] he is, in effect, anticipating Lorca's development of poetic drama. It is in the theater that Lorca's imagery finds a natural outlet for actualizing its dramatic potential. While Góngora's substitutions are static ("cristal" for water, "nieve hilada" for tablecloths of white linen and "volante nieve" for the white feathers of a bird),[102] Lorca's are dynamic. In *El maleficio de la mariposa*, "El aire me trae su aliento" means that Curianito is arriving. "Mi ilusión / está prendida en la estrella / que parece una flor" alludes to La Mariposa's fall to earth. "Estrella caída de un ciprés" not only symbolizes La Mariposa but also refers to her ominous descent into Curianito's life, and "llorando el rocío del amanecer" is an imagistic representation of how Curianito reacts to his unrequited love.

In his analysis of the poetic imagery of Góngora, Lorca stressed the expansion and blending of images, a method he used as a means of moving images out of the realm of static decoration and into the area of drama. Indications of the way this process functions in the later works appear as early as the first two plays that are so closely allied to Symbolism. In the passage cited earlier from *El maleficio de la mariposa* wherein Nigromántica is jolted out of her dream-like musings ("El prado está silencioso. / Ya parte el rocío a su cielo ignorado [675]), a "prado-rocío" image, rooted in the world of the senses, "escapes from itself" (words used by Raymond in *From Baudelaire to Surrealism*) by expanding to include the departure of the dew—a foreshadowing of what eventually happens to Curianito's love. This expansion of the imagery is part of an ongoing metaphorical process that began in the opening scene of the play when "rocío" and "labios de amores" were blended thus: "Sueño que las dulces gotas de rocío / son labios de amores que me dejan besos / y llenan de estrellas mi traje sombrío" (672). A similar expansion of metaphor occurs in Act III of *Mariana Pineda* when Mariana exclaims: "¡Ay, qué fragatita, / real corsaria! ¿Dónde está / tu valentía? / Que un famoso bergantín / te ha puesto la puntería" (878-879). The metaphor of the defense of the "fragatita" against the threat of the "bergantín" is one of the circles radiating outward from a central idea that appeared in Act II when Mariana confrontó Pedrosa in these words: "Sepa que yo no tengo miedo a nadie. / Como el agua que nace soy de limpia, / y no puedo manchar si usted me toca / pero sé defenderme" (854). Recalling Lorca's observation that Góngora chooses his narrative and then covers it with metaphors, we can state that in this instance, Lorca demonstrates an affinity with Góngora. That is to say, the basic idea that Mariana is engaged in a dangerous conflict has been maintained while being clothed in a scenario of images that point to the fatal consequences of her involvement in a conspiracy.

D. Lorca and the Traditional Spanish Ballad

With respect to Lorca's refinement of techniques of the ballads, the conclusion of Act I of *Bodas de sangre* immediately comes to mind. In a style reminiscent of a ballad, the rapidity and suddenness with which the act comes to a close leaves the reader imagining the circumstances surrounding an action that is not depicted onstage. At this moment in the drama, La Criada is speaking of the movements of a horseman she heard the previous night, and La Novia tersely expresses her disbelief. In an onrush of energy generated by only a few words—a characteristic of the ballads—a significant action is "viewed" through the "eyes" of characters who, in this instance, may be thought of as assuming the role of a *juglar*.

García-Posada has pointed out that the dynamic quality of Lorca's poetry owes much to simple syntactical structure, with the use of nouns and verbs as accelerators—a characteristic also present in the ballads.[103] This process appears in *Bodas de sangre* with respect to the image of "la navaja." For La Madre, the knife symbolizes death, and she repeats the word in phrases that assume the quality of a litany. However, the word is also carried forward by succinct mentions of related words such as "hoe," "pitchfork," "harvesters," "thorn," "needle" and "ax" that embed the original symbolically charged image ever deeper into dramatic context by contributing to a fundamental metaphorical continuity that repeatedly signals death in this drama.

When early in the first scene of *El maleficio de la mariposa* Nigromántica tells Doña Curiana about her feelings of foreboding, she narrates poetically ("vi una estrella roja toda temblorosa / que se deshojaba como una enorme rosa" [672]) and actualizes the event she is reporting by interspersing her poetic lines with dialogue she quotes from the vivid past ("'Amigas cigarras—grité—¿veis las estrellas?' / 'Un hada se ha muerto', respondieron ellas" [672]). This technique recalls the traditional ballads. In "Romance de don Tristán," for example, after Tristán has been wounded, the *juglar* continues his narrative and recreates the past event by including dramatic dialogue:

> Llegó allí la reina Iseo,
> la su linda enamorada,
> cubierta de paños negros,
> sin del rey dársele nada:
> <<¡Quien vos hirió, don Tristán,
> heridas tenga de rabia
> y que no hallase maestro
> que supiese de sanallas!>>
>   Júntanse boca con boca,
> juntos quieren dar el alma[104]

The very first scene of *Mariana Pineda* also illustrates Lorca's use of ballad techniques in a passage spoken by Angustias in reference to Mariana:

> Borda y borda lentamente.
> Yo lo he visto por el ojo de la llave.
> Parecía el hilo rojo, entre sus dedos,
> una herida de cuchillo sobre el aire. (783)

The anaphora at the beginning of the passage stresses the information that is communicated and sets the stage for the imagistic repetition of the information in the third and fourth lines that allude to the negative implications of Mariana's activity. Through an economy of words, repetitions, and the heightened presentation of a reported act ("Yo lo he visto por el ojo de la llave")—all characteristics of the traditional ballad—Lorca has introduced into the dialogue a small portion of the structure of the imagery that will gradually convey the tragic result of Mariana's clandestine embroidering. One might say that when Entwistle, writing about Calderón, stated that his plays lost sight of the narrative value of the *romance*"[105], he had in mind precisely what Lorca did do. That is, Lorca kept within his sight the narrative value of the *romance* so that it could help him write poetry and drama.

E. Lorca and Lope de Vega

As we have already indicated, Lorca learned from Lope de Vega the strategic use of popular songs to create a dramatic climate and to serve as what Lázaro Carreter called "plastic and almost orchestral illustrations."[106] For Lorca, however, the "orchestral" aspect of the popular song emanates from within the song itself and suffuses the general dramatic structure of the play; whereas for Lope, the song tends to remain an illustration. Popular songs, therefore, contribute to the dynamics of Lorquian imagery by furnishing vehicles for imagistic components of the metaphorical structure to adapt themselves to given dramatic contexts. For example, the song beginning "Amor, amor. / Entre mis muslos cerrados . . ." (982),[107] heard very early in *Perlimplín*, 1) occurs immediately upon Marcolfa's alluding to eroticism in marriage and 2) contains key words such as "amor" and "noche" that become embedded in the dialogue while Perlimplín becomes increasingly aware of the physical world of erotic love and Belisa approaches the inner world of the soul.

An example from Lope's *El caballero de Olmedo* will help place Lorca's achievement in perspective. In Act III, Alonso, on his way to Olmedo, hears a voice singing:

> Que de noche le mataron
> al caballero,
> la gala de Medina,
> la flor de Olmedo.[108]

Clearly, this refrain foreshadows the imminent death of Alonso and provides Lope with a very dramatic device for heightening our awareness of Alonso's plight. Like Lope, Lorca also uses songs to foreshadow as well as to describe or review the actions of principal characters. However, Lorca adapts the use of song to the purpose of creating his own style of poetic theater. He integrates songs with dialogue so that they can often be looked to for images or metaphors that constitute additional "information" concerning the course of action that is being played out by the characters. In its early stages, this process is present in *Mariana Pineda*; in later plays it is refined when songs such as that of the harvesters in *La casa de Bernarda Alba* or the nuptial songs in *Bodas de sangre* are more closely integrated with events transpiring in the drama.

In capsule form and in anticipation of a detailed analysis in a subsequent chapter, we can cite the "romancillo del bordado" from Act II of *Mariana Pineda* as one example of Lorca's way of incorporating a *romance* into the text of a play. Reciting to Mariana's children, Clavela begins: "Bendita sea por siempre / la Santísima Trinidad, / y guarde al hombre en la sierra / y al marinero en el mar" (822). This *romance* contains images associated with the sea that will become increasingly more important as signifiers in Mariana's drama, and it anticipates the words that Mariana will speak to Pedro in a scene shortly thereafter ("Como la enamorada de un marinero loco"). Thus, this *romance* inserted in the text in the natural setting of a bedtime story: 1) supplies the metaphor of a woman waiting on shore for her seaman to return, 2) makes Mariana's thoughts "visible" and 3) helps direct the action towards the development of the extreme agitation the protagonist will feel as the act progresses. One can say, therefore, that "la canción popular o popularizante" that was so common in the theater of Lope de Vega is for Lorca another means of providing imagery with access to the action at the human level, thereby becoming an integral part of the drama while still maintaining its cohesiveness and fluidity within the thematic or total metaphorical construct.

F. Lorca and Calderón

With respect to Lorca's affinity with Calderón, we turn our attention especially to the use of metaphor. Lorca's plays, like Calderón's, often contain "pilot metaphors" with plot and character underpinned by poetry. But we also note that by setting images in the dialgoue in a manner that reflects the on-going drama, Lorca goes beyond presenting metaphorical language as a support for thematic material. As the protagonists of *Doña Rosita, Bodas de sangre* and *La casa de Bernarda Alba* seek escape either into the imagination or into an illusory perception of reality, the imagery of these plays becomes actively involved in creating the narrative line of the dialogue through which the actual or imagined world is presented. One example of Calderón's setting imagery into a dramatic context occurs in *El médico de su honra* when light, which symbolizes both life and honor, is actually extinguished several times. The loss of honor for Don Gutierre motivates snuffing out the life of the woman who caused his dishonor—an action that is reflected in the image of plunging a room into darkness by snuffing out the flame of a candle. Imagery thus has its counterpart in action. A similar manipulation of metaphor occurs in the final scene of *Bodas de sangre* when two girls are winding a skein of red yarn. The girls' action, reminiscent of the image of the Fates controlling the life of Man, occurs in the play at the time when fate cuts the thread of life of Leonardo and El Novio. Lorca's image of the red yarn, however, does not linger at an "elevated" metaphorical level, because, 1) it is placed in the context of a domestic setting consisting of a natural activity engaged in by young girls of that time and 2) it appears naturally in the context of a song whose imagistic content ("roja," "jazmín," "laurel," "heridas," "cuchillo") is a natural outgrowth of imagery continuities previously organized into a metaphorical structure adapting itself to changing dramatic contexts.

As one follows the development of Lorca's theater, it becomes apparent that although Calderón provides Lorca with a model for incorporating metaphorical language into an unfolding drama, Lorca emphasizes the dramatic rather than the thematic possibilities of a metaphor. That is, Lorca stresses the human rather than the cosmic level of imagery. Perlimplín gives a "human" soul to Belisa who laments the absence of "el joven de la capa roja;" Doña Rosita is a withering flower in a domestic setting; and the dark waters in *Bodas de sangre* are engaged in an ominous struggle with a horse in the context of a child's lullaby. Although Calderón also presents key images that radiate through a text, he does not give them the same role to play in a drama. Calderón's images in the *autos*, for example, function basically in a larger-than-life context. Lorca's imagery, even when steeped in ideas pertaining to human destiny, are rooted in dramatic contexts at a human level.

In writing about the human dimension in Lorca's theater, Lázaro-Carreter explains Lorca's desire to put himself in contact with the people and to be true to popular means of expression. While Lorca endeavors to embrace human conflict of general dimensions, he stays within concrete, truthful social boundaries.[109] This is basically what Lorca says in one of his lectures on theater.[110]

The use of fused and expanding images by both Calderón and Lorca, and their role within the total structure of a play, can be seen in the following examples drawn from both playwrights. In the first act of *La vida es sueño*, Segismundo laments:

> Nace el ave, y con las galas
> que le dan belleza suma,
> apenas es flor de pluma,
> o ramillete con alas
> cuando las etéreas salas
> corta con velocidad,
> negándose a la piedad
> del nido que deja en calma:
> ¿y teniendo yo más alma,
> tengo menos libertad?[111]

In this passage, Calderón, by accumulating interlocking images associated with earth and sky (with "flor de pluma" as their focal point), takes the bird from its nest and gives it soaring flight, thereby creating an expanded image that, through contrast, serves to heighten Segismundo's frustration. Blended images ("flor de pluma," "ramillete con alas") form a vivid mental picture to illustrate Segismundo's thoughts. The imagery here, however, is static in the sense that the bird in this passage is an isolated element of a series ("el bruto," "el pez," "el arroyo") used by Calderón to *describe* Segismundo's mental and physical state. Within the confines of the passage, the bird image expands; but its effect serves the moment as an illustration. Although there are more bird images in the play (in Act II, for example, Clotaldo uses an eagle, "la reina de las aves," as an example of majesty when speaking to Segismudo), they also are illustrations rather than components of an imagistic continuity through which the drama is expressed at various stages in its development.

Lorca also employs the process of expanding images to embrace thematic material, yet during the course of a drama he gives them space to develop in such a way that they form a current of interactions that move in the direction of the action of the characters. In other words, there are imagery "continuities" (a term used by Brower in speaking of *The Tempest*) that relate the metaphorical language to the changing conditions in the dramatic line of the play. When El Tío tells Rosita at the close of Act II of *Doña Rosita* that he has cut the only remaining "rosa mudable" while it was still red and that if he had waited two hours more, "te la hubiese dado blanca" (1411), the red-white dichotomy in the rose image expresses what is transpiring at the human level of the drama. Fifteen years have passed, and Rosita, like the flower, is on the verge of turning white and withering. Further, the preservation of the flower ironically has depended on the fact that it was cut off from its life source—an image that lingers momentarily to fuse with a sea image that follows immediately to conclude the act:

Y aquel dulzor sutil
de mi ilusión fatal
a la luz de la luna
lo viste naufragar (1411)

The association between a severed rose and a shipwrecked illusion sustains a continuity in the metaphorical language expressing the protagonist's gradual awareness of the loss of hope with the passage of time.

In comparing Calderón and Lorca, we offer a final example in "light" as a component of imagery used by both playwrights. To follow the course of light in Calderón's *auto*, *La vida es sueño* is to follow a dialectical process between it and its arch enemy darkness in their struggle to control Man. When harmony is finally restored and Luz declares "Yo, a que siempre en mi Luz tenga / auxilios que le iluminen,"[112] the epic struggle is resolved. The symbolic nature of the characters has been preserved. Although their fortunes varied during the course of the drama, their allegorical function, supported by the metaphorical language, remained constant. To follow light through the first half of Act III of *Bodas de sangre* is to see not only the presence of death in the spectral light of the moon, but also lovers desperately seeking darkness as an escape into a world in which nothing exists except the love that inexorably draws them together. Thus, the light-darkness continuity parallels the hope-despair fluctuations that La Novia and Leonardo experience.

In summary, what emerges in comparing and contrasting Calderonian and Lorquian imagery in the theater is the sense that both poets as playwrights saw the dramatic possibilities of symbol and metaphor but from different points of view. What sometimes appears as cosmic in one becomes human and personal in the other. Nevertheless, the formalized structure of imagery in the Golden Age dramatist serves as background which helps set in relief the role of imagery in theater as conceived by an author of poetic drama in the twentieth century.

Notes

1. Virginia Higginbotham, *The Comic Spirit of Federico García Lorca* (Austin: Univ. of Texas Press, 1976), p.20.
2. Felicia Hardison Londré, *Federico Garcia Lorca* (New York: Frederick Ungar Publishing Co., 1984), pp.5, 12.
3. Bettina Knapp, *Maurice Maeterlinck* (Boston: Twayne, 1975), p.76.
4. *The Heritage of Symbolism* (London: Macmillan and Co., 1943), p.194.
5. Patricia W. O'Connor, *Gregorio and María Martínez Sierra* (Boston: Twayne, 1977), pp.32, 21.
6. Introduction to *The Cradle Song and Other Plays* by G. Martínez Sierra (New York: E.P. Dutton and Co., 1929), p.xviii.
7. Katherine Worth, *The Irish Drama of Europe from Yeats to Beckett* (Atlantic Heights, N.J.: Hamilton Press, 1978), p.24.
8. *Symbolisme from Poe to Mallarmé*, 2nd ed. (New York: Gordian Press, 1970), p.58.
9. W.B. Yeats, *Ideas of Good and Evil*. (New York: Russell and Russell, 1967), p.255.
10. "La imagen poética de don Luis de Góngora," in *Obras completas*, ed. Arturo del Hoyo, 12th ed. (Madrid: Aguilar, 1966), p.71.
11. Kermode, p.85.
12. Worth, pp.46, 61, 146.
13. "Charla García Lorca-Pablo Neruda," in *Obras completas*, ed. Arturo del Hoyo, 12th ed. (Madrid: Aguilar, 1966), p.146.
14. "Apuntes sobre el teatro de García Lorca," in *Federico García Lorca*, ed. Ildefonso-Manuel Gil (Madrid: Taurus Ediciones, 1973), pp.276-277.
15. "Introducción" to *Teatro I*. By Federico García Lorca (Madrid: Akal Editor, 1980), pp.17, 58-59.
16. *From Baudelaire to Surrealism* (New York: Wittenborn, Schultz, 1950), pp.6, 7, 124, 354.

17. Edward Engelberg, Introduction to *The Symbolist Poem* (New York: E.P. Dutton and Co., 1967), p.39.
18. Chiari, pp.37-38, 104, 120, 124, 145.
19. Engelberg, pp.39-40.
20. Arthur Symons, *The Symbolist Movement in Literature*, rev. ed. 1919 (New York: E.P. Dutton and Co., 1958), p.5.
21. *Ecos antiguos, estructuras nuevas y mundo primario de la lírica de Lorca* (Bahia Blanca: Cuadernos del Sur [Univ. Nacional del Sur], 1967), pp.12-13.
22. Roque Esteban Scarpa, *El dramatismo en la poesía de Federico García Lorca* (Santiago de Chile: Editorial Universitaria, 1961), pp.58, 71, 94.
23. "Teoría y juego del duende," in *Obras completas*, p.118.
24. "Imaginación, inspiración, evasión" in *Obras completas*, p.86.
25. Chiari, p.47.
26. Marie Laffranque, *Les idées esthétiques de Federico García Lorca* (Paris: Centres de recherches hispaniques; Institut d'études hispaniques, 1967), p.105 n.103.
27. *Verlaine y los modernistas españoles* (Madrid: Editorial Gredos, 1975), pp.44, 64, 68, 71, 166, 168, 182, 222, 250.
28. "La imagen poética de don Luis de Góngora," in *Obras completas*, p.65-66, 73.
29. "La imagen poética de don Luis de Góngora," in *Obras completas*, p.69.
30. "La imagen poética de don Luis de Góngora," in *Obras completas*, p.81.
31. André Belamich, *Lorca* (Paris: Éditions Gallimard, 1962), p.112.
32. Miguel García-Posada, *Lorca: Interpretación de "Poeta en Nueva York,"* (Madrid: Akal Editor, 1981), p.326.
33. Rafael Ferreres, *Verlaine y los modernistas españoles* (Madrid: Editorial Gredos, 1975), p.37.
34. "Imaginación, inspiración, evasión," in *Obras completas*, p.86.
35. "La imagen poética de don Luis de Góngora," in *Obras completas*, p.80.
36. E.M. Wilson, Introduction to *The Solitudes of Don Luis de Góngora* (Cambridge: The Minority Press, 1931), p.xii.
37. R.O. Jones, *A Literary History of Spain: The Golden Age Prose and Poetry* (London: Ernest Benn, 1971), p.153.
38. *Poesía y estilo de Pablo Neruda*, 3rd ed. (Buenos Aires: Editorial Sudamericana, 1966), pp.220, 222.
39. *Metaphor and Reality* (Bloomington: Indiana Univ. Press, 1962), p.72 ff.
40. *From Baudelaire to Surrealism*, pp.35, 287.
41. "The Metaphors of Luis de Góngora," *Publications of Univ. of Penn.* 25 (1933), p.90.

42. "Claridad y belleza de las *Soledades*", in *Soledades de Góngora* (Madrid: Revista de Occidente, 1927, p.15.

43. *Ecos antiguos, estructuras nuevas y mundo primario de la lírica de Lorca*, p.33.

Ramos-Gil summarizes: "Lenguaje e inspiración corren parejos. No se trata de un repertorio de emblemas o de eufemismos ilustradores del tema; nos hallamos ante una especie de rito o magia verbal, en el que la palabra-símbolo de múltiples resonancias en las misma gama—se funde con la situación y se convierte en elemento autónomo. Esto es más visible en las poesías insertas en su teatro." (33)

44. "Claridad y belleza de las Soledades," p.21.

45. "La imagen poética de don Luis de Góngora," in *Obras completas*, p.68. Among others, Lorca cites these examples from Góngora: "verdes voces," "Del verde margen otra, las mejores / rosas traslada y lirios al cabello, / o por lo matizado, o por lo bello / si aurora no con rayos sol con flores."

46. *Ecos antiguos, estructuras nuevas y mundo primario de la lírica de Lorca*, p.55.

47. *Lorca: interpretacíon de "Poeta en Nueva York"*, p.101.

48. "*Don Perlimplín:* Lorca's Theater-Poetry," *Kenyon Review*, 17, No. 3 Summer 1955, pp.343-345.

49. "El poeta García Lorca y su *Romancero gitano*," in Entrevistas y declaraciones in *Obras completas*, p.1805.

50. Among those who refer to Lorca and the ballad tradition are: García-Posada, *Lorca: interpretación de "Poeta en Nueva York"*, p.230.

William J. Entwistle, *European Balladry* (Oxford: Clarendon Press, 1939), p.187.

Francis Fergusson, *The Human Image in Dramatic Literature* (New York: Doubleday Anchor Books, 1957), p.88.

Edwin Honig, *García Lorca* (Norfolk, Conn.: New Directions Books, 1944), p.210.

Ramos-Gil, *Ecos antiguos*, p.17., also in *Claves líricas de García Lorca* (Madrid: Aguilar, 1967), p.230.

Juan Luis Alborg, *Historia de la literatura española*, 2nd ed. (Madrid: Editorial Gredos, 1966), I, p.241.

Roy Campbell, *Lorca* (New York: Haskell House Publishers, 1970), pp.12-13.

Warren Carrier, "Poetry in Drama of Lorca," *Drama Survey*, 2, No.3 (Feb. 1963), p.299.

51. Donald F. Fogelquist, *Juan Ramón Jíménez* (Boston: Twayne, 1976), pp. 41-42, 79.

52. Beverly DeLong, "Sobre el desarrollo lorquiano del romance tradicional," *Hispanófila*, No. 35 (Jan., 1969), p.56.

53. William J. Entwistle, *European Balladry* (Oxford: Clarendon Press, 1939), p.153.

54. "Tragic Themes in Spanish Ballads," in his *Spanish and English Literature of the 16th and 17th Centuries* (Cambridge: Cambridge Univ. Press, 1980), p.222.

55. Ramón Menéndez Pidal, *Flor nueva de romances viejos*, 16th ed. (Buenos Aires: Espasa-Calpe Argentina, 1967), pp.16, 24.
56. Margit Frenk Alatorre, *Cancionero de romances viejos*, 2nd ed. (México: Dirección General de Publicaciones, 1972), pp.xxxviii-xxxix.
57. DeLong, pp.51-52.
58. *European Balladry*, pp.25, 154, 156, 159.
59. *Flor nueva de romances viejos que recogió de la traadición antigua y moderna R. Menéndez Pidal* (Madrid: Tip. de la "Revista de archivos, bibliotecas y museos," 1928), p.30.
60. García-Posada, "Introducción" to *Teatro*, I. pp.17, 28.
61. "Lope de Vega en un teatro nacional," in Entrevistas y declaraciones in *Obras completas*, p.1749, 1750.
62. Edwin Honig, *García Lorca* (Norfolk, Conn.: New Directions Books, 1944), p.109.
63. Entwistle, p.186.
François Nourissier, *F. García Lorca, dramaturge* (Paris: l'Arche, éditeur, 1955), p.32.
J.B. Trend, *Lorca and the Spanish Poetic Tradition* (New York: Russell and Russell, 1971), p.168.
64. "The Exemplary Nature of *El caballero de Olmedo*," in his *Spanish and English Literature of the 16th and 17th Centuries*, p.190.
65. García-Posada, "Introducción" to *Teatro*, I, pp.62-63.
66. Lázaro Carreter, "Apuntes sobre el teatro de García Lorca," in *Federico García Lorca*, ed. Ildefonso-Manuel Gil (Madrid: Taurus Ediciones, 1973), p.278.
67. "Un fin de fiesta montado con un sello artístico," in Entrevistas y declaraciones in *Obras completas*, p.1741.
68. *Federico García Lorca*, (Madrid: Edaf, D.L., 1979), p.121.
69. *The Fields of Light* (New York: Oxford Univ. Press, 1962), p.119.
70. García-Posada writes in *Lorca: interpretación de "Poeta en Nueva York"*; "Símbolo y metáfora, metáfora y símbolo como rasgos dominantes: he aquí la gran síntesis que el lenguaje poético lorquiano lleva a cabo." (326)
71. "Un teatro en nuestro tiempo," in Entrevistas y declaraciones in *Obras completas*, p.1767.
72. Ricardo Arias, in the preface to *The Spanish Sacramental Plays* (Boston: Twayne, 1980), describes *autos sacramentales* as one act plays that are sermons written for the stage. They are in theological praise of a religious feast. A large number of *autos* have the Eucharist as their theme; and in them, theological questions are dramatized. "The logic of the *autos*," writes Arias, "is the logic of faith." (2, 3 of Preface).
73. "Introducción" to *Teatro*, I, pp.28-29.
74. *Lorca, the Theater Beneath the Sand* (London: Marion Boyars, 1980), p.23.
75. *García Lorca*, p.109.

76. "The Implicit Craft of the Spanish 'comedia'", in *Studies in Spanish Literature of the Golden Age Presented to Edward M. Wilson*, ed. R.O. Jones (London: Tamesis Books, 1973), p.342

77. "Góngora and Calderón," *Hispanic Review*, V (1937), pp.241, 244-248.

78. "The Four Elements in the Imagery of Calderón," in *Modern Language Review*, XXXI (1936), p.43.

79. Heinz Gerstinger, *Pedro Calderón de la Barca*, trans. Diana Stone Peters (New York: Frederick Ungar Publications Co., 1973), pp.21-22, 29, 44, 86.

80. Sister Francis de Salas McGarry, *The Allegorical and Metaphorical Language in the Autos Sacramentales of Calderón* (Wash. D.C., The Catholic Univ. of America, 1937), pp.50-61, 110, 115, 130.

81. "Calderón's Dramatic Poetry," in his *Spanish and English Literature of the 16th and 17th Centuries*, p.124.

82. "Charla sobre teatro," in *Obras completas*, p.150.

83. Bettina Knapp. *Maurice Maeterlinck*. (Boston: Twayne, 1975), p.175.

84. Katherine Worth, *The Irish Drama of Europe from Yeats to Beckett*. (Atlantic Heights, N.J., Humanities Press, 1978), p.96.

85. Concha Zardoya, "*Mariana Pineda*, romance trágico de la libertad," *Revista Hispánica Moderna*, 34 (1968), pp.489, 493.

86. Robert Barnes, "The Fusion of Poetry and Drama in *Blood Wedding*," *Modern Drama*, 2, No. 4 (1960), p.395.

87. *Symbolisme from Poe to Mallarmé*, p.38.

88. Francis Fergusson, *"Don Perlimplín"* Lorca's Theater Poetry," in *Lorca: A Collection of Critical Essays*, ed. Manuel Durán (Englewood Cliffs, N.J.: Prentice-Hall, 1962), p.171.

89. Zardoya, p.474.

90. *The Line in the Margin* (Madison, Wisconsin: The Univ. of Wisconsin Press, 1980), p.183.

91. C.M. Bowra, *The Heritage of Symbolism* (London: Macmillan, 1943), pp.5, 9.

92. "La nueva obra de García Lorca," in Entrevistas y declaraciones in *Obras completas*, p.1739.

93. "Galería, Federico García Lorca," in Entrevistas y declaraciones in *Obras completas*, p.1771.

94. "Art poétique," in *Oeuvres poétiques complètes*, ed. Jacques Borel (Paris: Éditions Gallimard, 1962), p.327.

95. All page numbers within parentheses that refer to *El maleficio de la mariposa* are from the following text: Federico García Lorca, *El maleficio de la mariposa*, in *Obras completas*, ed. Arturo del Hoyo, 12th ed. (Mardrid: Aguilar, 1966), pp.669-721.

96. James R. Lawler, *Form and Meaning in Valéry's "Le Cimetière marin"* (Carlton, Melbourne Univ. Press, 1960), p.39.

97. "La imagen poética de don Luis de Góngora," in *Obras completas*, p.81.

98. All page numbers within parentheses that refer to *Doña Rosita la soltera* are from the following text: Federico García Lorca, *Doña Rosita la soltera*, in *Obras completas*, ed. Arturo del Hoyo, 12th ed. (Madrid: Aguilar, 1966), pp.1351-1438.

99. "The Fusion of Poetry and Drama in *Blood Wedding*," *Modern Drama*, 2, No. 4 (1960), p.400.

100. *Ecos antiguos, estructuras nuevas y mundo primario de la lírica de Lorca*, pp.10, 58.

101. *El adjetivo de la lírica de Federico García Lorca* (Barcelona: Editorial Ariel, 1973), p.86.

102. Dámaso Alonso in "Claridad y belleza de las *Soledades*," p.15.

103. *Lorca: interpretación de "Poeta en Nueva York*," p.214.

104. "Romance de don Tristán," in *Flor nueva de romances que recogió de la tradición antigua y moderna R. Menéndez Pidal*)Madrid: Tip de la "Revista de archivos bibliotecas y museos," 1928, pp.73-74.

105. *European Balladry*, pp.186-187.

106. "Apuntes sobre el teatro de García Lorca," in *Federico García Lorca*, ed. Ildefonso-Manuel Gil (Madrid: Taurus Ediciones, 1973), p.278.

107. All page numbers within parentheses that refer to *Amor de don Perlimplín con Belisa en su jardín* are from the following text: Federico García Lorca, *Amor de don Perlimplín con Belisa en su jardín*, in *Obras completas*, ed. Arturo del Hoyo, 12th ed. (Madrid: Aguilar, 1966), pp.979-1018.

108. Lope de Vega, *El caballero de Olmedo*, ed. Francisco Rico, 6th ed. (Madrid: Ediciones Cátedra, 1985), p.197.

109. "Apuntes sobre el teatro de García Lorca," pp.281, 283.

110. "Charla sobre teatro," in *Obras completas*, p.150.

111. Pedro Calderón de la Barca, *La vida es sueño*, ed. Evangelina Rodríguez Cuandros, 8ª ed. Colección Austral (Madrid: Espasa-Calpe, 1987), pp.61-62.

112. *La vida es sueño: drama y auto sacramental*, ed. José María Valverde (Barcelona: Planeta, 1981), p.181.

Chapter 2
Lorquian Image Criticism

Critics have scrutinized images in Lorca's plays primarily as manifestations of themes or as symbols of the psyche of individual characters. The moon represents death or the unavoidable fate of man. Water symbolizes fecundity; thirst means sexual frustration, and a horse symbolizes sexual potency. Whiteness is interpreted as a veneer of perfection, and light symbolizes fruitfulness. Those who have studied Lorca's imagery tend to isolate a theme and then discuss a play's imagery as confirmation of its theme, rather than viewing the images as part of an on-going metaphorical "narrative" that recalls, underscores and foreshadows events in a drama. In other words, the critics' approach has generally been symbolic and thematic rather than dramatic. Although some have isolated imagistic leitmotifs and thereby alluded to and given examples of dynamic imagery, few have traced specific components of imagery throughout a play, relating images to each other and to the dramatic contexts of the unfolding conflict. In Lorquian studies, therefore, little attention is given to the manner in which continuities in the metaphorical language infuse the dialogue with what Brower calls "felt qualities." This is the aspect of imagery that makes us "feel the peculiar quality of what is taking place" as characters express their desires, illusions, ideals and dreams while following the dictates of their imagination.

In numerous studies by critics who maintain that Lorca's imagery in the theater reaffirms thematic content, two themes emerge as predominant frameworks for poetry in Lorca's theatrical output: 1) society versus the individual and 2) fantasy as a counterpoint to reality. Within these categories, one can include thematic variations such as an authority-liberty opposition and love that essentially takes the form of a dream of love which never becomes reality. Also the imagination is frequently singled out as an important means by which Lorca's characters seek to effect their escape from intolerable circumstances.

By turning our attention first to several critics who stress thematics and then to several who lead images in the direction of drama, we will arrive at the threshold of our study.

In an analysis of *Yerma*, Calvin Cannon stresses the symbolic nature of Lorca's images as they relate to the fundamental tension of the play. Lázaro Carreter explores the theme of authority versus liberty, and Ramos-Gil and Rafael Martínez Nadal see in Lorca's plays an opposition between reality and imagination. All of these approaches view imagery basically in terms of thematics. They do not explore imagery from the point of view of its symbiotic relationship to on-going dramatic contexts.

Cannon finds that the imagery of *Yerma* is an expression of the basic tragic tension of the play.[1] In *Yerma*, according to Cannon, images of lightness-darkness, water-dryness, and flowering and withering are directed towards the conflict between fruitfulness and barrenness that leads ultimately to Yerma's tragedy. Although Cannon does include situations in which images directly relate to the action of the drama, he stresses the dynamics of the imagery at a thematic rather than a dramatic level by underscoring the symbolic nature of the imagery. The sun, for example, symbolizes virility and penetrates the earth; fire represents eroticism and creativity; a woman with child is a woman with light; and María, whose child is a "palomo de lumbre," is a symbol of the Virgin Mary (122-125). Cannon, summarizing, says that the leading images state the fundamental issue of the tragedy: the barrenness of a woman in a Nature commanding fruitfulness (130). Thus, Cannon views this drama as if it were a poem with images presented in such a way that an overall static design can be discerned.

Sometimes Cannon straddles what we have been calling dynamic and static imagery when he comments on Lorca's ability to use one image to evoke another. For example, when the chorus prays "Señor que florezca la rosa, / no me dejéis en sombra," Cannon indicates that Yerma again is reminded of the light of birth and her earlier dream of a child in white. Also, when the Macho exclaims during his dance "¡Venid a ver la lumbre / de la que se bañaba!," light and water imagery are united in a dramatic reaffirmation of the fundamental tragic tension of the play (126-127). Yet Cannon's approach repeatedly stresses theme over dynamics. He points to examples of images of light and darkness, but never to instances of light *becoming* darkness as Yerma moves from hope to despair. The image of the luminous impregnation of the woman remains at the thematic level of the play as Yerma remains barren. Cannon stresses the verbal "statements" made by patterns of imagery as they "confirm and express" the basic tension of the play, instead of seeing them as additional or phantom characters playing a role in a subtext that parallels the evolving human relationships in the drama.

Lázaro Carreter places Lorca's theater within the general framework of the individual versus society—an approach taken by several other Lorquian critics.[2] For Lázaro Carreter, individuals in Lorca's plays are trapped in a society so diversified through political action that they become separated from the spiritual roots that nourish their individuality.[3] The critic clearly states that Lorca was never a politically "engagé" writer, but one who placed general problems of the human condition in specific milieus. According to Lázaro Carreter, Lorca's characters struggle within the context of man's destiny being controlled by fate, as evidenced by the presence of "la afirmación explícita del 'fatum'" in Lorca's theater beginning with *Mariana Pineda* and continuing onward to *Bodas de sangre*, *Yerma*, *Doña Rosita* and *La casa de Bernarda Alba* (273, 281, 284). What is particularly significant about Lázaro Carreter's point of view is his statement about the *manner* in which Lorca represents his ideas in the theater: "Nuestro gran poeta procede en el teatro y en la lírica, del modernismo" (276). This suggests a trajectory in the development of Lorca's techniques that makes important points of contact with our study.

When one combines Lázaro Carreter's belief that Lorca's characters are individuals trapped by society with his tenet that Lorca produced a modernista drama in *Mariana Pineda*, there emerges a view of Lorca's theater that spans a thematic and poetic trajectory reaching from Lorca's first success in the theater as far as, but not including, *La casa de Bernarda Alba*. Lázaro Carreter's exclusion of Lorca's final play can be explained by the fact that his general observations pertaining to both the poetic and dramatic aspects of Lorca's theater tend to place the poetry outside the dramatic conflict. In other words, the tendency is to view the poetry as "arias;" as an adjunct or adornment; as a counterbalance to the prose; as an intensifier of the conflict; as a creator of atmosphere; as "rupturas líricas del proceso drámatico." We, on the other hand, "hear" Lorca's poetry as if it emanated from an inner voice structuring images in such a way that in their interrelationships they express the dynamics of the human relationships. The latter is a process that Lorca begins to develop in *El maleficio de la mariposa* within the general framework of Symbolist theater and realizes fully in *La casa de Bernarda Alba* where the poetry is a less visible but important part of the expression of drama. An image such as dew in *El maleficio de la mariposa* (symbolizing love and evanescence and Curianito's attempt to grasp the elusive butterfly) already begins to play a role in the metaphorical language—a process that Lorca perfected with images such as those of heat and water through which the tensions of Bernarda Alba's daughters are expressed.

Lázaro Carreter's position does relate to the idea that Lorca's characters are frequently overcome by a desire to escape, but it does not stress the process and action that the word "escape" implies. This differs from our approach to thematics as they pertain to Lorca's imagery. In the plays we will discuss, many images are attached to the idea of escape—escape from a reality that the mind perceives as setting limits on the imagination. The element of escape not only bridges the authority-liberty, reality-fantasy points of view but also suggests that movement is involved in the activities of both the real world and that of the imagination—an idea that is crucial to the dynamics of imagery in Lorca's poetic theater.

The second major thematic line that is important to the shape of many of Lorca's imagery continuities consists of tension between fantasy and reality. Important comments by Ramos-Gil include the following: "La recreación popular de Lorca está hecha desde dentro;" "Lo peculiar al cantor [de las canciones populares] queda en la penumbra;" "El acierto de Lorca fue intuir aquella *intra-vida* en el canto de resonancias milenarias."[4] In a later essay entitled "Hacia una revisión del teatro loquiano," Ramos-Gil reiterates his basic position: "La aventura teatral de Lorca será, pues, una gradual aproximación, una comunión con la existencia, que haga tangible, cuando no concilie, el angustiado encuentro del ensueño y la realidad."[5] Nevertheless, within the context of "el anhelo de trascender las fronteras de lo humano" (a characteristic implied in statements made by others who have carefully observed Lorca's theater[6]), Ramos-Gil keeps Lorca's imagery at the symbolic level. Except for several instances such as the song of the washerwomen in *Yerma*, Ramos-Gil does not expand imagery to include its dramatic potential during the course of an entire drama. The moon is associated with fecundity in *Yerma* and with eroticism in *Bodas de sangre*. With respect to the latter, Ramos-Gil writes that the intervention of the moon serves to stimulate passion and desire in order to impel the conflictive characters toward their doom.[7] Similarly, "el río" ("orilla," "ribera," "juncos") is a symbol of eroticism, as exemplified by Adela's comment in *La casa de Bernarda Alba*: "El me lleva a los juncos de la orilla" (111). For Ramos-Gil, images are not engaged in an on-going dynamic interaction that parallels action in the evolving drama.

The conflict between imagination and the reality of life is also the thrust of Martínez Nadal's analysis of love as a vital force in the theater of Lorca.[8] If one is bent on examining the way Lorca manipulates images to show that a character is struggling to escape a repressive reality, Martínez Nadal's inclusion of a "polivalencia de símbolos" (p.208) is very important; and his analysis of the movement of the "caballo" image in *El Público* and *Bodas de sangre* (213-218) especially reveals the potentially dynamic role of an image in the representation of conflict. However, by not including other images that assume symbolic quality, Martínez Nadal minimizes the importance of the dynamic interplay of symbols in the playwright's metaphorical language.

Turning our attention from critics who have focused on the relationship between Lorca's metaphorical language and over-arching themes, we observe that others have indeed directed imagery towards dramatic involvement. However, they too fall short of our own approach to imagery continuities.

García-Posada sets Lorca's imagery in the direction of drama when he calls Lorca a great poet of metaphor. According to García-Posada, Lorca often spoke about the fusion of the lyrical and the narrative in his *romances* and always exhibited a tendency towards dramatization.[9] A significant clue to the mobility of Lorquian images in the theater is García-Posada's designation of a "polivalencia textual del símbolo" (whose prevalence he notices especially in *Poeta en Nueva York*) (108). Multiple connotations permit symbolic language to adapt itself to various stages of interaction among the characters. Referring specifically to *Bodas de sangre*, García-Posada cies the significant role of the symbol of the horse in the development of the drama. Early on, the horse is associated with Leonardo, and its galloping resounds through the work, from the beginning to the end.[10] Although García-Posada indicates that symbolic images "follow" characters through a play, he does not explore the symbiotic relationship between poetry and drama that results when imagery is consistently engaged in reflecting the action of the play as it unfolds.

The difference between imagery that employs symbols statically rather than dynamically can be seen in the manner in which two critics view Lorca's manipulation of the horse as a symbol in *Bodas de sangre*. According to Rupert Allen, the horse works symbolically on two levels. It is a solar horse that bears a day rider (El Novio) bringing fertility, and a night horse with a night rider (Leonardo) bringing sexual power and death to the drama.[11] Although Allen does relate the horse to other components of the drama (Leonardo, for example, is associated with the night horse of the lullaby), the reference is static. It refers to the general outline of the drama and does not move the horse through the unfolding temporal and dramatic space of the play. Even though Allen points out that the *nana* is simultaneously a lullaby and a description of Leonardo's activities and his fate, he does not connect the song directly to the stage in the development of the action at the time the *nana* occurs. Juan Villegas, on the other hand, makes contact with our study in an article entitled "El leitmotiv del caballo en *Bodas de sangre*. Villegas first articulates the importance of the dynamics of Lorca's imagery and then traces the dynamic quality of the multiple appearances of the horse as a recurrent symbol in *Bodas de sangre*:

> La abundante bibliografía acerca de la producción literaria de Lorca ha comprobado la importancia de los símbolos, motivos y mitos. . . . Tan importante como establecer los vínculos literarios y extraliterarios de este rasgo lorquiano, es examinar la función dramática o poética de cada uno de ellos en obras individuales. Estas conforman un mundo en sí. . . . El símbolo no vale por sí mismo sino que tiene sentido en cuanto forma parte del cosmos creado con la obra literaria en particular.[12]

For Villegas, the horse of the lullaby is a symbol of the horse-rider continuity throughout the play. He points out the number of times a horse is mentioned and associated with Leonardo and relates the appearance of this symbol to Leonardo's progression through the action of the play. In other words, the horse image appears in various contexts to reflect Leonardo's movement—from a state of containment and suffering in the first act, through his steps in the second act either to carry out or abandon his purpose with respect to La Novia and then to the ensuing violence in the third act (22-34). Thus, the symbol moves dynamically through the imagery and follows the course of the character with whom it has a symbiotic relationship. Villegas states that in Lorca's dramas, symbols are not static. They are related to the evolving action, accumulating nuances that have a purposeful function in the total structure (22). In our view, the foregoing observation is a confirmation that Lorca went beyond Symbolist theater to unite poetry and drama through images that recur not only to deepen one's impression of a character but also to reflect or express movement or a change in the character's thoughts and behavior. Villegas, however, does not further his argument by including other images, nor does he establish a trajectory that shows the evolution of Lorca's technique from the earliest to the final plays.

Writing about the theater of his brother Federico, Francisco García Lorca not only articulates a very important idea with which our study agrees, but also confronts critics of Lorca's plays with a challenge that we address. In the words of Francisco García Lorca: "And yet the overevaluation of *Bernarda Alba* in relation to the poet's other works is easy to explain. For one thing, it is a final point of reference. People have always seen in it something like the rectification of a poetical vision of the theater, and a step toward the type of realism that has come to be considered appropriate to 'normal' theater, theater *par excellence*, as opposed to 'poetic theater.' *Bernarda Alba* would be the final triumph of the playwright over the poet. To me this means that neither *Bernarda Alba* nor the rest of García Locra's theater has been properly understood."[13] We agree. García Lorca's theater is not a struggle between a playwright and a poet, but rather the evolution of a playwright who is also a poet. According to Francisco, however, "Those who study Federico's theater with the false idea of evolution will have to explain exactly how *Doña Rosita* can be the work that comes immediately before *The House of Bernarda Alba* and how the latter work could conceivably have announced the form of the theater that was to have followed. The continuous change and unified style of Federico's theater can only be explained by carefully studying his language, the technique of his dialogues, and the way he manipulates time, space, and other basic elements of theater" (p.233). Our study is precisely an analysis of the evolution of the way Lorca uses language, specifically in imagery, to create dialogues that make *La casa de Bernarda Alba* a product of tiny seeds planted as early as *El maleficio de la mariposa* and cultivated and nurtured in later plays, including *Doña Rosita la soltera*. The sounds, color and light that Francisco García Lorca traces thematically through *Bernarda Alba* resonate with Lorca's earlier use of sounds, color and light embedded in dialogues to reveal specific movements in drama.

As we have already stated, most critics approach Lorca's imagery through themes and symbols. Even in studies that open a wider view onto Lorca's imagery—studies by Sandra Cary Robertson, Dennis A. Klein, Antonio Cao, Virginia Higginbotham and C.B. Morris, to name a few— the scope of observation with respect to the on-going dynamics of the imagery is limited. Robertson rightly associates rain with tears in Acts II and III of *Mariana Pineda*;[14] but the observation is fleeting. Robertson does not explore the *intensification* of the rain-tears-sadness *continuity* in this play—a continuity that parallels the cumulative emotional stress that Mariana experiences. However, with respect to the opening *nana* of *Bodas de sangre* (pp.202-213), Robertson observes an important continuity in Lorca's imagery. Like Martínez Nadal[15], Robertson provides an excellent analysis of the role of the horse (introduced in the Act I *nana*) in the development of the drama. Noting the poetic opposition between "el agua," or the forces of "la sangre," and "el caballo," Robertson observes an evocation of this counterpoint when La Novia, in the final pages of the drama, describes Leonardo as "un río oscuro, lleno de ramas" (pp.202-213). However, in Robertson's analysis, the *nana* is presented in terms of a "forecasted tragedy," isolated and viewed as a play within a play. Both "plays" are seen as separate entities, with the *nana* summarizing, in effect, the longer play. The reader is not led in the direction of on-the-spot observation of the pulse of the drama that has already been set in motion through imagery. For Robertson, the horse of the lullaby becomes the central symbol of the play (p.211); but what Lorca does with the "symbol" as it interacts with other images throughout the drama is left essentially unexplored.

Klein touches upon the dynamics of Lorca's imagery, especially in *La casa de Bernarda Alba*. For example, when Adela questions the significance that tradition ascribes to a falling star, Klein concludes that Adela actively questions and transgresses traditions when she expresses her desire to see the light of the star.[16] Similarly, when an unusual noise in the night is explained as possibly "una mulilla sin desbravar," Klein states that the "mulilla" is really the untamed Adela (p.137). Nevertheless, apart from limited examples such as those cited above, Klein's observations concerning the imagistic connotations of flowers and horses, for example, remain at the level of symbols and allusions. The images remain as static rather than dynamic components of on-going dramatic dialogue. One might say the same of Cao's observations concerning the importance of "la imagen plurivalente" in Lorca's theater. For example, Cao indicates that water that is drunk in *Bodas de sangre* assumes an erotic connotation, citing these words in La Suegra's *nana*: "Duérmete, rosal, / que el caballo se pone a llorar. / . . . / La sangre corría más furete que el agua."[17] Yet Cao's conclusion—"Este trozo lírico encierra la casi totalidad de la temática de la obra" (p.89)—rests the imagery of the play on the foundation of thematics rather than on unfolding drama.

As is the case with the above-mentioned critics, Higginbotham also offers insights into Lorca's imagery; but she also tends to comment in generalized terms rather than to open scenes to the role of imagery in the dramatic flow of events. Higginbotham observes, for example, that the silence that Bernarda Alba demands is broken by occurrences such as the tolling of bells, songs, shouts, lullabies and the blast of a shotgun.[18] But this observation concerning silence and interrupting sound takes the form of summary rather than an analysis of the relationship between the sounds and silences and the dramatic action as it occurs. A similar example of cogent Lorquian criticism that also overlooks the *dynamics* of Lorca's imagery can be taken from Morris's commentary on María Josefa's role as the most articulate character in *La casa de Bernarda Alba*.[19] Except for a brief reference (p.91) to an echo of sea imagery at the end of Act I, Morris does not invest the imagistic components of María Josefa's words with the dynamics that relate them to imagery continuities through the entire play.

In this chapter, we have indicated that Lorquian studies have explored ways in which poetry plays an important role in the theater of Lorca. All have either implicitly or explicitly stated basic themes and then, to varying degrees, analyzed the poetry through which the themes emerge. Within thematic contexts, some critics stress the role of imagery in creating mood and atmosphere. Some see images as symbols of characters, emotions and forces beyond the control of individuals. Others "hear" Lorca's poetry in the theater as lyrical or descriptive passages like arias interspersed throughout a continuous narrative. Further, several critics, by tracing the path of selected images through a play, have suggested that Lorca's theater unites poetry and drama. In these instances, however, the images are essentially symbols. Consequently, Lorquian imagery criticism does little more than bring us to the threshold of process.

We will pick up where Lorquian imagery studies leave off. When we say that "sangre" in *Bodas de sangre* is a symbol of death, violence, sex, passion and lineage, we are providing an example of what García-Posada calls "la polivalencia textual del símbolo." But when we place "sangre" in specific contexts as it makes multiple appearances in the text, we carry "la polivalencia textual del símbolo" directly into the dramatic line of the play. Therefore, in the chapters that follow, Lorca's poetic theater will be viewed from the vantage point of the dynamics of imagery rooted in specific dramatic contexts for the purpose of binding metaphorical language to the human drama as it unfolds.

Notes

1. "The Imagery of Lorca's *Yerma*," *Modern Language Quarterly*, 21 (1960), p.122.

2. François Nourissier stresses revolt as the major aspect of the theme, with death being the price of that revolt (*F. García Lorca, dramaturge* [Paris: L'Arche, éditeur, 1955], p.137). With respect to *La casa de Bernarda Alba*, J. Rubia Barcia writes: "Lo que cuenta son las reacciones colectivas" ("El realismo 'mágico' de *La casa de Bernarda Alba*," *Revista Hispánica*, 31 [1965], p.396). According to André Belamich, from *El Público* to *La casa de Bernarda Alba*, characters are adjusted to the world but are prevented by society from obtaining happiness. (*Lorca* [Paris: Éditions Gallimard, 1962], p.78).

3. "Apuntes sobre el teatro de García Lorca," in *Federico García Lorca*, ed. Ildefonso-Manuel Gil (Madrid: Taurus Ediciones, 1973), pp.273-274.

4. *Ecos antiguos, estructuras nuevas, y mundo primario de la lírica de Lorca* (Bahia Blanca: Cuadernos del Sur [Univ. Nacional del Sur] 1967), pp.20, 23, 41.

5. In *Revista de Literatura*, XLII, No. 83 Enero-Junio de 1980, p.156.

6. Marie Laffranque has stated her position thus: "A chaque étape, son [de Lorca] esthétique est résolument à l'opposé du naturalisme. . . . la poésie est pour lui 'évasion' hors d'un monde difficile à vivre, soit vers la beauté objective et construite . . ." (*Les idées esthétiques de Federico Garcéa Lorca*, [Paris: Centre de recherches hispaniques; Institut d'études hispaniques, 1967], p.314). For María Teresa Babín, Lorca's theater is an extension of his poetry ("García Lorca, poeta del teatro," *Asomante* 4, No. 2, 1948, 48), which she characterizes thus: "La homegeneidad del mundo poético de García Lorca está lograda por un esfuerzo consciente de acoplar la realidad concreta con la irrealidad soñada y misteriosa" (*Estudios lorquianos*, 1st ed. [Barcelona: Colección Mente y Palabra, 1976], p.237). And in writing about *Yerma*, Gustavo Correa states: "In *Yerma* the act of conception acquires a lyrical sublimation; the purely physiological is abandoned and conception becomes enchanted, an act of magic—something that happens between singing participants" ("Honor, Blood, and Poetry in *Yerma*," trans, Rupert C. Allen, Jr.; *Tulane Drama Review*, 7, No. 2 [Winter 1962], 105).

7. *Claves líricas de García Lorca* (Madrid: Aguilar, 1967), p.252, n.109.

8. "*El público.*" *Amor, teatro y caballos en la obra de Federico García Lorca* (Oxford: Dolphin, 1970), p.139.

"En el teatro bajo la arena," writes Martínez Nadal, "[Lorca] va a explorar las raíces humanas del drama del amor imposible . . . [El poeta] va a empezar la galería de mujeres consumidas en inútil espera . . . el conflicto constante entre la imaginación, siempre virgen, a la dura realidad de la vida que pasa." (pp.53,143)

9. *Lorca: interpretación de "Poeta en Nueva York"* (Madrid: Akal Editor, 1981), pp.93, 230, 235.

10. "Introducción" to *Teatro* I, p.71.

11. *Psyche and Symbol in the Theater of Federico García Lorca* (Austin: Univ. of Texas Press, 1974), pp.168, 178-183.

12. In *Hispanófila*, No. 29 Jan. 1967, p.34.
13. *In the Green Morning: memories of Federico*, trans. Christopher Maurer (New York: New Directions, 1980), pp. 233-234.
14. *Lorca, Alberti, and the Theater of Popular Poetry* (New York: P. Lang, 1991), pp. 158-159.
15. *"El público." Amor y muerte en la obra de Federico García Lorca*, 3ª ed., ampliada e ilustrada (Madrid: Hiperión, 1988), pp. 218-224.
16. *"Blood Wedding," "Yerma," and "The House of Bernarda Alba:" García Lorca's Tragic Trilogy* (Boston: Twayne Publishers, 1991), pp. 125-126.
17. *Federico García Lorca y las vanguardias: hacia el teatro* (London: Tamesis, 1984), pp. 89-90.
18. "Lorca's Soundtrack: Music in the Structure of his Poetry and Plays," in *"Cuando yo me muera . . .": Essays in Memory of Federico García Lorca*, ed. C.Brian Morris (Lanham, Md.: University Press of America, 1988), p.204.
19. *García Lorca: "La casa de Bernarda Alba"* (London: Grant & Cutler in association with Tamesis Books, 1990), p.117.

Chapter 3
El maleficio de la mariposa

As we have indicated, *El maleficio de la mariposa* is a symbolist play in the tradition of Maeterlinck and Yeats, but it also begins to use imagery in a manner that will characterize the later poetic dramas of Lorca. Our initial impression of the imagery in *El maleficio de la mariposa* also reminds us of the evocative quality of lines from Verlaine, Marquina and Martínez Sierra, as well as the expanding images of Góngora. That is to say, the characteristic of layering images—especially as evidenced in works by Symbolists and Modernistas—permeates *El maleficio de la mariposa*. After examining affinities that this play has with the theater of Maeterlinck and Yeats and with Symbolist poetry, our study will provide an analysis of imagery continuities in this work, pointing out the predominantly Symbolist quality of the metaphorical language and then indicating where Lorca begins to use images in a more dynamic way. Thus, we will launch the trajectory leading to a complete fusion of poetry and drama in the later plays.

Lorca's first play introduces a theme that is present, with some variation, in almost all his plays: a character feels that the world of reality does not offer the conditions that would promote the happiness that he or she envisions. This causes unbearable frustration that leads to an attempt to escape and ultimately results in death. In *El maleficio de la mariposa*, the boy insect Curianito is a poet so enamored of his idea of love and beauty that he attempts to possess his ideal which is embodied in La Mariposa, a butterfly fallen from the sky. As the young poet withdraws further into his imagination, the magic spell cast by his ideal leads him to destruction. This story can therefore be placed in the context of what Mario Praz calls the ecstasy of the exoticist who, as an exile from his own person and from the present, pursues a fatal woman who is the embodiment of love as an imaginative projection of sexual desire.[1] Like Praz who states that in the magic and mystery of Keats's "La Belle Dame sans Merci" one observes the world of the Symbolists in embryonic form (202-203), we can say that Lorca's Curianito and La Mariposa also inhabit a world of mystery and magic expressed through evocative imagery.

During Curianito's fateful pursuit of his ideal of love and beauty, poetic imagery repeatedly refers to various aspects of his plight. The basic imagery continuities are associated with dew, stars, flowers, light-darkness, flight and dreams. These components of the imagery constitute the fundamental metaphorical language through which poetry expresses the drama. Taken singly and in combination, these words assume symbolic value and underscore the protagonist's movement from a creature hopeful of embracing his love to one profoundly disillusioned. For the most part, these elements of the imagery evoke or progressively help the reader penetrate the feelings or thoughts of the characters. But after examining this aspect of the imagery that recalls the spirit of the Symbolists, we shall see that the text also reveals moments in which techniques are employed for setting images not only in thematic contexts but in dramatic ones as well, thereby giving the first indications of the direction Lorca's imagery will take in plays that follow this first attempt.

The title Lorca gave his first play is an example of the use of images for thematic purposes. The connotative meanings of "maleficio" and "mariposa" and their subtle alliteration link them in the mind of the reader in a relationship marked by tension such as that that exists in this play between death and beauty, despair and love, earth and heaven—a situation that prevails in a tale of "une belle dame sans merci" and one that recalls Cipriano's pursuit of Justina in Calderón's *El mágico prodigioso* as well as Don Félix's desire to possess the phantasmagoric Elvira in Espronceda's *El estudiante de Salamanca*. The "maleficio-mariposa" opposition also underpins the image evoked by Curianito's first words after the appearance of the butterfly ("¡Oh qué pena tan honda en el alma me siento!" [698]), thereby adding another layer to the imagery that counterpoints joy with sorrow—an opposition exemplified in Nigromántica's comment that love killed the fairy of the earth and the sea, as well as in these words she utters prior to Curianito's outburst cited above: "Dulce estrella caída de un ciprés soñoliento, / ¿Qué amarga aurora vieron tus ojos al caer?" (698).

The prologue of *El maleficio de la mariposa* introduces many of the significant words whose imagistic qualities are explored during the course of the drama. Words such as "rocío," "flores," "estrellas," "anochecer," "luz," "muerte," "amor," "visión," "poeta," and "poesía" begin to insinuate

The Dynamics of the Imagery in the Theater 53
of Federico Garcia Lorca

themselves into the consciousness of the reader. Thus we are led to the entrance of a magical world of the senses inhabited by insects whose movements and perceptions, by dint of their living so close to the earth, have the effect of transforming a world of fantasy into a heightened awareness of the fate of living creatures in a down-to-earth environment.

The prologue of *El maleficio de la mariposa* sets the tone and mood of the play. Here we are introduced to the poet and his desire to transcend reality by bringing to life what is present in his imagination. In effect, Lorca engages Curianito in what John Porter Houston calls objectifying subjectivity or (referring specifically to Yeats) communicating an "état d'âme."[2] By extrapolating from Houston (32, 40), one could say that for Curianito, love and beauty occupy that transcendental place where being is at once "sensible but impalpable." Curianito uses images that give his consciousness imaginative flight in the contemplation of that ideal love. The fact that his desire is linked to disaster recalls Valéry's "La Jeune Parque" where the youngest of the Fates serves as a symbol of the poet's mind: "Je scintelle, liée à ce ciel inconnu . . . L'immense grappe brille à ma soif de désâstre."[3] In Lorca's play, Curianito, the embodiment of poetry, will "reach for the moon." His imagination leads him to seek something beyond the world of his fellow creatures who live as close to the earth as possible. Thus, Lorca at the outset establishes contact with a situation very often present in Symbolist works: something (a feeling, a thought, a person) is evoked and imbued with a sense of life that makes us as aware of its "presence" as we are of observable phenomena. A very young poet strives to fly towards a world of happiness that he has imagined, but in so doing, he has ironically permitted death to creep into his life in the world to which he is bound. As stated in the prologue: "Inútil es deciros que el enamorado bichito se murió. ¡Y es que la Muerte se disfraza de Amor!" (670). The prologue prepares the reader for a play that will explore the power of the imagination and indicates early the allusive and elusive nature of the metaphorical language through which Curianito's effort to escape into the imagination will be expressed. In addition to introducing key words that will comprise the imagery continuities, the poet who is the speaker of the prologue places one layer of imagination upon another by telling us that he had heard the story that is about to unfold from a character (an old sylph) that had emerged from the imagination of another poet (Shakespeare):

'Muy pronto llegará el reino de los animales

y de las plantas; el hombre se olvida de su
Creador, y el animal y la planta están muy
cerca de su luz; di, poeta, a los hombres
que el amor nace con la misma intensidad en
todos los planos de la vida; que el mismo ritmo
que tiene la hoja mecida por el aire tiene la
estrella lejana, y que las mismas palabras
que dice la fuente en la umbría las repite
con el mismo tono el mar; dile al hombre que
sea humilde, ¡todo es igual en la Naturaleza!' (670)

The prologue not only narrates the idea that even the smallest manifestations of nature are imbued with poetry but also clothes itself in poetry. Through subtle shifts in phrasing, the prologue has the flow or dream-like quality of a Symbolist poem, recalling lines from a poem like Verlaine's "En sourdine" which begins "Calmes dans le demi-jour / Que les branches hautes font, / Pénétrons bien notre amour / De ce silence profond."[4] Gentle shifts in rhythm help the prologue reach the mist of the imagination as preparation for the drama of the insect in the play who "fell in love with a vision that was very far from his life" ("se prendó de una visión que estaba muy lejos de su vida").

With respect to its narrative line, *El maleficio de la mariposa* is infused with the spirit of selected works by Maeterlinck and Yeats, as well as showing an affinity for a symbolist play like Martínez Sierra's *Pastoral*. In this work, the protagonist's entrance into a world of fantasy in his search for "la reina Sol" resonates with Curianito's desire to see his ideal of love and beauty. The children of Maeterlinck's *The Blue Bird* also reach into a world of fantasy that takes the form of a dream and sends them on a one year's journey in search of the Blue Bird of knowledge—a quest that brings them into the presence of the Joy of Seeing what is Beautiful, the Joy of Thinking, the Joy of Understanding and the Joy of Loving.

In Scene 2, it is Silvia who carries the theme of longing for something out of reach. Dropping the daisy she has been carrying, she asks:

¿Por qué sendero
de la pradera
me iré a otro mundo
donde me quieran? (679)

Her question has the effect of conjuring up the presence of the poet-protagonist as he was described in the prologue: "comedia rota del que quiere arañar a la luna y se araña su corazón;" ". . . hubo un insecto que quiso ir más allá del amor," "Se prendó de una visión que estaba muy lejos de su vida." This sense of reaching out to grasp something mysteriously threatening from another world permeates *El maleficio de la mariposa* as it does a Symbolist play like Yeats's *The Shadowy Waters*. Silvia's musings recall Dectora's words spoken to Forgael, the dreamer:

> I looked upon the moon,
> Longing to knead and pull it into shape
> That I might lay it on your head as a crown.
> But now it is your thoughts that wander away,
> For you are looking at the sea. Do you not know
> How great a wrong it is to let one's thought
> Wander a moment when one is in love?[5]

To set the earliest stages in Lorca's development of a dynamic use of metaphorical language, we provide further evidence of a Symbolist presence in Lorca's first play. This can be found in the way tension between poetic imagination and reality is communicated in *El maleficio de la mariposa* and *The Shadowy Waters*. In both plays, the tension takes the form of one character trying to dissuade another from a course thought to be foolhardy. In the first scene of *El maleficio de la mariposa*, the voice of poetry, through Nigromántica, insists on being heard even though Doña Curiana has made several attempts to focus Nigromántica's attention on the immediate surroundings and the dawn of a new day:

> Curiana Nigromántica (Como soñando):
>   Todas las estrellas se van a apagar.
> Doña Curiana:
>   No penséis en eso, vecina doctora,
>   mirad la alegría que nos trae la aurora.
> Curiana Nigromántica:
>   ¡Ay, lo que yo vi junto al encinar! (675)

A similar casting aside of the thoughts of one character by another occurs in Yeats's play:
> Forgael: . . . I never
>   . . . I never wake from sleep
>   But that I am afraid they [the birds] may
>   have passed; . . .

56   *The Dynamics of the Imagery in the Theater
of Federico Garcia Lorca*

> . . . .
> Aibric: Be satisfied to live like other men,
>   And drive impossible dreams away. The world
>   Has beautiful women to please every man. (98)

Continuing their argument, Nigromántica persists in speaking like a poet and dreamer, using images that link heaven and earth ("El prado está silencioso. / Ya parte el rocío a su cielo ignorado, / el viento rumoroso / hasta nosotros llega perfumado" [675]); and even when rebuked ("¿También sois poeta, doctora vecina?" [675]), she defends the presence of poetry in everyday life—a situation that Doña Curiana considers unacceptable and leads Nigromántica to exclaim: "Con razón te daba palos tu marido; / cocina y poesía se pueden juntar" (676). Under very different circumstances but in the same spirit, Yeats's Forgael and Aibric continue their argument, with the latter trying to rescue the "visionary" from his dream world:

> Forgael: Yet never have two lovers kissed but they
>   Believed there was some other near at hand,
>   And almost wept because they could not find it.
> Aibric: When they have twenty years; in middle life
>   They take a kiss for what a kiss is worth,
>   And let the dream go by. (98)

Similar words appear when Doña Curiana tries to restrain Silvia's flights of fancy:

> Curianita Silvia: Me queda
>   mucho tiempo que llorar
>   Yo me enterraré en la arena
>   a ver si un amante bueno
>   con su amor me desentierra. (679)
> Doña Curiana: Estás muy enamorada,
>   ya lo sé. Mas en mi época
>   las jóvenes no pedíamos
>   los novios a boca llena,
>   ni hablábamos en parábolas
>   como hablas tú. . . . (680)

The flight imagery associated with imagination, when placed in the context of this struggle between imagination and forces trying to keep thoughts earthbound, contributes to an intensification of the tension as

Nigromántica herself (who has been associated with poetic vision) tries to dissuade Curianito from a course he is unwilling to relinquish. "No la mires con ansias," she implores, "porque puedes perderte. Te lo dice tu amiga ya vieja y achacosa" (701). But Curianito is determined: "Me volaré tristeza sobre la noche oscura / y llamaré a mi madre como cuando era niño. / ¡Oh amapola roja que ves todo el prado! / Como tú de linda yo quisiera ser" (701).

Another point of contact between Lorca, Yeats and Maeterlinck appears in their dramatization of lurking dangers in those who do not comprehend someone possessed of a vision. In *El maleficio de la mariposa*, Alacranito, a diabolical scorpion, attacks the butterfly that embodies Curianito's ideal; but he is driven away by insects serving as guards. Similarly, in *The Blue Bird*, enemies in the form of animals and trees attack Tyltyl and Mytyl while they search for the Blue Bird; and in *The Shadowy Waters*, the threat comes verbally when the First Sailor says "Join with us; be our captain, Aibric. We are agreed to put an end to Forgael" (97).

Thus far, Lorca's imagery in the passages we have cited has remained primarily at the level of illustration, of deepening our understanding of a spirit that pervades the work—a spirit associated with an attempt by the imagination to soar above the commonplace. But when La Mariposa finally makes her appearance, she dramatizes the tension in the imagery between beauty as perceived by the imagination and as it manifests itself in reality. The butterfly's actual appearance, however, does not surprise us, because her presence as well as her relationship to Curianito has been strongly evoked in the metaphorical language. When Silvia asks Curianito in Act I, Scene 4 "¿Y dónde está tu estrella?", and he answers "En mi imaginación" (687), the star image provides us with a visualization of the roles that Curianito and La Mariposa play in the drama. With his reply, Curianito has said, in effect, that he, with his poetic vision, is imagination. He is the embodiment of a youthful search for love and beauty that extends beyond reality. He creates his own reality. He is the dreamer who is first introduced in the prologue and then takes shape in the consciousness of the reader who follows the course of the images that have alluded to the role the poet will play; and when he tells Silvia that he will sing the praises of the star that is in his imagination, he brings La Mariposa one more step closer to reality. When Silvia sadly comments "La estrella verás algún día" (687), the allusive language anticipates the appearance of the butterfly whose fall to earth will cast a malevolent spell like the darkness that befell Nigromántica when she saw a star die.

The butterfly image is another indicator of this playwright's early ties with the Symbolist-Modernista tradition. For example, we are reminded of this exchange that takes place in Martínez Sierra's *Pastoral* when Rosa María and Alcino are searching for "la reina Sol:"

> Rosa María: Mira, Alcino: la primera hoja
> que ha caído de un árbol; parece una
> mariposa.
> ....
> Alcino: En el verano no hay mariposas.
> ....
> No me hables de la mies ni di las eras;
> entre ellas ha caído el sudor de mi frente,
> y la reina Sol no ha querido venir.[6]

For Martínez Sierra, however, the butterfly image remains at the level of simile; whereas for Lorca, it will become dramatically significant with respect to the unfolding events.

In the metaphor of the butterfly, Lorca achieves dramatic and poetic equilibrium. La Mariposa, a beautiful winged creature, is the visual contrast to the detestable Alacranito who crawls along the surface of the earth devouring other creatures. Suddenly, something beautiful that implies escape with its capacity to become airborne has fallen among earth-bound creatures, and the joy that Curianito feels recalls that of Maeterlinck's Tyltyl when he first sees the Blue Bird in the Land of Memory.

To sustain our initial impression that Lorca's dramatization of Curianito's quest for an imagined ideal recalls the spirit of Maeterlinck and Yeats, we will turn our attention to patterns of imagery in this drama. This will help us bring into focus Lorca's early use of imagery primarily as a means of underscoring thematic material and creating an ambience reminiscent of Symbolist works. Against this background, the dynamic quality of Lorca's imagery—appearing briefly in this play and then developed and refined in later works—will stand out clearly.

Flight imagery becomes increasingly important as Curianito, like Maeterlinck's Tyltyl and Mytyl and Yeats's Forgael, orients his thoughts towards something (in this instance, the butterfly) that for him represents heaven's mystery. Images of flight reach their most intense level in the final scene when Curianito entreats the butterfly to remain with him: "Con besos curaré yo tus heridas / si conmigo te casas; / y un ruiseñor inmenso que es mi amigo / nos llevará volando en la mañana" (719). The elusiveness of his love, however, has already been transmitted through the flight imagery in words spoken earlier by La Mariposa: "Volaré por el hilo de plata"; "Voy hacia la niebla"; "la muerte me dio dos alas blancas" (708). The butterfly is insistent upon taking flight after emerging from the imagination to be temporarily treated as a creature of the real world; and the fact that she has effectively cast her evil spell in the dramatic action onstage is underscored by the vibrations emanating from images of flight ("Curianito," warns Nigromática, "tu suerte / depende de las alas de esa gran mariposa. / No la mires con ansias, porque puedes perderte" [701]) and reaching out towards Curianito's final words: "¿Quién me manda sufrir sin tener alas?" (721).

Further evidence that Lorca, in the choice of words and their allusive quality, evinces Symbolist characteristics appears in images drawn from nature that conjure up the overwhelming sense of happiness Curianito feels when reflecting upon his love. In the love poem that Curianito reads aloud in Act I, Scene 4, we hear phrases such as "Oh amapola roja que ves todo el prado;" "llorando el rocío del amanecer;" "Eres tú la estrella que alumbra a la aldea;" "¡Que cieguen mis ojos antes que te vea / con hojas marchitas y turbio color!" (685). Here one sees an affinity with *The Blue Bird*, for example, in which stars appear as beautiful young girls; the Dew dances joyfully, and myriads of blue birds fly among luminous stars.[7] Also Yeats's Forgael associates love with the stars and is himself called a morning star.[8] Further, the light-darkness continuity—dramatically focused when Nigromántica says "Todas las estrellas se van a apagar" (672)—has Symbolist counterparts. In Maeterlinck, Light accompanies the children searching for the Blue Bird hidden in Night; and from *The Shadowy Waters* we cite Forgael saying "Yet sometimes there's a torch inside my head / That makes all clear, but when the light is gone / I have but images, analogies" (99). Thus, through these and similar examples, we can affirm a Symbolist presence in Lorca's earliest play.

One of the fundamental conventions of Symbolism, from Baudelaire as a forerunner to Valéry as an exponent of its heritage, is that of the poet who is swept along by his art as a means of expressing what mysteriously always seems to lie one step beyond total comprehension. Curianito voices the poet's aspiration thus: "Mi ilusión / está prendida en la estrella / que parece una flor / . . . / Yo seré su cantor: / le diré madrigales / del dulce viento al son" (687). Baudelaire wrote "Car Lesbos entre tous m'a choisi sur la terre / Pour chanter le secret de ses vierges en fleurs."[9] Verlaine's "À Clymène" also expresses the spirit that is in the voice of Lorca's boy poet ("Puisque ta voix, étrange / Vision qui dérange / Et trouble l'horizon / De ma raison";[10] and one might even hear in Curianito's voice the rapture expressed in Valéry's "Orphée": " . . . Je compose en esprit, sous les myrtes, Orphée / L'Admirable! . . . / . . . / Il chante, assis au bord du ciel splendide, Orphée! / Le roc marche, et trébuche; et chaque pierre fée / Se sent un poids nouveau qui vers l'azur délire!"[11]

In addition to an affinity with the Symbolist theater of Maeterlinck and Yeats, *El maleficio de la mariposa* draws on a poetic technique that Lorca extolled in Góngora: i.e., expanding an image by having it radiate outward from the center. This is shown in the dew imagery that helps introduce into the text the idea of love and then radiates outward towards other aspects of the thematic content of the play. Initially the dew appears as a symbol of love: "Sueño que las dulces gotas de rocío / son labios de amores que me dejan besos" (672). Then like the circles caused by a pebble dropped in water, the dew extends its sphere of influence to include sadness ("Pintas sobre el cielo tu traje encarnado / llorando el rocío del amanecer" [685]); and then reaches the ailing butterfly when Nigromántica prescribes the following cure: "Dale el rocío añejo / y ponle un tibio paño . . ." (699). Finally, the expanded metaphor of dew as a manifestation of love draws the two principal characters within its orbit when we are told that Curianito "hablaba de unas alas de mariposa herida, / más digna del rocío que la carne del nardo" (704). Although the dew in these instances remains essentially descriptive and decorative as it radiates through the dialogue in various contexts, it serves the playwright's dramatic purpose by underscoring the sadness that will result from the love Curianito showers upon La Mariposa.

Through variation, expanded images can unify a text with their power to be all-pervasive. For a playwright who is creating a mood or evoking feelings through the accumulation of images that intensify the desired effect, the expanded image can be a valuable technique towards accomplishing his purpose. This is the case with Lorca in *El maleficio de la mariposa* and explains why Góngora, whom Lorca praised as a master of the expanding metaphor, could serve as a model in the application of this technique. Góngora's "Soledad primera" yields the following example of the process at work. Through seven stanzas, Góngora keeps alive the image of night approaching. As one image follows another, darkness thickens until it finally envelops the scene.

Viendo pues que igualmente les quedaba

para el lugar a ellas de camino
lo que al Sol para el lóbrego occidente . . .
. . . .
al pueblo llegan con la luz que el día
cedió al sacro volcán de errante fuego . . .
. . . .
. . . no alguna sea
de nocturno Featón carroza ardiente
y miserablemente
campo amanezca estéril de ceniza
    la que anocheció aldea. . . .
. . . .
    Tanto garzón robusto,
tanta ofrecen los álamos zagala,
que abreviara el Sol en una estrella
    por ver la menos bella . . .
. . . .
cruza el Trión más fijo el hemisferio
. . . .
Los fuegos—cuyas lenguas, ciento a ciento,
desmintieron la noche algunas horas
. . . .
Vence la noche al fin, y triunfa mudo
el silencio, aunque breve, del rüido . . .[12]

    As we already observed with Symbolists, we note that Góngora's "Soledades" are clothed in images replete with color, stars, dew, trees, night and the dawn. Moreover, the synesthesia so prevalent in Symbolist writings is also very evident in phrases such as these drawn from Góngora's "Soledad primera": "Durmió, y recuerda el fin, cuando las aves / — esquilas dulces de sonora pluma— / señas dieron süaves / del alba al Sol" (49-50); "los jaspes líquidos" (51); "centellas saca de cristal undoso" (65); "fanal es del arroyo cada onda, / luz el reflejo, la agua vidrïera" (69).
    Through images implanted in the text to create a strong *impression* of what is transpiring in relationships between and among characters, we are made aware of the intensity of Curianito's soaring poetic imagination and the thoughts of those who pull it back to earth. Many images are directed towards this opposition underlying Curianito's desire to take flight on the wings of his love for beauty and to follow the butterfly in escaping from an uncomprehending world. Throughout the text, this antagonism can be followed in selected passages:
    Nigromántica: Sueño que las dulces gotas de rocío

son labios de amores que me dejan besos
y llenan de estrellas mi traje sombrío.
(672)
. . . .
Cocina y poesía se pueden juntar (676)

Doña Curiana: ¿También sois poeta, doctora vecina?
Nosotras, las pobres, con nuestra cocina
tenemos bastante. (676)

Nigromántica: ¡Qué suerte de nosotras, repugnantes y tristes!
Acariciar tus alas de blanquísima seda
y aspirar el aroma del traje con que
vistes! (698)

Curianita 1ª: ¡Pero a mí qué me importa tanta y tanta tontuna!
Y de una mariposa, ¿por qué se ha
enamorado?
¿No sabe que con ella no podrá
desposarse? (704)

Gusano 3º: La gota que tú tragas
no vuelve sobre el prado;
como el amor, se pierde
en la paz del olvido.
Y mañana, otras gotas
brillarán en la hierba
que a los pocos momentos
ya no serán rocío. (713)

Curianito: ¿Qué haré sobre estos prados sin amor
y sin besos? (718)

As we begin to examine the imagery of *El maleficio de la mariposa* in more detail, we will bring to a sharper focus the close identification with allusive and evocative imagery of Symbolist and Modernista writers in addition to their techniques for incorporating them in a text. Thus we will firmly establish the framework into which Lorca introduces elements of dynamism that anticipate a coalescence of poetry and drama in the later plays.

The setting for Act I quickens the senses, stirs the imagination and strongly reminds us of scenes set by Symbolist and Modernista writers. It is a green meadow covered with dew and dominated by the shade of an enormous cypress tree. There are blue stones, a small path tracing an arabesque, splendid lilies and the burrows of insects, creating the appearance of a fantastic town of caves—all bathed in the red of dawn. Into this idealized setting, Lorca introduces a very old cockroach named Doña

The Dynamics of the Imagery in the Theater of Federico Garcia Lorca

Curiana who is missing one leg as a result of being maimed by a human being—a detail to store away as a slight counterpoint to the theme of love introduced in the prologue. The contrast created by a disfigured old woman in a "perfect" setting very subtly injects a "shadow" into the idyllic setting and lightly underscores the light-darkness ("mariposa-maleficio," illusion-disillusion, enchantment-disenchantment) continuity that will form part of the design of the imagery in this play.

When the visionary Nigromántica says in the opening scene "La [estrella] vi perecer / y sentí caer / en mi corazón / un anochecer" (672), one hears an echo from the voice of the prologue that began with a similar idea clothed in similar imagery: "La comedia que vais a escuchar es humilde e inquietante, comedia rota del que quiere arañar a la luna y se araña su corazón" (669). Through Nigromántica (early in the dialogue of Act I) Lorca embeds the prologue's revelation of a poet's unsuccessful escape into the projected world of love and beauty. When Nigromántica is asked who might have killed the fairy of land and sea, she replies unequivocally that love killed her. Thus, the imagery pertaining to the extinguished light of a star and the fairy killed by love begins to establish a poetic meta-narrative that carries forward information from the prologue relating to a poet's unsuccessful attempt to "scratch" the moon. We therefore anticipate the appearance of the protagonist. In other words, we sense the presence of Doña Curiana's son, because he has already "appeared" as a character in the imagery. When, in fact, Doña Curiana does say that her son is in love with something he will never have, we recall the image in the prologue of the poet who wounds his heart ("quiere arañar a la luna y se araña su corazón") as well as the image of the dead star that made such a strong impression on Nigromántica ("La vi perecer / y sentí caer en mi corazón / un anochecer"). Doña Curiana thus confirms what we have already begun to feel as layers of imagery are added to the meta-narrative.

Through the image of the poet "que quiere arañar a la luna," the prologue reaches even into the dialogue of minor characters. When, for example, the glowworm Gusano Tercero says in Act II, Scene 5 that an old wise man once told him to drink the drops of dew without ever asking where they came from, we are reminded of the poet Curianito who aspires to search for the origin of the light that illuminates him. Lorca has thus brought us back to the very first line of the prologue ("comedia rota del que quiere arañar a la luna y se araña su corazón") through the allusive quality of the language used by the glowworm. Through this technique of having one image subtly recall another, so common with the Symbolists,

Lorca has increased our awareness of the ultimate futility of the poet's quest introduced in the imagery of the prologue.

Step by step through images especially associated with a counterpoint between heaven and earth, Lorca underscores the gravitational pull that reality exercises on the imagination and the latter's struggle to follow its own inclination and escape from the constraints placed on it. When early in Act I Nigromántica begins to pursue the idea that love killed the fairy of land and sea, the next line spoken by Doña Curiana silences her by focusing attention on the natural surroundings ("Mirad cómo quiebra el primer albor" [673]). Gradually as one image follows another, the tension mounts between those who consider poetry a living, vital part of life, and those who see it as nonessential for existence. Curiana Nigromántica speaks with the voice of a poet when she says "Vengo de soñar que yo era una flor / hundida en la hierba;" whereas Doña Curiana speaks with a voice of one who is "unenlightened" when she declares "Nosotras, las pobres, con nuestra cocina / tenemos bastante" (675). While Nigromántica alludes to ominous events, expressed in terms of a darkness descending into her heart, Doña Curiana brushes aside any sign of impending tragedy: "Yo voy a barrer / mi puerta con brisa del amanecer." Even at the level of this casual conversation, the playwright begins to mobilize a sense of uneasiness that is fully confirmed when La Mariposa eventually declares that she is both beauty and death.

With the appearance of the evil scorpion, the storm clouds gathering in the baleful images in the text have a physical counterpart in a character participating in the drama. The poet's imagination that flies like a butterfly towards a distant star meets opposition. In Curianito's world, Alacranito is a brutal visual manifestation of malevolence that first made its appearance in the "maleficio" of the title of the drama and then gathered momentum in phrases such as "mi traje sombrío," "'Todas las estrellas se van a apagar,'" "y sentí caer / en mi corazón / un anochecer," "la mató el amor" and "Amor . . . Dicen que eres dulce y negro." One can also say that imagery anticipates comments made by the characters. When Silvia hears Curianito exclaim that he feels a pain in his heart, she simply says "El quiere ya a una estrella" (698). She does not have to say anything more, because the rich imagistic associations established between the word "estrella" and love, beauty and sadness fill out the meaning of this line.

Undaunted by verbal attacks by others who consider his words ridiculous, Curianito persists in his poetic vision and escapes further into his imagination. He has become so deeply affected by the butterfly who represents his ideal of beauty that he directs his thoughts away from the reality of his earthly existence. In this respect, he is like the dew that rises to the sky in the sunlight and the maimed wing that wants to fly. This tension between heaven and earth has been so strongly alluded to through images associated with words like "estrella," "alas," "sueños" and "corazón" that La Mariposa's first words, spoken as if from a dream, are in natural phase with the imagery:

¡Quiero
volar, quiero volar, el hilo es largo!
. . . .
El hilo va a la estrella
donde está mi tesoro;
mis alas son de plata,
mi corazón es de oro;
el hilo está soñando
con su vibrar sonoro . . . (699)

Having examined Lorca's metaphorical language in terms of the Symbolist spirit it evokes through layered images, we will now follow the course of five key imagery continuities: 1) stars, 2) light-darkness, 3) dew, 4) flowers and 5) flight. These are the elements which either singly or in combinations place this play in the mainstream of Symbolist theater and at the same time contain the seeds for the poetic drama Lorca develops in his later plays.

The very early appearance of the image of a star whose light has been extinguished, and its recurrence alone or in combination with flower and dew imagery, establish it as a prime indicator of the course taken by Curianito, the poet. In the opening moments of Act I, Lorca introduces several components of the basic imagery. Stars, flowers and the dew will be key elements of the heaven-earth opposition through which Curianito's ill-fated flight into poetic imagination is expressed. Very often these images work first at a static, symbolic level (representing love and beauty) and then at the level of foreshadowing events. In some instances, they are indicators of the changing relationship among the characters.

As the play begins, Nigromántica, a cockroach covered with dew and wearing a cone of stars, matches her fantastic appearance with these words: "Sueño que las dulces gotas de rocío / son labios de amores que me dejan besos / y llenan de estrellas mi traje sombrío" (672). Dew, love and the stars are therefore quickly linked to each other. Nigromántica then says that a swallow told her that all the stars are going to be extinguished and that she herself saw in the oak grove a trembling red star shedding its petals like an enormous rose:

> Mi alma tiene tristeza, ¡vecina!
> Me dijo ayer tarde una golondrina
> 'Todas las estrellas se van a apagar.'
> Dios está dormido, y en el encinar
> vi una estrella roja toda temblorosa
> que se deshojaba como una enorme rosa. (672)

A star losing its substance like a rose shedding its petals completes a linkage between dew, stars, flowers and love and becomes one layer of images that will infuse the text with the idea that the poet's ideal of love and beauty shining brightly in his imagination will finally disintegrate.

In the first scene of Act I, more phrases resonate with each other. Doña Curiana's words to Nigromántica "Amiga, / que el gran Cucaracho os pague en amor / y que en vuestros sueños se convierta en flor" (674) recall this phrase spoken earlier by Nigromántica: "Vengo de soñar que yo era una flor / hundida en la hierba" (671). Another layer is added to the star-flower-dew imagery at the beginning of Scene 4 in the poem composed by the boy insect:

> ¡Oh amapola roja que ves todo el prado,
> como tú de linda yo quisiera ser!
> Pintas sobre el cielo tu traje encarnado
> llorando el rocío del amanecer.
>
> Eres tú la estrella que alumbra a la aldea
> sol del gusanito buen madrugador.
> ¡Que cieguen mis ojos antes que te vea
> con hojas marchitas y turbio color!
> . . . .
>
> Pues mis besos tienen la tibia dulzura
> del fuego en que vive mi rara pasión;
> y hasta que me lleven a la sepultura
> latirá por ti este corazón . . . (685-686)

Curianito's love poem has imagistic elements that embed deeper into the text similar images in visionary words spoken earlier by Nigromántica.

Hearing Curianito's "Tu traje encarnado" recalls Nigromántica's "mi traje sombrío" (672). "Mis besos tienen la tibia dulzura / del fuego en que vive mi rara pasión" recalls "las dulces gotas de rocío / son labios de amores que me dejan besos" (672). As images begin to accumulate, this paean to love brings into focus the "something" that the poet Curianito is trying to express. By combining many images (flowers, colors, dew, heaven, earth, light, darkness, stars, dawn and the heart), the playwright makes more visible and thereby evokes the presence of a love so deep that for a young poet like Curianito life would be unbearable without it. The conviction with which Curianito speaks could be summarized by the poet Rubén Darío's "Yo soy aquel...": "Tal fue mi intento, hacer del alma pura / mía, una estrella, una fuente sonora, / con el horror de la literatura / y loco de crepúsculo y de aurora;"[13] or one may cite these lines from Verlaine as a reflection of Curianito's spirit: "—Que je meure, Mesdames, si / Je ne vous décroche une étoile."[14]

When Silvia asks Curianito directly when he intends to get married, the aspiring poet answers with imagery whose components 1) recall earlier passages and 2) add another layer to the star-flower relationship that moves the listener closer to a clearer visualization of love:

Mi ilusión
está prendida en la estrella
que parece una flor. (687)

The phrase "estrella que parece una flor" resonates with earlier lines ("flor hundida en la hierba," "las dulces gotas de rocío... llenan de estrellas mi traje sombrío," "¡Oh amapola roja.../... Eres tú la estrella que alumbra a la aldea") and further suffuses the dialogue with the presence of love in the form of heaven-earth imagery. The importance of the flower imagery to the evocation of love is further underscored when Silvia tells Curianito's mother that her son does not want to marry her because "Me dijo que él amaba / a una flor" (695).

As Act I draws to a close, Curianito feels within himself the heaven-earth duality limned in the poetic images. Realities of the flesh are beginning to stir in the young boy who wants to possess the love that he has thus far extolled through his imagination. In a fleeting evocation of "traje sombrío" and "turbio color," Curianito asks: "¿Por qué ya se marchita la flor de mi pureza, / mientras otra flor nace dentro del pensamiento?" (701). Again, a key image ("flor") evokes the presence of an abstraction— a process that began to gain momentum especially in the poem cited from

Scene 4 ("¡Oh amapola roja . . .") in which images charged with the senses ("amapola roja," "traje encarnado," "llorando el rocío," "estrella que alumbra a la aldea," "tibia dulzura del fuego") join one another to summon the "presence" of the protagonist's abstract love as expressed in the culminating phrase "mi rara pasión." Again one can cite an affinity with Verlaine in this process that Lorca employs of having Curianito continue to verbalize what he pictures in his mind so as to draw forth its presence. In "Clair de Lune," the poet evokes a lady's soul, beginning with "Votre âme est un paysage choisi" and then proceeding to accumulate images of sound and sight—"Jouant du luth et dansant;" "Tout en chantant sur le mode mineur / L'amour vainqueur;" "Et leur chanson se mêle au clair de lune, / "Au calme clair de lune triste et beau"—until the culminating phrase "sangloter d'extase" strikes a chord that brings all the notes together and expresses "votre âme."[15]

El maleficio de la mariposa also reflects the Symbolist tradition in its use of synesthesia—a device often used by the Symbolists (and, as we have already seen, by Góngora) to engage the senses. In this play we read "el viento rumoroso / hasta nosotros llega perfumado," "la tibia dulzura del fuego;" "amarga aurora;" "el aroma del traje con que vistes;" "el hilo está soñando / con su vibrar sonoro;" "cegó la fuente de mi seda;" "¿No te ha quemado la luz de mis palabras?" One by one, images associate themselves with the senses; and because of the resultant density of sensorial stimuli, when Nigromántica refers to La Mariposa as "Dulce estrella caída de un ciprés soñoliento" (698), we "feel" the presence of beauty tinged with sadness.

Act II of *El maleficio de la mariposa* places the stars, flowers and the dew deeper into the thematic core of the play by maintaining the relationship between these images and love as well as the tension they help create in a heaven-earth opposition that develops during the course of the play. In the opening scenes of this act, the words "rocío" and "flor" become associated with the butterfly herself when Curiana Santa says "[Curianito] hablaba de unas / alas de mariposa herida, / más digna del rocío que la carne del nardo" (704) and when Doña Curiana adds: "Ella viene del alba. Es una flor errante" (705). Even minor characters help bind the dew imagery to love, such as when three glowworms speak of the dew as a mysterious manifestation of love that descends upon the earth at night only to evaporate in the morning ("Los viejos / sabemos que el amor / es igual que el rocío" [713]). Along with the symbolism of the dew in this brief episode with the glowworms, Lorca keeps the heaven-earth counterpoint alive, because the words are spoken by earthly creatures who "emit light" but do not understand nor feel the phenomena they describe. These creatures are, therefore, on the opposite end of a polarity with the ethereal butterfly who says that she understands the mystery of the dew: "Yo he sentido / como las claras gotas / hablaban dulcemente, / contándose misterios / de campos infinitos" (714).

One might say that La Mariposa, along with the reader (and through a process similar to that described in "Clair de Lune"), has been listening to the song of the flowers, the stars and the dew without failing to perceive their melodic line. Further, when the butterfly says "pero todas las voces, / y los cantos que escuches, / son disfraces extraños / de un solo canto" (715), she speaks as if she were listening to herself being sung by the poet Curianito who promised earlier to sing the praises of the star of his imagination. Like the reader, La Mariposa has been "listening" to a song whose metaphorical language, as we have thus far observed, is allusive and evocative rather than dynamically expressive of the action in the drama. Gradually, the author of *El maleficio de la mariposa* shapes the image of love which is projected in the imagination of Curianito the poet. From this point of view, the imagery remains in the realm of contemplation rather than becoming actively engaged in expressing drama.

Lorca's use of imagery to heighten our awareness of thematic material is especially demonstrable in the penultimate scene when Curianito describes the world where he feels happiness lies as "el mundo del rocío donde el amor no acaba" (718). Here, in the closing moments of the play, "rocío" releases all the thematic force it had accumulated since its first appearance in the opening moments of the play when Nigromántica explained her dream. Curianito's use of the word "rocío" in his description of the world of love increases the metaphorical value of the dew image. The ephemeral nature of the dew underscores both the futility of his attempt to keep La Mariposa from flying away as well as the realization that the only way to hold onto his love is by taking flight to the realm he can picture in his mind. Thus, the essence of the conflict in this drama has been crystallized in the imagery. Curianito has fallen in love with a beautiful creature who descended upon the earth like the dew only to tantalize him with a morning freshness that is destined to disappear. One might say that Curianito will suffer what ails Keats's knight-at-arms in "La Belle Dame sans Merci," espressed in these words:

   I see a lily on thy brow

With anguish moist and fever dew,
And on thy cheeks a fading rose
Fast withereth too.[16]

The fact that the love for beauty that Lorca's protagonist feels assumes the form of a mysterious creature, an "unobtainable woman" here symbolized by a butterfly, is further contact between Lorca and Symbolist and Modernista writers. Since this Romantic poetic convention appears frequently in works of writers not far removed in time from *El maleficio de la mariposa*, it is likely that verses in the spirit of Verlaine or Darío echoed in the mind of the boy poet—verses such as the following:

Je fais souvent ce rêve étrange et pénétrant
D'une femme inconnue, et que j'aime, et qui
   m'aime[17]

Yo adoro a una sonámbula con alma de Eloísa,
virgen como la nieve y honda como la mar;
su espíritu es la hostia de mi amorosa misa,
y alzo al són de una dulce lira crepuscular.[18]

The butterfly image is especially recurrent in verses by Darío:

Mi pobre alma pálida
era una crisálida.
Luego, mariposa
de color de rosa.[19]

¡Divina Psiquis, dulce mariposa invisible
que desde los abismos has venido . . . [20]

For the poet Curianito who is completely star struck, La Mariposa is the incarnation of that elusive "something" that has kept him apart from those who surround him. She is the beloved to whom he has been addressing his poetry. "Amapola," he declares, "ya he visto mi estrella misteriosa" (700). The flower-star imagery that previously shaped Curianito's love ("¡Oh amapola roja que ves todo el prado, / . . . / Eres tú la estrella que alumbra a la aldea" [685]) is now linked to the figure of a butterfly whose actions will produce the sad outcome anticipated in images such as "vi una estrella roja toda temblorosa / que se deshojaba como una enorme rosa" (672). La Mariposa, the embodiment of love and beauty, falls to earth, casts her spell, and leaves the heart forever yearning to possess her. She herself confirms what we have felt through the textual images of beauty tinged with sadness:

Porque soy la muerte
y la belleza. (709)

Again in the dramatization of the butterfly's spell, one hears an echo from Symbolism; in this instance, from Mallarmé's "Hérodiade" in the scene between Hérodiade and La Nourrice:

... O femme, un baiser me tûrait
Si la beauté n'était la mort ... [21]

The presence of profound sadness which the imagery has been evoking is also confirmed by an image used by La Mariposa to describe herself in the conclusion to her soliloquy in Act II, Scene 3: "Que la gota de lluvia se asombre / al resbalar sobre mis alas muertas" (709). Through the words "lluvia" and "muertas," the image links the presence of the butterfly to the fate of Curianito whose final question ("¿Quién me manda sufrir sin tener alas?" [p..721] is the culmination of a series of questions ("¿Duerme la casta reina de este prado? / ¿La que el rocío cuaja? / ¿La que sabe el secreto de la hierba / y el canto de las aguas?" [719]) that recall earlier images imbued with the spirit of La Mariposa and bring into even sharper focus the image of "el hada del campo y del mar" who cast her spell in the text before she appeared on stage.

The feeling that death is linked to love and beauty in this play emerges also through a light-darkness opposition in the imagery, beginning in the opening moments of Act I. Light, expressed in words such as "mañana clara," "primer albor" and "llenan de estrellas," quickly gives way to dimness ("traje sombrío;" "Todas las estrellas se van a apagar.") and reaches the point of expressing a sense of doom when Curianito laments his broken heart in the final scene of the drama:

¿Por qué si tiene el agua
fresca sombra en estío y la tiniebla
de la noche se aclara
con los ojos sin fin de las estrellas
no tiene amor mi alma? (720)

To clarify what Lorca does with the light-darkness opposition, we recall Maeterlinck's *The Blue Bird* in which similar imagery is used for a different purpose. In that play, Light accompanies the children, because it knows that Night hides the Blue Bird. For Maeterlinck, both light and darkness remain at the level of opposition for their symbolic value, whereas Lorca has them "interact" to create a sense of disaster; a feeling that Curianito's vision will be plunged into darkness by the spell cast by the butterfly. In other words, the light-darkness continuity for Maeterlinck in *The Blue Bird* is more the expression of an idea than a feeling. For Lorca, this continuity, appearing early on when Nigromántica says "Me dijo ayer tarde una golondrina: / 'Todas las estrellas se van a apagar'" (672), sets a tone for Curianito's fatal quest. Through an accumulation of phrases such as "y sentí caer / en mi corazón / un anochecer;" "negro tu caparazón / como noche sin estrellas;" "Caerá toda la noche sobre su pobre frente," and "Hilé mi corazón sobre carne / para rezar en las tinieblas," Lorca heightens the feeling that the light in Curianito's mind will be extinguished.

In *El maleficio de la mariposa*, Lorca has placed poetry at the heart of the drama. Every manifestation of nature is invested with a potential for speaking to the human heart, and a poet like Curianito receives its vibrations through "las puntas divinas de sus antenas." The spirit which permeates this play is that which stirred Baudelaire:

> La Nature est un temple où de vivants piliers
> Laissent parfois sortir de confuses paroles;
> L'homme y passe à travers des forêts de symboles
> Qui l'observent avec des regards familiers.[22]

It is the spirit that stirred Rubén Darío:

> ...El gran bosque
> es nuestro templo; allí ondea
> y flota un santo perfume
> de amor....[23]

And it is the spirit that stirs La Mariposa:

Lo que dice la nieve sobre el prado
lo repite la hoguera;
las canciones del humo en la mañana
las dicen las raíces bajo tierra. (709).

Thus, the text of the sad tale of the insect poet brings us back to Symbolism. Curianito's senses, his "antenas," are so acute that they listen to nature's music like the poet in Verlaine's verses:

Les sanglots longs
Des violons
   De l'automne
Blessent mon coeur
D'une langueur
   Monotone.[24]

El maleficio de la mariposa, however, does step out of its Symbolist framework at several points where images are placed in the text in such a way that they become dynamically active in dramatic contexts that do not merely foreshadow events. In these instances, the images become active in the narrative of the drama and therefore begin to set Lorca's course away from Symbolism and in the direction of the more dynamic involvement that imagery assumes in subsequent plays.

In the first scene of Act I, Nigromántica and Doña Curiana engage one another in a battle of words, with the former defending poetry and the latter rejecting it as a component of daily life. As the scene draws to a close, Nigromántica declares: "Cocina y poesía se pueden juntar" (676) and then leaves; whereupon Doña Curiana says: "Que la luz os guíe. Yo voy a barrer / mi puerta con brisa del amanecer" (676). In this instance, Lorca has invested a surrealistic image with dramatic potential. Sweeping the doorway with a breeze of dawn is an image that is consonant with the drama as it is beginning to unfold. To demonstrate this point, we can offer a series of images that might be unleashed in one's mind at the instigation of the phrase spoken by Doña Curiana: broom—sweeping—breeze—clearing—dawn—renewal—continuance. Doña Curiana does in fact want to start the new day by continuing to give her customary attention to daily household activities instead of being bothered by "useless" matters such as the defense of the merits of poetry. Further, her use of a poetic image to indicate that she is about to undertake her daily chores recalls the idea contained in Nigromántica's assertion that "cocina y poesía se pueden juntar." Thus, the battle lines are drawn between those who defend the presence of poetry in one's life and those who sweep it out of the house. In this case, the imagery does not foreshadow as much as it indicates what is transpiring between the characters. It is not statically evocative but rather dynamically engaged in expressing an element of the drama.

In Act I, Scene 2, Doña Curiana wants Silvia to give her reasons for her sadness, whereupon Silvia asks: "¿Por qué sendero / de la pradera / me iré a otro mundo / donde me quieran?" (679). Her question, in effect, anticipates Curianito's desire to take flight with the butterfly and reflects her growing concern that she, like Curianito "que quiere arañar a la luna," will not be able to find happiness in the world of reality. Again, the imagery is intimately connected with the dramatic context at that moment.

Curianito's first words, delivered in an aside, confirm what Silvia's imagery anticipated; i.e., that Curianito is outside the circle of his fellow creatures who are destined to crawl along the face of the earth. His first utterance states explicitly that he does not want to get married—"¡Que no me caso, madre! / Ya os he dicho mil veces / que no quiero casarme" (684)—thereby not only rejecting a course set for him by others but also confirming the apprehension that Silvia conveyed in the images she used while talking to Doña Curiana.

Another example of the dynamic use of imagery occurs in Act I, Scene 5, when Nigromántica gives this prescription for curing La Mariposa:

> Dale el rocío añejo
> y ponle un tibio paño
> con emplastos de ortigas
> y polen de azucenas.
> . . . . .
> Además le receto baños de luna y siesta,
> allá entre las umbrías de la vieja floresta.
> (699-700).

The butterfly who is the visual manifestation of love and beauty has a broken wing, so Nigromántica's prescription for a cure includes love ("rocío") and light ("baños de luna") that appeared earlier in the imagery associated with Curianito. The boy poet is, therefore, "present" in the prescription. Further, Nigromántica's cure for La Mariposa mixes poetry with "practical sense," thus making her prescription a "living example" of what she meant in Scene 1 when she told Doña Curiana "cocina y poesía se pueden juntar." Again, images are related to what a character is either doing or thinking at the point in the drama when the words are spoken.

An example of metaphorical language that straddles the Symbolist use of images to evoke a feeling and a playwright's use of imagery to represent a stage in the dramatic development of the relationship of the characters appears in the third scene of Act II. There La Mariposa concludes her soliloquy by saying "que la gota de lluvia se asombre / al resbalar sobre mis alas muertas" (709). Instead of "gota de rocío" which a reader might expect because of the repeated appearances of dew as a symbol of love, the playwright has written "gota de lluvia," and in so doing, he has fused the image of love already embedded in the phrase "gota de rocío" with the feeling of sadness that inheres in "gota de lluvia." By repeating the phrase "gota de," Lorca has used its suggestive power to recall Curianito's love and to look ahead to the tears that he will shed when he is unable to break the spell cast by the butterfly. The image of rain thus serves the theme (love-death), the tone (sadness) and the action (Curianito's crying) as it adds one more visual impression in our mind of a scenario in which beauty remains only a creature in the poet's mind because the butterfly will not submit to being "defined" through capture.

An outstanding example of a phrase that is an early indicator of the role imagery plays in poetic drama in Lorca's later plays appears at the beginning of Act II. Here, through the word "filament" ("hilo") that has appeared at various points in the text, the heaven-earth and imagination-reality dualities that have already been implanted in the imagery to describe Curianito's yearning and the butterfly's mysterious attraction make direct contact with the relationship between the characters at this stage of its development. Curianita Primera, a field insect, describes Curianito's behavior with an image that is almost surrealistic: "Yo le vi columpiarse sobre un hilo de araña" (702). The word "hilo" was previously associated with La Mariposa in Act I, Scene 5, when she said "El hilo va a la estrella / donde está mi tesoro; / . . . / el hilo está soñando / con su vibrar sonoro" (699). By "listening" to an inner voice speaking from the subtext, the reader is informed that this mysterious thread is the butterfly's link to the ultimate value and power of her beauty. Through words such as "estrella," "soñando," and "vibrar sonoro" that recall images used by Curianito ("¿Y dónde está tu estrella?" / "En mi imaginación" [687]; "Yo seré su cantor: / le diré madrigales / del dulce viento al son" [687]), the spider's filament becomes linked to the poet who is in love with an ideal in his imagination. The fact that Curianito, as reported by Curianita Primera, is swinging on "un hilo de araña" bears dramatic credence with respect to the action of the play, because his total attention is indeed now focused on La Mariposa. The image used by Curianita Primera has thus communicated a sense of how deeply Curianito has actually been affected by the appearance of the butterfly. In addition, the thread image receives even more dramatic weight when shortly thereafter Curianita Primera foreshadows events with these words: "Sobre un hilo de araña nadie vive" (702). Although La Mariposa will be able to fly away from the world by means of the filament ("Un hilo me llevará a los bosques / donde se ve la vida" [715]), Curianito's only means of escape will remain in his imagination—a realization that leads him ultimately to death. Thus, when we hear "Yo le vi columpiarse sobre un hilo de araña," we "hear" that: 1) Curianito is enraptured by La Mariposa, and 2) the fate of his ecstasy is linked to the mysterious thread drawing La Mariposa heavenward, away from the boy poet.

Despite these early stirrings of a dynamic use of imagery with respect to the unfolding events, *El maleficio de la mariposa* remains essentially a dream play in the tradition of Maeterlinck's *The Blue Bird* and Yeats's *The Shadowy Waters*. Through layers of images bearing a sense of otherworldliness that began to form in the reader's mind during the prologue, Lorca increases the tempo of enveloping the play in a dream:

Vengo de soñar que yo era una flor (671)

que el gran Cucaracho os pague en amor
y que en vuestros sueños se convierta en flor (674)

Dulce estrella caída de un ciprés soñoliento (698)

vigilando los sueños de la blanca durmiente (707)

Los [poetas] quemará el olvido (708)

como el amor, se pierde
en la paz del olvido (713)

The elusive love "sung" by the poet assumes a shape through an accretion of images and submits to an embrace only in the poet's imagination—a condition not unlike that which inheres in the following verses by Verlaine in which repetitions and subtle variations produce a mesmerizing effect one often attributes to music:

Je fais souvent ce rêve étrange et pénétrant
D'une femme inconnue, et que j'aime, et qui m'aime
Et qui n'est, chaque fois, ni tout à fait la même
Ni tout à fait une autre, et m'aime et me
    comprend.[25]

    By giving *El maleficio de la mariposa* the shape of a fable clothed in dream, Lorca, in effect, captures the butterfly that eludes Curianito; but the capture takes place in the imagination. In other words, the beauty that Curianito wants to possess physically on earth is attainable only in imagination; and his attempt to escape from reality in order to live in the world he envisions leads to disaster. This is the thematic content of the play that is supported by the symbolist imagery. Thus we conclude that like works within the tradition of Symbolist theater and poetry, Lorca's earliest play deals with allusion and illusion, evocation, "felt" qualities, elusiveness and an attempt to make visible that which is incorporeal. Nevertheless, this play does yield passages in which images are closely associated with what is happening in the relationships among the characters. Although such passages surface only briefly, they launch Lorquian imagery on a trajectory leading to the dynamic involvement of imagery in drama. But in the final analysis, one observes that in *El maleficio de la mariposa*, images that are infused with a dynamic quality are engulfed by evocative imagery. The mood of the play drifts further into the mists of imagination as La Mariposa continues to slip away into the dream world from which she seemed to emerge. "¿Por qué me turbáis mi sueño?", she asks (716). For the butterfly, a vibrant life exists beyond the beautiful meadow in a place in the imagination to which she has access through a silver thread. "El hilo / de plata va a los campos / donde se ve la vida," she says (716), and thus adds another image to those which have engaged our mind's eye in the process of forming a visual impression of what exists in the imagination of the characters.
    When La Mariposa begins to dance in anticipation of her flight away from Curianito, she leaves behind a dying dreamer who attempted to capture the love and beauty that he has been singing of with the voice of poetry. Through Curianito's attempt to possess La Mariposa, Lorca brings to the theater what Verlaine urges in his "Art poétique:"

Que ton vers soit la chose envolée
Q'on sent qui fuit d'une âme en allée
Vers d'autres cieux et d'autres amours.

78   The Dynamics of the Imagery in the Theater
       of Federico Garcia Lorca

....
Que ton vers soit la bonne aventure
Eparse au vent crispé du matin.[26]

Although the butterfly in *El maleficio de la mariposa* breaks the heart of the only creature who sought love in her beauty, we remember the poetic flights of the poet under her spell, because the imagery, through its cumulative effect, has impressed them very deeply in our mind.

Notes

1. *The Romantic Agony*, trans. Angus Davidson (London: Oxford Univ. Press, 1933), pp.197, 202.
2. *French Symbolism and the Modernist Movement* (Baton Rouge: Louisiana State Univ. Press, 1980), pp.19, 20.
3. "La Jeune Parque," in *Oeuvres*, Vol. 1, ed. Jean Hytier (Paris: Éditions Gallimard, 1957), p.96.
4. "En sourdine," in *Oeuvres poétiques complètes*, ed. Jacques Borel (Paris: Éditions Gallimard, 1962), p.120.
5. *The Shadowy Waters*, in *The Collected Plays of W.B. Yeats* (New York: Macmillan, 1953), p.107.
6. *Pastoral*, in *Teatro de ensueño* (Madrid: Renacimiento, S.A., 1911), p.84.
7. Maurice Maeterlinck, *The Blue Bird*, trans. Alexander Teixeira de Mattos (New York: Dodd, Mead and Co., 1965), pp.112-113, 118-119.
8. *The Shadowy Waters*, pp.102, 109.
9. "Lesbos" from *Fleurs du Mal* in *The Flowers of Evil*, trans. Francis Duke (n.p.: Univ. Of Virginia Press, 1961), p.200.
10. "À Clymène," in *Oeuvres*, p.116.
11. "Orphée," in *Oeuvres*, pp.76-77.
12. *Soledades*, ed. Dámaso Alonso (Madrid: Revista de Occidente, 1927), pp.67-69.
13. "Yo soy aquel . . .", in *Antología/Rubén Darío*, ed. Carmen Ruiz Barrionuevo, Colección Austral (1987), Literatura (Madrid: Espasa-Calpe, 1992 [?]), p.117.
14. "Sur l'Herbe," in *Oeuvres*, p.108.
15. Verlaine, "Clair de Lune," in Oeuvres, p.107.
16. *La Belle Dame sans Merci: A Ballad*, in *Complete Poems/John Keats*, ed. Jack Stillinger (Cambridge, Mass.: The Belknap Press of Harvard Univ. Press, 1982), p.270.
17. Verlaine, "Mon Rêve familier," in *Oeuvres*, p.63.
18. Rubén Darío, "Ite, missa est," in *Antología/Rubén Darío*, p.85.
19. "Dice Mía," in *Antología poética/Rubén Darío*, ed. Arturo Torres Rioseco (Berkeley: Univ. of California Press, 1949), p.32.

20. "Divina Psiquis," in *Antología/Rubén Darío*, p.134.
21. "Hérodiade," in *Selected Poems by Stéphane Mallarmé*, trans. C.F. MacIntyre (Berkeley: Univ. of California Press, 1957), p.28.
22. "Correspondances," from *Fleurs du Mal*, in *The Flowers of Evil*, p.18.
23. "El año lírico," from *Azul...* in *Azul.../Cantos de vida y esperanza*, ed. Álvaro Salvador, Colección Austral (Madrid: Espasa-Calpe, 1992), p.148.
24. "Chanson d'Automne," in *Oeuvres*, p.72.
25. "Mon Rêve familier," in *Oeuvres*, p.63.
26. "Art poétique," in *Oeuvres*, p.327.

Chapter 4
Mariana Pineda

In *Mariana Pineda*, Lorca dramatizes the story of a woman who escapes reality by transforming personal love and political involvement into an act of heroism that becomes legend. The imagery, therefore, is shaped by the playwright's presentation of Granada's heroine both from within, at the personal level, and from a distance, with her story set into narrative frames that lend the air of a *romance* or legend to her drama.

To establish a mood and to make Mariana's feelings palpable for the reader, Lorca employs prominent characteristics of the metaphorical language of his first play, *El maleficio de la mariposa*: gradual accumulation of allusive and evocative language, fused images, expanded metaphors and words that speak directly to the senses. As in the earlier play, *Mariana Pineda* contains images whose total effect creates an awareness of the protagonist's state of mind and the mood that surrounds her—images that radiate through the text in a manner similar to the process involved in the development of an expanding metaphor as described by Lorca in "La imagen poética de don Luis de Góngora." In the incremental presentation of images that form a total impression of the protagonist in her circumstances, *Mariana Pineda*, like *El maleficio de la mariposa*, also shows a strong affinity for Symbolist and Modernista writings as exemplified by works of Maeterlinck, Verlaine and Yeats as well as Antonio Machado, Martínez Sierra and Marquina. But within this Symbolist-Modernista context, Lorca leads images in the direction they will take in his later plays where he achieves a symbiotic relationship between poetry and drama, a development that owes much to the use of the traditional Spanish *romance* in *Mariana Pineda*.

Popular songs and traditional ballads, used very frequently by dramatists such as Lope de Vega in the Golden Age and Marquina in a period closer to Lorca's works for the theater, form a significant part of the metaphorical structure of *Mariana Pineda*. This was Lorca's successful play and an early attempt to bring dynamism to images used in dialogue. In this play, the *romances* not only bear thematic material and frame various stages of the drama but also provide the narrative with a poetic technique for fusing the personal and human drama with the legendary quality of Mariana's story. Even Mariana herself assumes what might be called the role of the *juglar* in telling her own story.

Before exploring Lorca's dynamic use of *romances* in *Mariana Pineda*, we will direct our attention to the prominent imagery continuities, because 1) they look back to *El maleficio de la mariposa* and 2) they anticipate Lorca's use of imagery in later plays. As in *El maleficio de la mariposa*, the imagery continuities in *Mariana Pineda* interact primarily to create a feeling of sadness and impending tragedy that permeates the play. As the drama develops, rain becomes linked to tears, trembling and mourning; red thread becomes associated with blood and death; the sea provides images of drowning and hopes lost on shore; and light, having yielded to twilight and then to night, returns as Mariana escapes into an imagination that provides her with a means of transcending gloomy reality.

With respect to the dynamic quality of the imagery, *Mariana Pineda* firmly sets Lorquian drama on a course in which imagery continuities not only foreshadow events, illustrate a theme or evoke and heighten an awareness of the presence of emotions in the characters, but also coalesce with dramatic contexts that make the reader feel what is taking place at various stages in the interaction of these characters. The imagery in *Mariana Pineda* is anchored in five key continuities—rain and tears, blood, the sea, light-darkness and dreams—with each one contributing to the characterization of Mariana as a woman who suffers personal anxieties so intensely that she transcends the reality of her life by consciously transforming herself into the protagonist of a legend.

The general tone of this play is set in the opening *romance* which introduces several elements of the key imagery continuities:

¡Oh, qué día tan triste en Granada,
que a las piedras hacía llorar
al ver que Mariana se muere
en cadalso por no declarar!

Marianita sentada en su cuarto
no paraba de considerar:

"Si Pedrosa me viera bordando
la bandera de la Libertad."

¡Oh, qué día tan triste en Granada,
las campanas doblar y doblar! (781-782)

"Triste," "llorar," "se muere" and "la Libertad" are words that can and will be applied to Mariana, expressing the sadness in her life, her death and the legend in which she is a symbol of Liberty.

This play is filled with images of rain and tears that create a sense of Mariana's personal grief as well as the collective lament evidenced in the *romance* that sings of her fate. In Act I, Scene 4, Lucía makes what is ostensibly a casual comment: "Hay nubes por Parapanda. / Lloverá, aunque Dios no quiera" (794); yet when taken as one increment among many in an imagery continuity, Lucía's comment begins to implant in the text a feeling of sadness that emanates from the rain-tears imagery. This soft "voice" acquires more volume in Act II, Scene 6, when the stage directions state "Fuera se oye la lluvia y el viento" (834) and when Conspirador 2° says shortly thereafter: "La lluvia, como un sauce de cristal, / sobre las casas de Granada cae" (835). The rain becomes more persistent as the act progresses as evidenced in the stage direction indicating that the rain should be heard especially in moments of silence between Pedrosa and Mariana. "¡Qué manera de llover!", exclaims Pedrosa (850)—an observation that is echoed at the close of the act when Angustias tells Mariana: "Tu niña llora. / Tiene miedo del aire y de la lluvia" (859). The persistent rain thus sets the tone for the mounting tension in Mariana's household. This heightened awareness of an emotional state, expressed in terms of a manifestation of nature that makes its presence felt in the dialogue, has a counterpart in the theater of Maeterlinck. When Pelléas and Mélisande meet at "la fontaine des aveugles," the water and its mysterious clarity and depth becomes a third character, beckoning the lovers towards an imagined source of understanding that binds them to each other:

> Oh! l'eau est claire . . . Elle est fraîche . . . On entendrait dormir l'eau . . . Je voudrais voir le fond de l'eau . . . Elle est peut-être aussi profonde que la mer . . . Si quelque chose brillait au fond . . . Je voudrait toucher l'eau . . . Vos cheveux ont plongé dan l'eau . . . J'ai vu passer quelque chose au fond de l'eau . . . Il [l'anneau] est tombé dans l'eau! . . . elle est si loin de nous! . . . Il ne faut pas inquieter ainsi pour une bague . . .[1]

As the rain intensifies in *Mariana Pineda* to the point of frightening Mariana's child, the imagery associated with tears insinuates itself more forcibly into the text: "Me siento vestida de temblor y llanto" (806); "Pues si mi pecho tuviera / vidrieras de cristal, / te asomaras y lo vieras gotas de sangre llorar" (813). This series of rain-tears imagery that pervades the text and evokes Mariana's increasing sadness and apprehension recalls Mélisande who describes her constant weeping as something beyond her control and also reminds one of Pelléas who says, when Mélisande tells him that she loves him, "on dirait qu'il a plu sur mon coeur!" (Act IV, Scene 3). The rain-tears-sadness continuity in *Mariana Pineda* is one indicator that in this play Lorca continues to use metaphorical language having the allusive, evocative quality of the imagery of *El maleficio de la mariposa*. Thus, the playwright maintains a strong connection to Symbolist imagery, recalling lines like Verlaine's famous "Il pleure dans mon coeur / Comme il pleut sur la ville."[2]

Lorca also expands the imagery associated with the tears that are shed in Mariana's heart to include a collective grief ("sobre los barcos lloraba / toda la marinera" [844]); and in this context, Mariana gives the impression of being consciously aware of composing her own story. "Mírame y llora," she says. "¡Ahora empiezo a morir!" (859) In this regard, Mariana acts as a character whose imagination leads her to perceive her life as if it were already the subject of a drama. Like Hamlet as explained in Lionel Abel's work on Shakespearean metatheater[3] and Perlimplín in Philip Silver's analysis of several "metaobras dramáticas" of Lorca,[4] Mariana sometimes views herself from a vantage point that permits her to see herself as a character in a drama. Of Lorca and metatheater Silver writes:

> La 'poesía' que está en todas partes—incluso en *Yerma* y en *La casa de Bernarda Alba*—no es el verso dramático, sino la representación, en los papeles de los principales personajes, de que *esta* vida, esta cosa insustancial, es un sueño, y que ellos están atrapados en un 'drama' que sólo incidentalmente tiene que ver con las cosas de este mundo: en una palabra, que representan un papel en una obra que excede los límites de la pieza en que actúan. (175)

As if she were aware that she was destined to become a legend, Mariana says in the final moments of the play "Salvo a muchas criaturas que llorarán mi muerte" (889)—words that not only resemble but seem to confirm the comment made by Lucía in Act I ("Lloverá, aunque Dios no quiera" [794]). Thus, the playwright brings the rain-tears imagery full circle in its role of establishing the mood and tone of this drama.

The fact that images accumulate in *Mariana Pineda* in a way that gradually shapes for the reader a "character" in the mind's eye places this drama in the tradition of Symbolist and Modernista works. In this respect, one can cite similarities from works that preceded Lorca's play and with which it has an affinity. In Act III of *Pelléas et Mélisande*, one image sweeps another along until the reader cannot escape the overwhelming feeling that mystery and death are present: "Voici l'eau stagnante," "Sentez-vous l'odeur de mort qui monte!," "Il y a là un air humide et lourd comme une rosée de plomb, et des ténèbres épaisses comme une pâte empoisonée."[5] Similarly, in Yeats's *The Land of Heart's Desire*, the struggle for Mary's soul is clothed in the mystery of a wind that inevitably sweeps her away: "I had no sooner hung it on the nail / Before a child ran up out of the wind;" "No one's child at all. / She often dreams that some one has gone by, / When there was nothing but a puff of wind;" "For I would ride with you upon the wind;" "The wind blows out of the gates of the day, / The wind blows over the lonely heart."[6]

Lorca's use of imagery to establish a pervasive mood is also akin to what Antonio Machado accomplishes in "La tierra de Alvargonzález" where images produce a sense of decay, cold and death: "la luna llena manchada / de un arrebol purpurino;" "los viejos [pinos] cubiertos de blanca lepra, / musgos y líquenes canos;" "Larga es la noche y el frío / arrecia. Un candil humea / en el muro ennegrecido."[7] Also, by means of a series of images that subtly intensify a feeling, Martínez Sierra gradually underpins *Cuento de labios en flor* with melancholy: "Me gustaría ir vestida de musgo;" "Si nunca hiciese frío ni lloviese, podría uno andar siempre por esos mundos . . .''; "negra como la noche fué su tristeza, y su llanto amargo como el agua del mar;" "estoy contenta de llorar;" "Yo quisiera vivir en el agua."[8] Further, the imagery associated with tears in *Mariana Pineda* also recalls Marquina's *La ermita, la fuente y el río* whose text contains many references to tears that help sustain the feeling of Deseada's sadness. As in these examples from other playwrights, *Mariana Pineda* contains abundant evidence that the fate of a character is expressed through layered images that evoke a feeling or mood that is palpably present as one scene follows another.

In addition to permeating the text with a mood of sadness, Lorca also layers images to create the feeling that Mariana's fate is linked to tragedy. Images associated with blood, wounds and death appear frequently, beginning with Mariana's active participation in the conspiracy by embroidering a flag:

> Borda y borda lentamente.
> Yo lo he visto por el ojo de la llave.
> Parecía el hilo rojo, entre sus dedos
> Una herida de cuchillo sobre el aire. (783)

By expanding the central image ("Parecía el hilo rojo") to include Mariana ("entre sus dedos") and to link her with the idea of bloodshed ("una herida de cuchillo"), Lorca demonstrates the technique of the expanding metaphor he described in "La imagen poética de don Luis de Góngora." Tracing this technique back to Góngora, we can cite a brief example from Modernista theater—Marquina's *La ermita, la fuente y el río*. In this instance, a metaphorical element expands until a human feeling is made "visible." Deseada, repressing her kindled love for Manuel, begins a metaphor thus:

> Me gustaría, Manuel,
> que no fuéramos parientes;
> ¡[sic] verte siempre y que las gentes
> te vieran, bravo y cruel,
> con el tallo de un clavel
> apretado entre los dientes; ...

She then expands the "bravo-cruel" "clavel-dientes" images:

> y cada vez que le dieras
> mordiéndolo un restregón,
> sufrir yo muerte y pasión, ...

Then she intensifies the feeling evoked by the beauty-violence counterpoint with this intensification in the imagery:

> como si con las tijeras
> de tus dientes me partieras
> las venas del corazón.[9]

For a masterful example of an expanding image, we return to Góngora, citing the image of the daughters of the Duque de Feria as "hijas del ruiseñor" in the sonnet entitled "En la muerte de tres hijas del Duque de Feria":

Entre las hojas cinco, generosa
si verde pompa no de un campo de oro,
prendas sin pluma a ruiseñor canoro
degolló mudas sierpe venenosa.
Al culto padre no con voz piadosa,
mas con gemido alterno y dulce lloro,
armoniosas lágrimas al coro
de las aves oyó la selva umbrosa.
Lloró el Tajo cristal, a cuya espuma
dio poca sangre el mal logrado terno,
terno de aladas cítaras süaves.
Que rayos hoy sus cuerdas, y su pluma
brillante siempre luz de un Sol eterno,
dulcemente dejaron de ser aves.[10]

Góngora expands the image "hijas del ruiseñor" through words associated with music and space until a final transformation occurs ("dulcemente dejaron de ser aves"). The word "ruiseñor" gives birth to "aladas cítaras" which in turn leads to "cuerdas" and "pluma" that become transformed into "rayos" and "luz." Through a fusion of images heavily dependent on the senses, Góngora permits us to "see" an idea: i.e., the heavenward ascent of the soul of the three daughters upon their death.

Although the aesthetic in Góngora's poem is very different from that of Lorca's play, the technique of interlocking images so that their cumulative effect concretizes an abstraction is similar. Lorca expands the images of blood, a wound and a blade that appeared in the opening *romance* of *Mariana Pineda* so that an increasing sense of tragedy accompanies the intensifying mood of sadness created by the rain-tears imagery. In subsequent passages, "el hilo rojo" in Angustias's description of Mariana embroidering becomes ". . . la vena . . . más ancha, / por donde brota la sangre / más caliente y encarnada;" and "una herida de cuchillo sobre el aire" takes the form of "¡Noche temida y soñada; / que me hieres ya de lejos / con larguísimas espadas!" as one image follows another in the evocation of the feeling of tragedy:

Si toda la tarde fuera
como un gran pájaro, ¡cuántas
duras flechas lanzaría
para cerrarle las alas! (795)

¡Noche temida y soñada;
que me hieres ya de lejos
con larguísimas espadas! (796)

Pedrosa conoce el sitio
donde la vena es más ancha,
por donde brota la sangre
más caliente y encarnada. (799)

Pues si mi pecho tuviera
vidrieras de cristal
te asomaras y lo vieras
gotas de sangre llorar. (813)

¡Libertad, aunque con sangre llame
a todas las puertas! (831)

Mi sangre se agita y tiembla,
como un árbol de coral
con la marejada tierna. (871)

... Doy mi sangre,
que es tu sangre y la sangre de todas las
   criaturas. (889)¡

Yo soy la Libertad, herida por los hombres! (891)

What Góngora does with interlocking images to evoke an idea, Lorca does to evoke a feeling. One might say, therefore, that Lorca seems to take what he perceives to be a great strength of Góngora—namely, the expanding metaphor, and uses it for drama.

By giving metaphorical language room to expand in the direction of dramatic action, there begins to stir in Lorca a sense of imagistic movement that is missing in Symbolist plays such as *Pelléas et Mélisande* and *The Shadowy Waters*. However, before we begin to explore in detail the dynamic qualities of the imagery in *Mariana Pineda*, we will continue our study of the key imagery continuities and point out more affinities with Symbolism that set Lorca on a course which develops the dramatic possibilities of imagery.

In order to create a well-defined image of a trembling figure destined to die, Lorca uses the Symbolist technique he employed to create an atmosphere charged with sadness and impending disaster. That is to say, images follow one another until their total effect is felt by the reader. Early in Act I, Mariana's trembling is described in a series of images drawn from nature, steeped in the senses and aimed towards making human feelings visible. Fluttering wings, rippling water and shimmering light describe Mariana's agitated appearance as related by Amparo:

> ... Dijo que en tus ojos
> había un constante desfile de pájaros.
> Un temblor divino, como de agua clara,
> sorprendida siempre bajo el arrayán,
> o temblor de luna sobre una pecera
> donde un pez de plata finge rojo sueño. (790)

By expanding the eye-bird image to include water ("como de agua clara"), land ("el arrayán") and sky ("luna"), and then by fusing the water and moon images through "pez" and "plata" to create a surrealist image ("donde un pez de plata finge rojo sueño"), Lorca uses nature to infuse Mariana's human reaction (trembling) with an unearthly quality that befits the legendary aura surrounding the heroine. The foregoing imagery in a description of Mariana not only anticipates her trembling during the play but also heightens our awareness of the general state of agitation alluded to in images of tears and blood. After indicating in a series of stage directions that Mariana is becoming increasingly agitated ("turbada," "impaciente," "ansiosamente," "está como en vilo," "llena de angustia," "palidísima y en acecho"), the playwright provides Mariana with these phrases that help us visualize the emotional feeling elicited in Amparo's description: "Me siento vestida de temblor y llanto" (806); "Mi sangre se agita y tiembla, / como un árbol de coral / con la marejada tierna" (871). Gradually the poetry moves closer to expressing the elusive emotional reality that Mariana experiences. Gradually, through the metaphorical language, Mariana's trembling becomes a "visible" inner state of being.

In addition to images of rain, tears and blood, the playwright sets water imagery in the text to express the insidious presence of fate accompanying Mariana as she becomes more deeply immersed in a dangerous situation, drifting further away from reality towards an awareness of having already met that fate:

> Ahora los ríos sobre España
> en vez de ser ríos son
> largas cadenas de agua. (801)

Acecho un mar oscuro, sin fondo ni oleaje,
en espera de gentes que te traigan ahogado. (832)

Pedro, mira por mí. Sé muy prudente,
que me falta muy poco para ahogarme. (840)

Ya soy como la estrella sobre el agua profunda,
última débil brisa que se pierde en los álamos. (886)

Like the accumulating images in a Symbolist poem drawing us closer to an elusive "something," each image of malevolent waters makes Mariana's apprehension—her fear of "drowning"—more palpable.

It is in the light-darkness imagery continuity, however, that *Mariana Pineda* shows the strong affinity for Symbolist imagery that Lorca demonstrated earlier in his first play, *El maleficio de la mariposa*. As day yields to night, Mariana slips deeper into her commitment to a cause that will prove fatal for her; and as radiant light replaces darkness, Mariana places herself outside reality by imagining herself transformed by her love into the embodiment of Liberty.

The most concentrated expression of the light-darkness imagery appears in Act I, Scene 5, when night descends on Granada and on Mariana's heart—an event that is foreshadowed when Mariana describes the happiness of her friends as "La misma alegría que la viejecilla / siente cuando el sol se duerme en sus manos / y ella lo acaricia creyendo que nunca / la noche y el frío cercarán su casa" (790). Night finally does arrive for Mariana, and in it she senses the extent of the danger to which she has exposed herself: "¡Noche temida y soñada, / que me hieres ya de lejos / con larguísimas espadas!" (796). Lorca, like many Symbolist and Modernista writers, imbues dusk with a sense of magic. As darkness overcomes the waning light, a natural setting is provided for Mariana's contemplative attitude and evokes images from such poets as Verlaine and Mallarmé. In Verlaine's "Crépuscule du soir mystique" we read:

> Le Souvenir avec le Crépuscule
> Rougeoie et tremble à l'ardent horizon
> De l'Espérance en flamme qui recule
> Et s'agrandit ainsi qu'une cloison
> Mystérieuse . . . [11]

Mallarmé also charges twilight with a mysterious vibrancy:

Une fraîcheur de crépuscule
Te vient à chaque battement
Dont le coup prisonnier recule
L'horizon délicatement.
Vertige! . . . [12]

A correspondence between waning light and contemplation is also present in lines from Antonio Machado: "Yo iba haciendo mi camino, / absorto en el solitario crepúsculo campesino,"[13] as well as in the following verses from Rubén Darío and Juan Ramón Jiménez:

En las pálidas tardes
yerran nubes tranquilas
en azul; en las ardientes manos
se posan las cabezas pensativas.[14]

y el crepúsculo vago, que cambia
    las verdades,
pone en todo, al rozarlo, no sé qué
    gasas húmedas.[15]

However, when one compares Symbolist-Modernista passages like those cited above with Lorca's use of the image of "crepúsculo" in the scene that reveals Mariana's growing apprehension and inner tensions, it becomes apparent that in *Mariana Pineda*, Lorca takes a very significant step to move away from imagery that is relatively static. This development that takes Lorca away from Symbolism is especially demonstrable if we compare Lorca's treatment of twilight in *Mariana Pineda* with Maeterlinck's use of a light-darkness continuity in the metaphorical language of *Pelléas et Mélisande*. Darkness hangs heavily over the principal characters in both plays, suggesting a stifling atmosphere and impending doom. For Maeterlinck, the presence or absence of darkness, however momentary, serves to reveal the unspoken feelings of characters that appear to move *through* rather than act *in* a haunting and almost haunted landscape. Images of light gradually evoke the presence of the love between Pelléas and Mélisande. "Donnez-moi la main," says Pelléas to Mélisande in Act II, Scene 3, "ne tremblez pas, ne tremblez pas ainsi. Il n'y a pas de danger, nous nous arrêterons au moment que nous n'apercevrons plus la clarté de la mer."[16] In Lorca, on the other hand, the presence or absence of darkness is more directly tied to the dramatic moment in the narrative line of unfolding events. Although both playwrights create a network of imagistic associations between man and nature so that even fragments of scenes contain an imagistic structure that heightens or illuminates the feelings, thoughts and actions of the characters, what is predominantly evocative for Maeterlinck begins to ally itself with drama for Lorca.

The dramatic potential of images in *Mariana Pineda* appears fleetingly as well as in more complex contexts. One example of a relatively uncomplicated image that fulfills this potential in the context of light and darkness occurs in Act II, Scene 9 when Mariana tells Pedrosa "La noche estaba triste / y me puse a cantar" (850). Instead of saying directly "Yo estaba triste," Mariana expresses her present emotional state by using "noche," a word that previously was charged with foreboding. Thus, the brief appearance of the darkness continuity slightly accentuates Mariana's growing agitation. A more complex example appears in Act II when the playwright, sustaining the darkness continuity, turns to the sea imagery that is linked to changes in Mariana's relationship with Pedro. In Pedro's presence, a radiant Mariana has confirmed her love for him to such a degree that at this moment she feels that the intensity of that love can transcend life:

> Ahora puedo perderte, puedo perder tu vida.
> Como la enamorada de un marinero loco
> que navegara eterno sobre una barca vieja,
> acecho un mar oscuro, sin fondo ni oleaje,
> en espera de gentes que te traigan ahogado. (831-832)

This awareness of her love-death relationship with Pedro then proceeds to find direct expression in the dramatic context of Pedro and Mariana awaiting news from a messenger:

> Mariana: Ahora llega.
> Pedro Y al fin sabremos algo.
> Conspirador 3°: Bien venido, si buenas cartas trae.
> Mariana (Apasionada, a Pedro): Pedro, mira por mí.
> Sé muy prudente,
> que me falta muy poco para ahogarme. (840)

Thus, through "te traigan ahogado" in the first passage quoted above and "ahogarme" in the second, the dramatist has 1) linked two scenes related in tone (if not in intensity) and 2) alluded to the idea that the fate of one character is linked to that of the other.

In the twilight scene of Act I to which we have already referred, Lorca activates the image of dusk so that it not only reflects Mariana's mood but also anticipates action. In the gathering dusk, Mariana becomes pensive:

> Tardecillo es. . . .
> [Mariana atraviesa rápidamente la escena y mira la hora en uno de esos grandes relojes dorados, donde suena toda la poesía exquisita de la hora y el siglo. Se asoma a los cristales y ve la última luz de la tarde.] (795)

She becomes increasingly agitated before Fernando arrives:

> ¡Con qué trabajo tan grande
> deja la luz a Granada!
> . . . . . .
> ¡Y esta noche que no llega! (796)

When Mariana's hated enemy, Pedrosa, is mentioned, the stage direction indicates that the scene has "una dulce penumbra," and the dialogue continues:

> Fernando: ¡Bien supo el rey lo que se hizo
>   al mandarlo aquí a Granada!
> Mariana: Ya es noche. ¡Clavela! ¡Luces! (800)

Thus, before Pedrosa appears, his presence and its fearful effect on Mariana is already felt through the allusive expanding metaphor of night descending on Granada; and when she says "Ya es noche," she punctuates her fears with an expression of the inevitable. Although this expanding image of nightfall reminds one of lines from Góngora's "Soledad primera" ("Vence la noche al fin, y triunfa mudo / el silencio, aunque breve, del rüido")[17] and Verlaine's "L'Heure du berger" ("Blanche Vénus émerge, et c'est la Nuit"),[18] it begins to break away from the confines of static imagery in the sense that it is related to what is happening to the characters.

An imagery-character relationship is also present when darkness descends on the convent in Act III. Images with a light-darkness counterpoint accumulate to anticipate Mariana's resolve to turn her back on the reality of night and to imagine a dawn that will reflect her death as a triumph: " . . . y al alba / por cada estrella que muere / nace diminuta flauta" (880); "yo soy como la estrella sobre el agua profunda, / última débil brisa que se pierde en los álamos" (886); "Nos espera una larga locura de luceros / que hay detrás de la muerte" (888); "Pero ¡qué bien entiendo lo que dice esta luz!" (889); "...Libertad verdadera, / enciende para mí tus estrellas distantes" (890).

In *Mariana Pineda*, light, or its absence, becomes associated with anxiety ("¡Noche temida y soñada; / que me hieres ya de lejos / con larguísimas espadas!" [796]); foreboding ("Y no me importa que el día / con la noche enturbiara" [813]); desire ("sobre tu cuello blanco, que tiene luz de luna" [832]); death ("Muy de noche lo mataron / con toda su compañía [843]); and faith ("Nos espera una larga locura de luceros / que hay detrás de la muerte" [888]). The light-darkness continuity, therefore, changes with the hope-despair fluctuations that Mariana experiences. This is different from the use of light in *Pelléas et Mélisande* where light remains at the level of symbolizing the deepening love between Pelléas and Mélesande. Lorca uses the gradual onset of night as an overarching metaphor for Mariana's movement towards disaster. Suggesting fear and danger, images of approaching darkness assume a dynamic quality as they help to express the intensification of Mariana's troubled and unsettled thoughts; and in her command for light following her firmly stated realization that night has finally arrived ("Ya es noche, ¡Clavela! ¡Luces!" [800]), one can sense the fervent determination that begins to take hold and finally place her beyond reality in the intense light of legend.

The element of dream and fantasy, of other-worldliness, is the final imagery continuity that we will trace as it follows Mariana's escape from the darkness of disillusionment into her imagination and finally into legend. Through images related to the world of dreams and the realm of the imagination, Mariana expresses feelings that move from apprehension ("Noche temida y soñada" [795]) towards longing (¡Ay, quién pudiera / en esta realidad estar soñando!" [803]), to resolution ("Y no me importa que el día / con la noche enturbiara" [813]) and self-knowledge ("Que yo también estoy dormida, niños, / y voy volando por mi propio sueño" [826]). Doubt and pain momentarily take over, but they are then replaced by affirmation ("¡Pedro!, cuando se quiere / se está fuera del tiempo" [831]; "Y yo me muero de sueño" [849]) and hope ("vendrá por la madrugada / por la madrugada fresca, / cuando sobre el cielo oscuro / brilla el limonar apenas [869]; "¡Morir! ¡Qué largo sueño sin ensueños ni sombras!" [886]). Finally, the image of "ensueño" which has been increasing our awareness of Mariana's ability to visualize herself in a world beyond reality is used to express the idea that Mariana completely enters the world of imagination: "Y ahora ya no te quiero [a Pedro], porque soy una sombra. / . . . / . . . ¡Ya no conozco a nadie! / ¡Voy a dormir tranquila!" (887). In effect, Mariana appears to be telling her own story, acting as a dramatist revealing the emotional state of a protagonist whose actions are taking place first in the imagination of her creator and then in the mind's eye of the reader. In this respect, we can cite what Philip Silver has written concerning Lorca and metatheater: "Es un hecho, además, que en muchas de las obras teatrales de Lorca la acción dramática que presenciamos *es* el sueño del personaje principal."[19]

In an analysis of Yeats's theater, Katherine Worth writes that the playwright had to find theatrical means of not only drawing us into the world of a dream but also permitting us to stand outside the mind of characters who are dreaming.[20] That is to say, the reader "enters" or "experiences" a dream but also retains an awareness of observing a character experience the dream. If we expand this idea to include the *technique* of presenting images, we may apply it to what Lorca achieves in *Mariana Pineda* by incorporating *romances* and techniques of the traditional Spanish *romance* in the presentation of the drama. The ballad provides Lorca with a means for 1) stepping "outside the dreaming mind" to depict Mariana as a figure moving through sequential events of a drama and 2) establishing a milieu for metaphorical content through which the protagonist reveals and reflects upon her emotional state. In other words, Mariana is presented as a character playing out a drama as well as acting as if she were outside the drama, witnessing the enactment of her own story. In addition to the first-person statements made by the protagonist ("Me siento vestida de temblor y llanto;" "también estoy dormida;" "ya estoy muerta;" "voy a dormir tranquila"), an important reason for our impression that Mariana's story has already been "actualized" before unfolding in the mind of the reader is Lorca's use of *romances* that refract the heroine's story and frame various portions of the drama. Narrative poetry provides Lorca with a means of infusing this play, heavily steeped in poetic imagery, with a sense of continuous movement without disturbing the evocative mood established by the metaphorical language.

In Act I, dream imagery begins to lead Mariana in the direction of transcending the disastrous consequences of her clandestine activities ("¡No la quisiera abrir!", exclaims Mariana referring to a letter from Pedro. "¡Ay, quién pudiera / en esta realidad estar soñando!" [803]). In effect, Mariana begins to sing the *romance* that tells her story:

Como dicen por Granada,
¡soy una loca mujer! (809)
. . . .
Pero mi vida está fuera,
por el aire, por la mar,
por donde yo no quisiera. (809)

Mariana, like the reader of her drama, "hears" the sadness that will envelop Granada. When Pedro tells Mariana (Act II, Scene 5) that he cannot love her unless his heart has the freedom to do so, he prompts a radiant Mariana, swept further away from reality, to reactivate the dream imagery heard earlier ("Voy volando por mi propio sueño" [826]) by saying "cuando se quiere / se está fuera del tiempo" (831)—another comment that leads the reader to feel that Mariana is aware of another reality, i.e., her existence in a *romance* that narrates her story.

Due to the swiftness with which the playwright sets the mood as Mariana awaits news that will determine whether or not she will be rescued by her co-conspirators, the second scene of Act III gives us the feeling that we are listening to narrative poetry in addition to providing a setting for the reappearance of a dream-reality continuity. The scene begins thus:

Mariana: ¡Hermana!
Carmen (Volviéndose): ¿Qué desea?
Mariana: ¡Nada!
Carmen: ¡Decidlo, señora!
Mariana: Pensaba . . .
Carmen: ¿Qué?
Mariana: Si pudiera
quedarme aquí, en el Beaterio,
para siempre.
Carmen: ¡Qué contentas
nos pondríamos!
Mariana: ¡No puedo!
Carmen: ¿Por qué? (864-865)

At this point in the dialogue, Mariana answers as if she were already outside reality: "Porque ya estoy muerta;" and shortly thereafter, as if she were a *juglar* interrupting the narrative of the *romance* with a personal exclamation, she says "¡Ay, qué buen soñar!" (865). Now the reader feels that Mariana possesses self-knowledge with respect to her legendary status—a situation that she describes in these words: "Este silencio me pesa / mágicamente" (865). Thus, the dialogue contains a feeling of movement that is a characteristic of a *romance* while retaining the inward-looking, dream continuity which is an important component of the metaphorical language.

As Act III unfolds, there are more indications that Mariana "listens" to her own story as she becomes legend. In a segment very reminiscent of the scene in Lope de Vega's *El caballero de Olmedo* in which Don Alonso hears a voice singing about his fate, Mariana hears someone singing:

A la vera del agua,
sin que nadie la viera,
se murió mi esperanza. (871)

This voice confirms Mariana's statement earlier in the act ("ya estoy muerta") and anticipates a repetition of this phrase ("¡Ya estoy muerta, Fernando! [886]) that reaffirms our feeling that Mariana is composing her own *romance*. Due to this sense of narrative movement, Mariana's repetitions appear to be less static than, for example, Mélisande's mesmerizing repetitions that evoke her state of mind.

In the final moments of the play, Mariana's words resonate with various elements of the imagery continuities that have been "telling" her story through "felt qualities" emanating from the text. To conclude her *romance*, Mariana expresses herself through images of water, light, darkness and dreams: ". . . Tus palabras me llegan / a través del gran río del mundo que abandono. / Ya soy como la estrella sobre el agua profunda . . ."; "¡Morir! ¡Qué largo sueño sin ensueños ni sombras!" (886). By crying out to the absent Pedro "Y ahora ya no te quiero, porque soy una sombra" (887), Mariana has already become absorbed into the *romance* that sings her memory; and when she proudly declares "Amas la Libertad por encima de todo, / pero yo soy la misma Libertad" (889), she elevates herself to the transcendental level of "Libertad" as expressed in the *romance* at the beginning of the drama. By repeating the opening *romance* at the conclusion of the play, Lorca not only provides a frame for the drama, but also reinforces the feeling we have that Mariana is actively engaged in reciting her own *romance*. In a phrase that recalls Hamlet's "Absent thee from felicity awhile, / And in this harsh world draw thy breath in pain, / To tell my story,"[21] Mariana herself sets the stage for the reappearance of the opening *romance* when she tells those to whom she bids farewell: "Contad mi triste historia a los niños que pasen" (890). By reminding us that we are "listening" to a *romance*, the playwright has again confirmed our feeling that there is narrative movement in a play whose poetry places it in the tradition of Symbolist-Modernista theater.

To stress the importance of Lorca's dynamic use of *romances*, we can look back briefly for a point of contrast. Lázaro Carreter has written that *Mariana Pineda* can be classified as Modernista theater thematically and structurally especially because of its heavy dependence on material drawn from history and on lyrical elements, either elegiac (such as Mariana's musing "Si toda la tarde fuera / como un gran pájaro") or descriptive (for example, the "romance" of the bullfight in Ronda)—elements that appear in the form of arias removed from the dramatic process.[22] If considered primarily from the point of view of structure, with the *romance* as a prominent feature, *Mariana Pineda* can, indeed, be compared with a Modernista play such as Marquina's *La ermita, la fuente y el río*. Like *Mariana Pineda*, Marquina's drama relies heavily on the *romance*. The action of each of the three acts revolves around an idea contained in an extended poetic passage, with a cypress tree at a hermitage, a fountain and a river supplying the central images. The protagonist summarizes each as follows:

> La ermita, para empezar
> una mañana a vivir;
> la fuente, para sufrir,
> y el río, para llorar.[23]

Lorca, however, unlike Marquina, does not use narrative poetry merely to illustrate or frame an idea. For Lorca, a *romance* also becomes a "narrative repository" for images that limn Mariana's story.

The *romance* provides Lorca with a means of keeping alive the narrative line of a drama whose text is replete with metaphorical continuities that are mood-setting, allusive and evocative. *Mariana Pineda*, therefore, avoids dramatic stasis that occurs in a play like *Pelléas et Mélisande* that depends very heavily on the effect produced by the evocation of inner thoughts and emotions. Further, if we say that Lorca's heroine gives us the feeling that she is the *juglar* singing portions of the ballad as the drama unfolds, we can conclude that the popular Spanish *romance* has given Lorca what Worth calls "theatrical means of standing outside the dreaming mind as well as of registering the process of dreaming."[24]

By using *romances* and popular songs to frame action, foreshadow events and present the narrative line of a drama in capsule form, Lorca continues a tradition that includes Lope de Vega as one of its greatest exponents as well as a more recent dramatist such as Marquina who used the *copla* to reflect a character's state of mind or prefigure events.[25] The example that follows will help place Lorca's use of the *romance* in perspective.

In Act II of Lope's *El caballero de Olmedo*, Tello addresses Inés:

> Oye una glosa a un estribo
> que compuso don Alonso,
> a manera de responso,
> si los hay en muerto vivo.
>   "En el valle a Inés
>   la dejé riendo:
>   si la ves, Andrés,
>   dile cuál me ves
>   por ella muriendo."[26]

Tello then proceeds to give this refrain a *glosa* whose central idea has two roots: 1) imagery associated with "estrellas-flores" ("Andrés, después que las bellas / Plantas de Inés goza el valle, / Tanto florece con ellas, / Que quiso el cielo trocalle / Por sus flores sus estrellas") and 2) two sets of counterpoints: "mirar-matar," and "vivir-morir" ("Yo la vi de amor huyendo, / Cuanto miraba matando"; "Pues da vida a cuantos mata"). Both the refrain and its gloss contain the idea of death that foreshadows the fate of Alonso, Tello's master. But their dramatic effect for this play is dissipated, because they do not relate to the *development* of the unfolding drama as much as they repeat a description of Alonso's emotional state that had already been revealed at the beginning of the act. Tello's recitation of Alonso's poem, nevertheless, serves the drama in at least two important ways: 1) it gives Tello an opportunity to describe Alonso's condition directly to Inés, and 2) it provides a highly dramatic moment. However, if the purpose of the song had been to relate imagery to the dramatic moment, we could say that Tello's recitation seems to arrest the action momentarily, because the words do not reflect movement with respect to Alonso's predicament.

Lorca, on the other hand, does not give us the feeling that dramatic momentum has been lost. In *Mariana Pineda* he begins to expand the use of the *romance* by making it a vehicle for carrying imagery continuities further along with the drama. The relationships that characters have with each other and the emotions behind those relationships find in ballads and popular songs a milieu for interaction among components of the metaphorical language through which they are expressed. In other words, through narrative poetry, a playwright can tie poetic elements of a text to the narrative line of a drama. This is the development that clearly emerges from *Mariana Pineda*.

Mariana's fateful struggle with Pedrosa and her flight into legend is fleshed out against a background established in the *romance* of the prologue in which the setting is Granada, the mood most somber ("¡Oh, qué día tan triste en Granada, / que a las piedras hacía llorar" [781]) and the struggle one of personal determination ("Marianita sentada en su cuarto / no paraba de considerar: / 'Si Pedrosa me viera bordando / la bandera de la Libertad,'"). In this *romance*, an event takes place ("Marianita se muere") caused by specific actions ("bordando la bandera," "por no declarar") associated with a cause ("Libertad") for which the protagonist is willing to die.

The playwright then opens the drama with dialogue that immediately places Mariana in the context of the *romance* of the prologue. Doña Angustias tells Clavela that she has observed a solitary Mariana embroidering a flag, and then she enshrouds this action in foreboding: "Parecía el hilo rojo, entre sus dedos, / una herida de cuchillo sobre el aire" (783). Thus, very quickly, the protagonist and the somber setting of the opening *romance* are echoed in the human drama. Another echo from the opening *romance* is heard in Act I, Scene 5, when Fernando introduces the name of Pedrosa into the conversation as night gradually approaches (" . . . pero Pedrosa / ya buscará su garganta. / Pedrosa conoce el sitio / donde la vena es más ancha, / por donde brota la sangre / más caliente y encarnada" [799]). For the reader who still "hears" the opening *romance*, Fernando's words seem to complete these lines of that *romance*: "'Si Pedrosa me viera bordando / la bandera de la Libertad.'" The scene in the dying afternoon in Granada thus engages the *romance* in the dialogue of the drama that begins to enact what was related in the *romance*. Further, when Mariana says that Granada stubbornly resists night as it approaches ("¡Con qué trabajo tan grande / deja la luz a Granada!" [796]), one also recalls the portion of the opening *romance* that refers to Marianita's determination never to surrender. Thus, the image of twilight receives a dramatic impulse set in motion by the opening *romance*.

The opening *romance* also makes its presence felt at the end of Act I when Angustias reports that the children, after having found the flag that Mariana has been embroidering in secret, are pretending to be dead and have wrapped themselves in the flag. In this incident that links death with the flag, Lorca has taken from the opening *romance* the idea that Mariana's clandestine activities are fraught with danger and has clothed it in an image related to a specific dramatic context. One can also say that at this point in the drama, Mariana, like the children playing with the flag, has enveloped herself with the "flag" of "Libertad" that could become her shroud. Through what Lorca called a "salto ecuestre" which takes place in the mind of the reader who is following the course of the metaphorical language, the image of the children wrapped in the flag associates itself with the image of Mariana engaging in activities which, as we were told in the *romance*, lead to her death.

The narrative voice of the opening *romance* is also "heard" in Act II, Scene 5 when Pedro makes his first appearance:

> La bandera que bordas temblará por las calles
> entre el calor entero del pueblo de Granada.
> Por ti la Libertad suspirada por todos
> pisará tierra dura con anchos pies de plata.
> Pero si así no fuese; si Pedrosa . . . (829)

At this instant, Pedro is interrupted by a terrified Mariana ("¡No sigas!"); and the reader who still "hears" echoes of the *romance* in the prologue may speculate that perhaps Mariana is also "listening" to the sad narrative of the *romance* and expects Pedro to complete his sentence with almost the exact words of this couplet from the *romance*: "'Si Pedrosa me viera bordando / la bandera de la Libertad.'" Again the playwright sets an evocative image in motion ("La Libertad . . . pisará tierra dura con anchos pies de plata") by placing it in a context associated with the dramatic line of a *romance*.

The importance of the opening *romance* in the dramatic structure of this play is borne out again at the close of Act II when Mariana expresses her own attitude at this point in the drama with words that bring the opening *romance* into the action of the play:

> Yo bordé la bandera con mis manos;
> con estas manos, ¡mírelas, Pedrosa!
> y conozco muy grandes caballeros
> que izarla pretendían en Granada.
> ¡Mas no diré sus nombres! (857)

Mariana is now in control of the *romance*. She acts as if she were the *juglar* narrating the tale that elicits tears in Granada. "¡Ahora empiezo a morir!", she tells Angustias at the conclusion of Act II; and like a *juglar*, she repeats a significant phrase: "Mírame y llora. ¡Ahora empiezo a morir!" (859). Mariana knows, as do those who have heard the *romance* of the prologue, that the sadness of Granada is intimately linked with her fate. As the bells of the convent begin to toll at the conclusion of the drama, their sound vibrates with lines from the popular *romance* sung by the children ("¡Oh, qué día tan triste en Granada, / las campanas doblar y doblar!" [782]). Even the final stage direction ("No cesa el campaneo") reinforces the quality of an oft-told tale that lingers in the air after having pervaded the text of a drama concerning a protagonist who is conscious of her own withdrawal into legend.

Apart from the opening *romance* that frames the entire play, our study of Lorca's dynamic use of *romance* in *Mariana Pineda* takes us to the first sustained use of narrative poetry in the play. This occurs in Act I, Scene 4, when Amparo describes the bullfight in Ronda. The playwright has placed the description of an exciting bullfight dominated by the feats of the great matador, Cayetano, in a dramatically feasible moment in the action; for it serves as a diversion from the tension that Amparo and Lucia sense in their friend Mariana. Midst a series of images of violence and beauty—bulls and flowers, beasts and butterflies, the smell of blood and that of the mountainside—Amparo draws Mariana into her description with exclamations such as "Yo pensaba siempre en ti; / Yo pensaba: si estuviera / conmigo mi triste amiga, / mi Mariana Pineda" (792-793). By introducing Mariana into the context of poetic imagery depicting beauty in the presence of death, the dramatist has linked this narrative interlude to the ominous tone set at the opening of the act when an image associated with blood was introduced into a description of Mariana's embroidering ("Parecía el hilo rojo, entre sus dedos, / una herida de cuchillo sobre el aire [783]). By means of images in Amparo's description—"de risas blancas y negras," "parecía que la tarde / se ponía más morena," "En la punta de su estoque / cinco flores dejó abiertas," "como una gran mariposa / de oro con alas bermejas," "La plaza, al par de la tarde, / vibraba fuerte, violenta / y entre el olor de la sangre / iba el olor de la sierra" (793-794)—Lorca maintains the flow of the imagery continuities of light-darkness, blood and trembling. This is accomplished in the setting of a poetic narrative that is more a part of the natural flow of dialogue than a set "aria" or a poetic interlude such as those that occur in a Modernista play like Marquina's *La ermita, la fuente y el río*.

After the description of the bullfight in Ronda which associated Mariana with courage in the face of death, the next sustained use of a *romance* sets another stage in the metaphorical presentation of Mariana's journey into legend. Again, the placement of a *romance* makes it resonate with a dramatic context. At the beginning of Act II, the "Romance del duque de Lucena" anticipates Pedro's arrival at Mariana's home by creating an image of Mariana as if she were the woman in the *romance* waiting on the shore for the arrival of her "marinero." Whereas the narrative of the bullfight in Ronda alluded to Mariana's courage, this *romance* frames the portion of the play that places Mariana in direct contact with the man she loves. Also the "Romance del duque de Lucena" links Act II with both the opening *romance* and the end of Act I, with "bandera" supplying the connection. In this Act II *romance* we hear "Una niña bordando. / . . . / bordaba una bandera" (822-823)—words recalling the phrase "bordando la bandera" from the opening *romance* in addition to the image of the children wrapped in the "bandera" at the conclusion of Act I. Further, the "Romance del duque de Lucena" establishes a base for the sea imagery that appears later. In "marinero en el mar" and "la verde, verde orilla," we see the beginning of a series of sea images that extends from the next scene ("Rezaremos / la oración de San Juan y la que ruega / por caminantes y por marineros" [826]), through the act ("Como la enamorada de un marinero loco / que navegara eterno sobre una barca vieja" [832]; "que me falta muy poco para ahogarme" [840]) and into Act III ("A la vera del agua, / sin que nadie la viera, / se murió mi esperanza" [872]; "Porque yo soy hija / de un capitán de navío" [874]; "¡Ay, qué fragatita, / real corsaria! ¿Dónde está / tu valentía?" [878]). Again, the narrative line of a *romance* has given images a point of reference, thereby leading them away from stasis and in the direction of an association with the dramatic line.

After Mariana's tense wait for events related to the conspiracy to take place, the narrative of the death of Torrijos in Málaga which the Fourth Conspirator relates in Act II, Scene 8, places Mariana in another *romance* frame: i.e., an awareness of death. In addition to its self-contained story, this passage is another example of Lorca's use of narrative poetry both as a "relater" and a "conveyor." The lengthy narrative of the death of Torrijos in the form of a *romance* joins the opening *romance*, the description of the bullfight in Ronda and the "Romance del duque de Lucena" as a means of adding another layer to the metaphorical language which brings death more into the consciousness of the reader. The setting in this narrative is Andalucía by the sea—a fact that keeps the interlocking "orilla-mar" imagery intact ("Y se acercó, satisfecho / con sus buques, a la orilla" [843]). Darkness, a principal component of the metaphorical language, is recalled ("Grandes nubes se levantan / sobre la tierra de Mijas" [844]) as are images of tears ("Sobre los barcos lloraba / toda la marinería, / y las más bellas mujeres, enlutadas y afligidas / lo iban llorando también / por el limonar arriba" [844]), of blood ("y muerto quedó en la arena, / sangrando por tres heridas" [844]) and dreams ("La muerte, con ser la muerte, / no deshojó su sonrisa" [844]). Moreover, in light of the fact that Mariana views herself as a character in a drama that depicts her as the personification of "Libertad," it is significant that she herself hears this *romance*; for she, the lonely woman waiting on shore, is closely identified (through Pedro and his cause) with the courageous Torrijos who is struck down when he resolutely sets foot on shore. In effect, Mariana is a "participant" in the *romance* as well as a listener to the outcome of her own *romance*. She will also meet the fate of the fallen hero who dies with unfailing belief in the justness of his cause. The Torrijos *romance* thus provides 1) an expanded metaphor for Mariana's story and 2) a repository for images that constitute continuities in the metaphorical language of the play.

Mariana is so profoundly moved by the Torrijos narrative that she keeps its spirit alive through sea imagery, saying while raising her wine glass: "'Luna tendida, marinero en pie'", / dicen allá, por el Mediterráneo, / las gentes de veleros y fragatas" (846). Then, as if referring to herself, she repeats in a dream-like state: "Luna tendida, marinero en pie." When Pedro responds "Que sean nuestras casas como barcos" (846), he brings the lingering sea imagery into direct contact with their lives. Because these images were generated by the Torrijos *romance*, they retain a residual association with that *romance* and thus lose some of their quality as mere reverie. In other words, there is a point of contact between them and a narrative line.

The song of the "Contrabandista" is the final *romance* to frame a stage of Mariana's life in this drama. We first saw Mariana as the protagonist of the opening *romance*. She then "stepped out" of the *romance* to reenact her story, gathered courage (as expressed in the description of the bullfight in Ronda), received Pedro in her home (anticipated in the "Romance del duque de Lucena"), and waited for news of events that place her in the presence of death (exemplified in the *romance* of Torrijos). Now, with the song of the "Contrabandista," Mariana slips back into legend (subtly supported by a shift in the metaphorical language from "hilo rojo" at the beginning of Act I to "hilo negro"). When we think of Mariana as reciting her own *romance*, the fact that it is she who sings the song of the "Contrabandista" is significant, for it identifies her more closely with a figure of legend:

> Yo que soy contrabandista
> y campo por mis respetos
> a todos los desafío,
> pues a nadie tengo miedo.
>   ¡Ay! ¡Ay!
> ¡Ay muchachos! ¡Ay muchachas!
> ¿Quién me compra hilo negro?
> Mi caballo está rendido
> ¡y yo me muero de sueño! (848-849)

With the phrase "a todos los desafío, / pues a nadie tengo miedo," Mariana reminds us of the determined heroine of the opening *romance*, the brave bullfighter in Ronda, the patient woman waiting for the "marinero" and the valiant warrior who faces death in his determination to set foot on shore. "¡Ay! Caballo, que me muero," she exclaims in another moment of self-awareness just before Pedrosa appears. "La canción del Contrabandista" is so charged with the emotional tensions and foreboding that Lorca has embedded in the text that when the stage direction indicates that Mariana sings it with "admirable y desesperado sentimiento," one is led to conclude that the heroine has already heard the *romance* of which she is the protagonist and that now she is passionately singing a segment of it herself.

Lorca expands the dramatic potential of the song of the "Contrabandista" in the scene that follows when Mariana confronts Pedrosa, showing her contempt with words provided by the song. "Sepa que yo no tengo miedo a nadie," she tells Pedrosa (854), recalling these lines from the song: "a todos los desafío, / pues a nadie tengo miedo." Again, *Mariana Pineda* demonstrates that the popular *romance* for Lorca not only provides a frame for a stage in the development of a character but also a means of keeping the metaphorical language alive without arresting the action of the drama.

In the context of Mariana's receding more into her imagination by reflecting on the legendary nature of her role in the conspiracy, Lorca uses a *copla* (Act III, Scene 6) that gives the protagonist the opportunity to 1) penetrate her own feelings (creating a static situation reminiscent of scenes in Symbolist theater) and 2) act like a *juglar* narrating events with the use of elements from the metaphorical language of this play.

Mariana opens scene 6 thus: "Recuerdo aquella copla que decía / cruzando los olivos de Granada," and then she continues with the lament "'¡Ay, qué fragatita, / real corsaria! ¿Dónde está / tu valentía? / Que un velero bergantín / te ha puesto la puntería.'" (878)—a refrain that she almost immediately repeats with sadness. The *copla* not only contains a metaphor for Mariana's predicament at that moment ("fragatita" = Mariana; "velero bergantín" = Pedrosa) but also gives her an opportunity to look backward and forward to the dramatic action. By recalling the olive groves of Granada, Mariana underscores the close identification she has with Granada as indicated in the opening *romance* ("¡Oh, qué día tan triste en Granada"); and by enveloping Mariana's struggle in sea imagery, this *copla* reminds us most notably of the "romance del marinero" in Act II. Looking ahead, the futility inherent in the metaphor of a "fragatita" facing the onslaught of a "velero bergantín" alludes to the tragic outcome of Mariana's struggle. The sea image then radiates towards the words "mar" and "brisa" that follow immediately in these lines of the dialogue: "Entre el mar y las estrellas / ¡con qué gusto pasearía / apoyada sobre una / larga baranda de brisa!" (878). Thus, the *copla* has multiple value for the drama, because its imagery 1) expresses Mariana's sense of helplessness at this point in the drama 2) contains an image (a "fragatita" attacked by a "bergantín") that reflects and heightens Mariana's plight with respect to Pedrosa, and 3) underpins subsequent dialogue pertaining to the unfolding human drama. Lorca takes what we might call a "copla lopesca" and integrates it into the action of a drama.

In addition to serving as frames for various segments of the play and milieus for expanded metaphors that radiate through the dialogue, the *romances* in *Mariana Pineda* provide an ebb and flow to a drama whose multi-layered evocative imagery and scenes of contemplation and reflection recall the relatively static nature of Symbolist theater in the tradition of Maeterlinck. Images such as "un pez de plata finge rojo sueño," "cuando el sol se duerme en sus manos," "cadenas de agua," "vestida de temblor y llanto," "sauce de cristal," "un techo de violetas," "fragatas de sombra y seda" and "fuego en la verde brisa" show a strong affinity for

Symbolism and Modernismo. However, phrases such as "borda y borda lentamente," "¡Con qué trabajo tan grande / deja la luz a Granada!," "larga locura de luceros," "¡Qué silencio el de Granada!", "¡Ay, qué buen soñar!" display techniques from the traditional Spanish *romance* (repetitions, anaphoras, intercalated exclamations) that give the metaphorical language a sense of movement and dramatic immediacy. Layered imagery thus combines with narrative poetry to help flesh out a character who gradually removes herself from a reality steeped in shadows, blood and tears and enters legend with dream-like equanimity.

To conclude our analysis of how Lorca incorporates the craft of a *juglar* into *Mariana Pineda* and to reaffirm the importance of *romances* in the total design of this play, we can compare passages with lines from "Rosaflorida," a popular *romance*. In "Rosaflorida" this straight-forward narrative passage appears:

> Dentro estaba una doncella
> que llaman Rosaflorida,
> siete condes la demandan,
> tres duques de Lombardía[27]

In *Mariana Pineda*, poetic narration occurs in passages such as the following:

> Borda y borda lentamente.
> Yo lo he visto por el ojo de la llave.
> Parecía el hilo rojo, entre sus dedos,
> una herida de cuchillo sobre el aire. (783)

> ¡Ay, Marianita
> rosa Y jazmín de Granada,
> que está esperando a su novio,
> pero su novio se tarda! (879)

The *juglar* of "Rosaflorida" interjects a comment about what is being narrated:

> a todos los desdeñaba,
> ¡tanta es su lozanía!
> Prendóse de Montesinos,
> de oídas que no de vista. (115)

Exclamations which momentarily draw one's attention to the "narrator's" feeling vis á vis what is narrated also punctuate Lorca's text:

> porque este cuello, ¡Oh, qué cuello!
> no se hizo para la pena (794)
>
> y otras veces finge en mí
> una larga cabellera
> ¡Ay, qué buen soñar! (865)

The narrator of "Rosaflorida" makes the narrated event more vivid and immediate by including dialogue:

> —¿Qué es aquesto, mi señora,
> qué es esto, Rosaflorida?
> o tenedes mal de amores
> o estades loca perdida.
> —Ruégate, mi camarero,
> que de mí tengas mancilla,
> lleváseme aquestas cartas
> a Francia la bien guarnida,
> déselas a Montesinos. (115)

As in the following passage from the scene in which night descends on Granada, Lorca gives Mariana's musings the appearance of a dialogue and thus injects a dynamic quality into contemplative moments:

> Se enreda entre los cipreses
> o se esconde bajo el agua.
> ¡Y esta noche que no llega!
> ¡Noche temida y soñada;
> que me hieres ya de lejos
> con larguísimas espadas! (796)

Similarly, Mariana addresses her children even though they are not physically present:

> Dormir tranquilamente, niños míos,
> mientras que yo, perdida y loca, siento
> quemarse con su propia lumbre viva
> esta rosa de sangre de mi pecho. (826)

Also, in Act III, Scene 4, Mariana addresses Pedro as if he were present:

Y aunque tu caballo pone
cuatro lunas en las piedras
y fuego en la verde brisa
débil de la primavera,
¡corre más! ¡Ven a buscarme! (871)

Thus, our study of elements of the traditional Spanish *romances* in *Mariana Pineda* leads to the conclusion that at a very early stage of his development as a playwright, Lorca is beginning to look beyond Symbolism for techniques to permeate a text with images that reach deep into the imagination without losing contact with the dramatic-narrative line of the human drama. Lorca has infused *Mariana Pineda* with imagery continuities that create moods and penetrate the innermost feelings of a figure of legend; yet the poetry shows evidence of becoming more integrated into dramatic contexts, especially through the use of the traditional Spanish *romance*. Lines such as "una herida de cuchillo sobre el aire," ". . . finge en mí / una larga cabellera," "fuego en la verde brisa" contain images associated with darkness, blood and dreams whose cumulative effect evokes feelings experienced by Mariana up to the moment she faces death and imagines herself transformed by love into a symbol of Liberty. By surrounding these images with the feeling that one is listening to a long *romance*, Lorca has acquired an important technique for insuring that images do not overwhelm and thereby arrest the development of the dramatization of the events narrated in the opening *romance* that outlines the drama. The playwright has succeeded in giving a feeling of movement to what are essentially frames of various stages in the development of a drama of a woman who escapes the reality of being left alone to face death by viewing herself as a legendary embodiment of an ideal; and he has accomplished this while also retaining evocative and allusive imagery that permits us to "hear" the inner cry of this courageous woman.

Notes
1. Maurice Maeterlinck, *Pelléas et Mélisande* (Paris: Fasquelle Éditeurs, 1950), pp.41-50.
2. "Ariettes oubliées" (III), in *Romances sans paroles* in *Oeuvres poétiques complètes*, ed. Jacques Borel (Paris: Éditions Gallimard, 1962), p.192.
3. *Metatheater* (New York: Hill and Wang, 1964), pp.40-58.
4. *La casa de Anteo*, versión española de Salustiano Masó (Madrid: Taurus Ediciones, 1985), pp.177-180.

5. Maeterlinck, pp.89-93.
6. The Land of Heart's Desire, in *The Collected Plays of W.B. Yeats, Revised Edition* (New York: Macmillan, 1953), pp.37, 39, 41.
7. "La tierra de Alvargonzález," in *Poesías completas*, 3rd ed. (Madrid: Espasa-Calpe, S.A., 1977), pp. 174, 178, 180.
8. *Cuento de labios en flor*, in *Teatro de ensueño* (Madrid: Renacimiento, S.A., 1911), pp. 228, 231, 252, 258, 261.
9. *La ermita, la fuente y el río*, in *En Flandes se ha puesto el sol/La ermita, la fuente y el río*, ed. Beatriz Hernanz Angulo (Madrid: Castalia, 1996), p.200.
10. In *Sonetos completos*, ed. Biruté Ciplijauskaité (Madrid: Editorial Castalia, 1969), p.213.
11. "Crépuscule du soir mystique," in *Oeuvres*, p.70.
12. "Autre Éventail," in *Selected Poems by Stéphane Mallarmé*, trans. C.F. MacIntyre (Berkeley: Univ. of California Press, 1957), p.68.
13. *Soledades (1899-1907)* (XIII, "Hacia un ocaso radiante . . ."), in *Poesías completas*, 3rd ed. (Madrid: Espasa-Calpe, S.A., 1977), p.84.
14. Rubén Darío, "Autumnal," from *Azul...* in *Azul.../Cantos de vida y esperanza*, p.158.
15. Juan Ramón Jiménez, "Tenebrae," from *Melancolía*, in *Segunda antolojía poética (1898-1918)* (Madrid: España-Calpe, 1959), p.140.
16. Maeterlinck, p.68.
17. "Soledad primera," in *Soledades de Góngora*, ed. Dámaso Alonso (Madrid: Revista de Occidente, 1927), p.69.
18. "L'Heure du berger," in *Oeuvres*, p.73.
19. *La case de Anteo*, p.175.
20. *The Irish Drama of Europe from Yeats to Beckett* (Atlantic Heights, N.J.: Humanitas Press, 1978), p.47.
21. William Shakespeare, *Hamlet*, in *The Tragedies of Shakespeare*, Vol. 2, The Modern Library (New York: Random House, n.d.), pp.686-687.
22. "Apuntes sobre el teatro de García Lorca," in *Federico García Lorca*, ed. Ildefonso-Manuel Gil (Madrid: Taurus Ediciones, 1973), p.277.
23. Marquina, p.258.
24. *"The Irish Drama of Europe from Yeats to Beckett*, p.47.
25. Two examples follow from *La ermita, la fuente y el río*, pp.196, 226:
"A la romería fui, / ¡ay! . . ., a la romería. / Y en el corazón, por ti, / ¡ay! . . ., me clavé una espina." (196).
<<Cada gotita del llanto / que se te cae de la cara, / brilla engarzada en el manto, / como una estrellita clara.>> (226).
26. *El caballero de Olmedo*, ed. Francisco Rico, 6th ed. (Madrid: Ediciones Cátedra, 1985), p.150.
27. "Rosaflorida," in *Flor nueva de romances que recogió de la tradición antigua y moderna R. Menéndez Pidal*, pp.115-116.

Chapter 5
Amor de don Perlimplín con Belisa en su jardín

Amor de don Perlimplín con Belisa en su jardín marks a significant point of transition in the evolution of Lorca's poetic drama from its pronounced Symbolist beginnings to theater whose imagery is integrated with dramatic contexts. *Perlimplín* combines the atmospheric, dream-like quality of *El maleficio de la mariposa* and *Mariana Pineda* with a more dynamic use of imagery that began to develop especially in the latter. The result is a drama dominated but not engulfed by its metaphorical language. Many evocative poetic images recall the allusive quality of Symbolist imagery; but due to Lorca's more complex use of songs and elements of the traditional Spanish *romance*, the imagery in *Perlimplín* moves further in the direction of expressing the narrative line in dramatic contexts than was the case in earlier plays.

Like Curianito and Mariana Pineda, Perlimplín embodies the power of the imagination to create an inner world so real that he is willing to accept death as a consequence of escaping from the reality that surrounds him. Indeed, Perlimplín, like Mariana Pineda, stages his own death. As he becomes more captivated by the delights of earthly pleasures represented by Belisa, Perlimplín's imagination strives to hold onto the aspects of love that are felt in the heart by carrying out a plan to sacrifice his life in order to initiate Belisa into the realm of love that touches the soul. This inner-outer opposition constitutes the salient continuity in the metaphorical language of this play and is related to the various dramatic stages leading to the tragic resolution of the conflict. The poetry follows Perlimplín as he becomes aware of the physical pleasure of love and Belisa as she realizes the spiritual nature of love. To achieve a relationship between poetry and drama, Lorca refines two techniques: 1) metaphorical language that sustains an outer-inner continuity which "narrates" Perlimplín's withdrawal into the imagination and 2) the use of songs and *romance* techniques to carry the imagery in the direction of the narrative line of the drama.

The tension between what is revealed and what remains secret, unawareness and discovery, the body and the soul, joy and pain, love and death is expressed through images that accumulate to reveal the soul beneath Perlimplín's farcical exterior and to penetrate Belisa's preoccupation with sensuality and eroticism. Also, like the *romances* in *Mariana Pineda*, songs frame scenes and thus provide a means for underscoring thematic material and for "freezing" in the mind's eye what Fergusson has called the ceremonious quality of the various scenes.[1] However, in *Perlimplín* Lorca takes components of the traditional ballad and the images they contain beyond the limits placed on them by dramatists very familiar to him (notably Lope de Vega, in *comedias* such as *El caballero de Olmedo*, *Peribáñez* and *Fuentovejuna*, and Marquina as evidenced in *La ermita, la fuente y el río*). In Lorca's play, song elements are a more integral part of dramatic contexts. Poetry assumes a more specific role in drama than the more generalized poetic effect that Fergusson observes especially in the transition from one scene to another (344).

In its general tone and thematic material, *Perlimplín* demonstrates that at this stage in his theatrical output, Lorca still shows a strong affinity for Symbolism and Modernismo. The use of synesthesia in passages such as "¡Qué música! ¡Como el plumón caliente de los cisnes!" (989) and "Jazminero flotante y sin raíces, el cielo caerá sobre mi espalda sudorosa . . . ¡Noche!, noche mía, de menta y lapislázuli" (1012) recall French Symbolist and Hispanic Modernista poetry. Also, Perlimplín's self-sacrifice in the name of love for a woman much younger than he brings to mind Deseada, Marquina's protagonist, who sacrifices herself rather than create unhappiness for a man younger than she. In Perlimplín's insistence that love requires a beautiful soul to sustain it, one hears echoes from the mysteriously spiritual world inhabited by Maeterlinck's Pelléas and Mélisande as well as Yeats's Forgael and Dectora. Indeed, the following passage from *The Shadowy Waters* is extremely close to the task Perlimplín's imagination sets before him; namely, to make Belisa, who understands only the world of physical love, offer love as an expression of what she feels in her soul:

> Dectora: I understand you now.
> You have a Druid craft of wicked music,
> Wrung from the cold women of the sea—
> A magic that can call a demon up,

Until my body give you kiss for kiss.
Forgael: Your soul shall give the kiss.[2]

The outer-inner, body-soul opposition in *Perlimplín* functions on two levels: 1) as an over-arching motif in the theme of love, and 2) as a continuity in the metaphorical language comprised of images set out in such a way as to provide the characters with language expressing various stages of their relationship with each other. The duality between the body and soul is placed in a human, intimate drama; not at a cosmic level as was sometimes the case in the theater of Calderón. This is very important to the idea that Lorca's imagery in the theater develops a symbiotic relationship with the action of the drama. In other words, passages in *Perlimplín* rooted in expressions of the opposition between palpable reality and the realm of imagination are not perceived primarily as abstractions articulating the conflict between the body and the soul, but rather as indications of a struggle between Perlimplín and Belisa playing out their emotions. The metaphorical language, therefore, reflects an ebb and flow in an ongoing human drama:

Perlimplín: Yo con mis libros tengo bastante. (981)
Perlimplín: ¿En qué mundo me vas a meter? (986)
Belisa: El que me busque con ardor me encontrará. Mi sed no se apaga nunca. (989)
Perlimplín: He aprendido muchas cosas, y sobre todo puedo imaginarlas. (1002)
Perlimplín: Jamás he visto un hombre en quien lo varonil y lo delicado se den de una manera tan armónica. (1005)
Belisa: ¡No es tu alma lo que yo deseo!, sino tu blanco y mórbido cuerpo estremecido! (1007)
Perlimplín: Antes no podía pensar en las cosas extraordinarias que tiene el mundo. (1009)
Perlimplín: Y para que sea tuyo completamente, se me ha ocurrido que lo mejor es clavarle este puñal en su corazón galante. (1015)
Perlimplín: Yo soy mi alma y tú eres tu cuerpo . . . Déjame en este último instante, puesto que tanto me has querido, morir abrazado a él. (1017)

The above passages "declare" the body-soul continuity which expresses the conflict between Perlimplín and Belisa, but as we explore the text we shall see that it is the imagery that makes us "feel" the conflict. In *Perlimplín*, as in *El maleficio de la mariposa* and *Mariana Pineda*, thematic material and dramatic events are often underscored, foreshadowed or confirmed by language that is evocative and allusive; but in this play, Lorca integrates the imagery more fully and naturally with the dialogue and action than was apparent in the two plays we have already examined.

The inner-outer opposition appears first in the prologue and then becomes a continuity that makes us feel the presence of Perlimplín's imagination as it gradually proves to Belisa that love can be felt in one's soul. Shortly after the curtain rises, Perlimplín tells Marcolfa "Cuando yo era niño una mujer estranguló a su esposo. . . . Siempre he pensado no casarme" (981), whereupon the servant responds: "El matrimonio tiene grandes encantos, mi señor. No es lo que se ve por fuera. Está lleno de cosas ocultas" (981). Also in the prologue, the foregoing brief exchange of dialogue reappears in an altered form when Marcolfa very succinctly refers to Belisa as "Hermosa doncella," prompting Perlimplín to reply "Como de azúcar . . . , blanca por dentro. ¿Será capaz de estrangularme?" (987). Thus, by means of an image associated with an opposition between internal and external reality, Lorca implants in natural, fluid conversation the idea that an outer sweetness may have an inner potential for causing harm —an idea that the playwright dramatizes in the relationship between Belisa who is overtly captivated by sexual delights and Perlimplín, the possessor of an imagination that leads him to plan and triumphantly execute a love-death.

The images in Perlimplín's speech at the beginning of Act I add another layer to the inner-outer continuity. First he describes Belisa in visual terms ("Belisa, con tantos encajes pareces una ola" [998]), and then he turns slightly inward in reference to himself ("Desde que tú viniste de la iglesia está mi casa llena de rumores secretos" [988]). In addition, Perlimplín extends the water image associated with Belisa ("pareces una ola") by saying "y me das el mismo miedo que de niño tuve al mar," a phrase with a bodeful undertone like that which we heard earlier in the prologue ("una mujer estranguló a su esposo;" "¿Será capaz de estrangularme?"). The shadow cast over the outer-inner, body-soul opposition (i.e., the Belisa-Perlimplín counterpoint) is further reinforced in Act II when Belisa tells Perlimplín that her secret admirer (Perlimplín) has written letters to her in which he has said:

> El alma es patrimonio de los débiles, de los héroes tullidos y las gentes enfermizas. Las almas hermosas están en los bordes de la muerte, reclinadas sobre cabelleras blanquísimas y manos macilentas. Belisa, ¡no es tu alma

lo que yo deseo!, ¡sino tu blanco y mórbido cuerpo estremecido! (1006-1007)

By associating words like "débiles," "tullidos," "enfermizas," "macilentas" and "mórbido" with the body-soul dichotomy, the dramatist makes us feel that death is more palpably a factor in the plan taking shape in Perlimplín's imagination. Finally, death does surface, first in the metaphorical language through the body-soul continuity ("El te querrá con el amor infinito de los difuntos y yo quedaré libre de esta oscura pesadilla de tu cuerpo grandioso" [1015]) and then in the action (Perlimplín's actual death from a self-inflicted wound) expressed also by the body-soul continuity in Perlimplín's final words:

> Yo soy mi alma y tú eres tu cuerpo . . .
> Déjame en este último instante
> puesto que tanto me has querido,
> morir abrazado a él. (1017)

Perlimplín's final request to Belisa has the effect of creating imagistic characters out of the body-soul, outer-inner continuity. In the declaration "Yo soy mi alma y tú eres tu cuerpo," the mind's eye sees these oppositions as counterparts of the characters engaged in the human drama. Through this connection between metaphorical language and elements of the drama, the playwright provides us with an indelible impression of the triumph of Perlimplín's imagination. By having Perlimplín say "morir abrazado a él" rather than "morir abrazado a ti," Lorca has sustained the power of Perlimplín's imagination by effecting the union of the body and soul—and linking them with death—within the metaphorical language at the same time that the "real" death-in-love is transpiring at the human level. Therefore, it is difficult to separate what is happening in the drama from the language in which it is expressed.

The reader of *Perlimplín*, as was the case with *El maleficio de la mariposa* and *Mariana Pineda*, senses the presence of impending sorrow through interlocking images; but in this later play, Lorca further develops his use of poetry in the theater by giving images, including those with surrealist tendencies, settings in dialogue that is more natural to characters interacting with each other at a very human level—this despite the fact that a play like *Mariana Pineda* is more "realistic" at the surface level of the action. The atmospheric tone set by images of light and darkness in *El maleficio de la mariposa* and *Mariana Pineda* now gives way to more images that invest the lines delivered by the characters with a dynamic quality. When Perlimplín's senses begin to awaken to Belisa's beauty, he asks: "¿Será capaz de estrangularme?" (987)—a rather startling question but one that is kept within the bounds of human activity by conjuring up the familiar image of "une belle dame sans merci." When the action progresses to the point at which Perlimplín marries Belisa, Perlimplín begins to talk to his bride quite naturally in more intimate terms ("Yo no había podido imaginarme tu cuerpo hasta que lo vi por el ojo de la cerradura cuando te vestías de novia" [991]), yet the metaphorical language is carried into this stage of his relationship with Belisa when he reminds us of his earlier fear of death ("¿Será capaz de estrangularme?") by adding "Y entonces es cuando sentí el amor. ¡Entonces! Como un hondo corte de lanceta en mi garganta" (991). As the action continues to unfold, further allusions to inflicting pain, especially with reference to "la garganta," adapt themselves to changing dramatic contexts. "Debe tener la piel morena y sus besos deben perfumar y escocer al mismo tiempo como el azafrán y el clavo" (1002), says Belisa of her unseen admirer; and when she speaks of the contents of letters from other admirers, she includes phrases such as "corazones heridos" and "héroes tullidos." Gradually, and in contexts that have a familiar ring with respect to the "belle dame sans merci" male-female relationship established in this play, the dramatist intensifies the feeling of impending violence through images associated with injury, reaching a high point when Belisa expresses her desperation in trying to restrain her husband from killing her unknown admirer ("Voy a atravesar la garganta de mi marido" [1016]). Linked by the word "garganta" which recalls Perlimplín's earlier question ("¿Será capaz de estrangularme?"), elements in the metaphorical language relating to violence continue to appear and to express an intensified feeling of approaching danger without interrupting the flow of natural dialogue.

Even when poetic elements can be considered a direct intrusion upon natural dialogue, one does not lose sight of the narrative line—a characteristic that is reminiscent of the "Soledades" of Góngora in which imagery clothes the narrative. An example of this occurs when Perlimplín, as Belisa's secret admirer, tells her that her husband stabbed him with an emerald dagger: " . . . pero me ha matado . . . Con este ramo ardiente de piedras preciosas" (1017). Substituting one object for another, the language directly conveys the information yet extends the reader's perception of Perlimplín's imagination with an image that is both aptly descriptive and allusively erotic. In a more complex passage, the metaphorical language reaches even further into the subtext while preserving the linear progression of the human drama. In Act I, five doors leading to five balconies are referred to as "cinco frías camelias de madrugada":

> Duende 1°: Vamos. Ya siento un dulce fresquillo por mis espaldas.
> Duende 2°: Cinco frías camelias de madrugada se han abierto en las paredes de la alcoba.
> Duende 1°: Cinco balcones sobre la ciudad. (996)

Through the central image of "cinco frías camelias de madrugada," the poetry conveys the fact that the cool breeze of the morning enters the bedroom through the five doors left open by five lovers who have left the room. But as the image of "frías camelias" radiates outward from its nucleus evoking cold and whiteness, it emits the idea that a light breeze of death has also insinuated itself into the room along with Belisa's lovers. This ominous note struck beneath the text will be heard more insistently as the drama progresses. The tragic outcome of Perlimplín's relationship with Belisa begins to take shape from within the poetry used to express what is happening as the characters interact. Again we observe that although the allusive and sensual imagery of this play reminds us of the Symbolist tradition, it is tied more closely to immediate dramatic contexts than was the case with much of the imagery in *El maleficio de la mariposa* and *Mariana Pineda*.

The outer-inner continuity that follows Perlimplín's successful attempt to create a reality through his imagination is sometimes simply declared, such as Belisa's references to her persistent admirer: "Tampoco he conseguido verlo. En mi paseo por la alameda venían todos detrás menos él" (1002); "Yo no le he visto la cara . . . Pero no se deja ver" (1005). In a less obvious but no less natural statement at the conclusion of the play, the hidden-revealed continuity is rooted in a dramatic context yet produces an allusion to the soul-body opposition that underpins the metaphorical language. In response to Belisa's desperate question after the death of Perlimplín ("Pero ¿quién era este hombre? ¿Quién era?" [1018]), Marcolfa's reply ("El hermoso adolescente al que nunca verás el rostro" [1018]) is a reference to the hidden face of the soul. In staging his own death, Perlimplín had concealed his body beneath his cape in order to reveal his soul to the woman he loves. Marcolfa's allusive response is, therefore, the hidden-revealed, outer-inner imagery continuity expressing what has, in fact, taken place in the human drama.

A more extensive example of the playwright's adding increments to the outer-inner continuity that expresses the tension in this drama between body and soul occurs in Act I in a playful exchange between two *duendes* who treat the action as a play within a play:

> Duende 2°: ¿Y qué te parece? Siempre es bonito tapar las faltas ajenas.
> Duende 1°: Y que luego el público se encargue de destaparlas.
> Duende 2°: Porque si las cosas no se cubren con toda clase de precauciones . . .
> Duende 1°: No se descubren nunca.
> Duende 2°: Y sin este tapar y destapar . . .
> Duende 1°: ¿Qué sería de las pobres gentes?
> Duende 2°: (Mirando la cortina.)
> Que no quede ni una rendija.
> Duende 1°: Que las rendijas de ahora son oscuridad mañana. (Ríen.)
> Duende 2°: Cuando las cosas están claras . . .
> Duende 1°: El hombre se figura que no tiene necesidad de descubrirlas.
> Duende 2°: Y se va a las cosas turbias para descubrir en ellas secretos que ya sabía. (993-994)

While the *duendes* are talking about the relationship between a play and its audience, we, as "listeners," are "hearing" the tension inherent in repeated references to an inner-outer opposition ("tapar-destapar," "cubrir-descubrir," "oscuridad-claridad")—a continuity in the metaphorical language which expresses the plan that takes shape in Perlimplín's imagination; i.e., "tapar el cuerpo para destapar el alma." Thus, the metaphorical language which is central to the text of this play shapes "natural" dialogue even in an "unnatural" setting (in this instance, a scene in which *duendes* appear). In *Perlimplín*, an imagery continuity is tied more to the immediate dramatic moment than if it were merely a foreshadowing, an illustration or a means for creating a mood. Poetry, including songs, is not inserted in this play only in moments of high dramatic intensity, nor does it serve simply as contrast for prose dialogue. In *Perlimplín*, Lorca calls upon poetry to condense narrative material and to expand the imagination (a "protagonist" in this play.) The poetry informs a dramatization of the power of the imagination to draw a character out of reality and to place him totally within its domain.

Lorca also uses songs to help the outer-inner continuity express Perlimplín's successful plan to make Belisa aware of the spiritual aspect of love. The playwright's tentative use of elements of song in *El maleficio de la mariposa* and his extensive use of the *romance* in *Mariana Pineda* lead to *Perlimplín*, another stage in his development of total poetic drama. In *Perlimplín*, songs do not stand out primarily as 1) moments of foreshadowing like the song heard by Lope's "caballero de Olmedo" 2) recapitulations such as the song sung by musicians in Act II of *Fuenteovejuna*, 3) elements of local traditions as evidenced by the wedding song of *Peribáñez* or 4) commentaries or reflections upon a state of mind like the *copla* that reflects Deseada's feelings towards the end of Act I of Marquina's *La ermita, la fuente y el río*. Although the songs in *Perlimplín* do frame the various stages of Perlimplín's flight into his imagination, they also convey and link various elements of the imagery expressive of the drama.

The first appearance of a song comes in the prologue when Belisa sings offstage:

> Amor, amor.
> Entre mis muslos cerrados,
> nada como un pez el sol.
> Agua tibia entre los juncos,
> amor.
> ¡Gallo, que se va la noche!
> ¡Que no se vaya, no! (982)

With respect to the narrative line of the play, the obvious eroticism of the song sets the opening frame; i.e., Belisa's preoccupation with sexual love (and hence her embodiment of the polarity in the imagery pertaining to physical pleasures that will contend with their opposite, the soul). However, the imagery in the song is not only descriptive of Belisa but also expressive of the dramatic context; for at this point in the drama, Perlimplín is beginning his initiation into the sexual aspects of love. Further, Lorca's placement of the song is appropriate dramatically, because it 1) follows Marcolfa's erotically suggestive comments to Perlimplín ("El matrimonio tiene grandes encantos, mi señor. No es lo que se ve por fuera. Está lleno de cosas ocultas. Cosas que no están bien que sean dichas por una servidora" [981]) and 2) leads directly to Marcolfa's prophetic statement—"Verá mi señor la razón que tengo" (982). The song also contains images which, when linked to others, evoke the carnal pleasures represented by Belisa. The sexual image of "Entre mis muslos cerrados, / nada como un pez el sol" echoes the close of Act I when Perlimplín tells Belisa "Nunca había visto la salida del sol . . . Es un espectáculo que . . . parece mentira . . . , ¡me conmueve! (1000). "Agua tibia entre los juncos" anticipates in Act III "Por las orillas del río / se está la noche mojando" (1011); and "¡Gallo, que se va la noche! / ¡Que no se vaya, no!" anticipates this image also from Act III: "La noche canta desnuda / sobre los puentes de marzo" (1011). Thus, Lorca has used the Symbolist technique of following one allusive and suggestive image by another to make an abstraction visible (i.e., the "outer" erotic manifestations of love represented by Belisa); but he has combined this poetic technique with one favored by earlier Spanish dramatists, especially Lope de Vega: namely, the use of popular songs in drama.

If we compare Lorca's use of Belisa's song with the manner in which Lope uses a song in *Peribáñez*, for example, we will see that Lorca has refined the technique to produce a different effect. In Act II of *Peribáñez*, Llorente's song, like Belisa's, is charged with sexual suggestiveness:

. . . . . .
Trébole de la soltera,
que tantos amores muda;
trébole de la viuda,
que otra vez casarse espera,
tocas blancas por defuera
y el faldellín de color.
Trébole, ¡ay Jesús cómo güele!
Trébole, ¡ay Jesús, qué olor![3]

The imagery in Llorente's song does not insinuate itself further into the text, but rather serves the dramatist very well by heightening the moment in which the Commander enters Casilda's room and by reflecting his less than honorable intentions. Belisa's song, on the other hand, fulfills another purpose. It contains phrases that resonate with others in the text, thereby helping to stamp in our mind the image of a woman who represents the physical aspects of love that will be counterbalanced by Perlimplín's commitment to matters of the heart.

More evidence of Lorca's method of including an extended poetic passage without interrupting the basic narrative line appears at the conclusion of Act I when Perlimplín, seated on the edge of Belisa's bed, says:

Amor, amor
que está herido.
Herido de amor huido;
herido,

muerto de amor.
Decid a todos que ha sido
el ruiseñor.
Bisturí de cuatro filos,
garganta rota y olvido.
Cógeme la mano, amor,
que vengo muy mal herido,
herido de amor huido,
¡herido!
¡muerto de amor! (1000)

The opening words ("Amor, amor") immediately echo the beginning of Belisa's song ("Amor, amor. Entre mis muslos cerrados") setting the protagonists who embody the outer-inner continuity into what we might refer to as a contrapuntal relationship. But at the same time, the metaphorical language of Perlimplín's lament expresses the present stage in his development as a character vis à vis his relationship with Belisa. What was ecstasy for Belisa is now a wound for Perlimplín. Not only is the outer-inner continuity advanced through an evocation of Belisa's earlier, contrasting song, but we begin to feel the presence of death in their relationship more forcefully as well. Phrases from Perlimplín's lament—"Herido de amor huido," "muerto de amor," "bisturí de cuatro filos," "garganta rota," "mal herido"—have counterparts in phrases that occur later in the drama: "el azafrán y el clavo" (1002); "corazones heridos" (1006); "se mueren de amor los ramos" (1011), "clavarle este puñal en su corazón galante" (1015); "voy a atravesar la garganta de mi marido" (1016); "la sangre gloriosa de mi señor" (1018). The imagery in Perlimplín's lament is also linked to earlier phrases such as "una mujer estranguló a su esposo" (981) and "¿Será capaz de estrangularme?" (987). Thus, the metaphorical language of Perlimplín's lament communicates the transition that he is experiencing at this moment. His awakening to physical desire has led to his suffering the pangs of love—a process that ultimately leads to his death in a garden of "cipreses y naranjos" which allude symbolically to the love-death motif that captivated Perlimplín's imagination. By recalling past apprehensions and alluding to a future course, Perlimplín's "set-piece" or "aria" keeps continuities in the metaphorical language alive while expressing the protagonist's thoughts at that moment.

Lorca's expanded use of a song is especially evident in Act III when Perlimplín hears a sweet serenade:

	The Dynamics of the Imagery in the Theater of Federico Garcia Lorca	121

Voces: Por las orillas del río
  se está la noche mojando.
  Y en los pechos de Belisa
  se mueren de amor los ramos.
Perlimplín: ¡Se mueren de amor los ramos!
Voces: La noche canta desnuda
  sobre los puentes de marzo.
  Belisa lava su cuerpo
  con agua salobre y nardos.
Perlimplín: ¡Se mueren de amor los ramos!
Voces: La noche de anís y plata
  relumbra por los tejados.
  Plata de arroyos y espejos.
  Y anís de tus muslos blancos.
Perlimplín: ¡Se mueren de amor los ramos! (1011-1012)

First we can say that with its highly evocative imagery steeped in the senses, this song shows a strong affinity for characteristics of Symbolism and Modernismo that were present in *El maleficio de la mariposa* and *Mariana Pineda*. The image contained in "se mueren de amor los ramos" resonates with these lines from Verlaine's poem that begins "L'ombre des arbres dans la rivière embrumée / Muert comme de la fumée, / Tandis qu'en l'air, parmi les ramures réeles / Se plaignent les tourterelles."[4] The song in *Perlimplín* also recalls Marquina's use of water imagery at the height of Deseada's expression of love in *La ermita, la fuente y el río*:

  <<¡Ya te han querido; es bastante!>>
  . . . .
  si hoy es de ella, antes que mío,
  como es del mar ese río
  y, al paso, da vida a un huerto.[5]

The song in Perlimplín's garden, however, goes beyond Symbolism and Modernismo. It not only foreshadows Perlimplín's death but links elements of the outer-inner imagery continuity as well. This song marks the third stage in the protagonist's movement towards a love-death. After Belisa's song which was the centerpiece of the action surrounding Perlimplín's arousal to sensual pleasures, and after Perlimplín's lament which expressed his wounded love, the song in the garden serves to indicate that Perlimplín's love has taken him closer to death. Also, the metaphorical language in the song reaches back into the text and brings the body-soul continuity into the present situation in the unfolding drama. In the song heard by Perlimplín, we hear echoes emanating from Belisa's song in the prologue. "Tus muslos blancos" recalls "mis muslos cerrados;" "se está la noche mojando" can be counterpointed with "nada como un pez el sol;" and "Belisa lava su cuerpo / con agua salobre y nardos. / ¡Se mueren de amor los ramos!" echoes "Agua tibia entre los juncos, / amor." By recalling Belisa's song (and hence Belisa as the embodiment of sexual love) at the time when Perlimplín is most determined to carry out his plan to make Belisa love her unknown admirer (Perlimplín) more than she loves her own body ("Yo necesito que ella ame a ese joven más que a su propio cuerpo" [1010]), the playwright intensifies the body-soul opposition close to the final outcome of the plan wrought in Perlimplín's imagination. Thus the metaphorical language directs its power to bear upon Perlimplín's expression of triumph when he says finally "yo soy mi alma y tú eres tu cuerpo . . . Déjame en este último instante, puesto que tanto me has querido, morir abrazado a él" (1017). We "feel" Perlimplín's final wish because the body-soul continuity that permeates the text has made us aware of the weight of the conflict facing the protagonist.

Through erotic imagery associated with the pleasures of night, the song in the garden also reminds us of an earlier comment made by Marcolfa—"El matrimonio tiene grandes encantos . . . Está lleno de cosas ocultas. Cosas que no están bien que sean dichas por una servidora" (981); and the water imagery recalls Perlimplín's ominous observation: "Belisa, con tantos encajes pareces una ola y me das el mismo miedo que de niño tuve al mar" (988). Finally with respect to the resonance this song has with other elements of the text, Perlimplín's refrain ("¡Se mueren de amor los ramos!") links the middle portion of the play with the prologue, Perlimplín's lament at the conclusion of Act I and, as we have already observed, the closing segment. Thus, in *Perlimplín*, Lorca continues to transform the *copla lopesca* (and in this instance the traditional *estribillo*) into a means for embedding poetry into dramatic contexts, thereby moving the trajectory of his development of poetic drama closer to a complete fusion of both elements.

To provide a sense of movement to this brief theater piece that is the enactment of a flight into the imagination, Lorca also employs characteristics of the traditional *romance*. Repetitions, refrains and sudden outbursts in *Perlimplín* remind us of rhetorical devices in the traditional *romances*. As a "sounding board," we can cite the final three stanzas of a traditional ballad entitled "Canción de una gentil dama y un rústico pastor":

—Mas es que la de la nieve
de mi cuerpo la blancura;
rostro de leche y coral;
delgadita en la cintura.

—"Mucho bueno poco dura"
—responde el villano vil—;
tengo el ganado en la sierra,
y a mi ganadico me quiero ir.
 —El cuello tengo de garza,
los ojos de un esparver,
las teticas agudicas,
que el brial quieren romper...
—No me puedo detener
por más que tengas ahí.
Mi ganado está en la sierra,
y a mi ganadico tengo de ir.
⎡Desecha de la dama, ⎤
⎣ que dice con enojo:⎦

 —¡Oh, malhaya el vil pastor
que dama gentil le ame
y le requiebre de amores,
y él se vaya aunque se llame!
—"El buey suelto bien se lame"
—respondió el villano al fin—,
y por más que me dijeres,
con mi ganadico me quiero ir.[6]

To illustrate alliterative passages in *Perlimplín* that evoke techniques used by the *juglares*, we cite the following:

Marcolfa:	Dígame, señor mío, las causas de ese no.
Perlimplín:	Dime tú, doméstica perseverante, las causas de ese sí. (980)

Marcolfa:	He decidido que vamos...
Perlimplín:	Hemos decidido que vamos... (984)

Perlimplín:	Habla sin miedo.
Belisa:	Hablan de mí..., de mi cuerpo...
Perlimplín:	¡De tu cuerpo! (1006)

With respect to the use of anaphora, Lorca's text yields these passages:

    Perlimplín: ¿Qué dice, Marcolfa? ¿Qué dice? ¿Y qué es esto que me pasa? ¿Qué es esto? (987)

    Perlimplín: ¡Sí! Yo te he besado... Pero...
                  si te hubiera besado alguien más...,
                  si te hubiera besado alguien más... (999)

    Belisa: Pero ¿quién era este hombre? ¿Quién era?
                  ....
                  ... le quiero, le quiero con toda
                  la fuerza de mi carne y de mi alma.
                  Pero ¿dónde está el joven de la capa roja?... Dios mío; ¿dónde está?
    Marcolfa: Don Perlimpín, duerme tranquilo... ¿La estás oyendo?... Don Perlimplín..., ¿la estás oyendo? (1018)

Also, exclamations like the following resonate with those we often hear in the traditional *romances*:

    Belisa: ¡Ay, qué música, Dios mío! ¡Qué música! (989)

    Belisa: ¡Amor!... ¿Quién te ha herido en el pecho? ¿Quién te abrió tus venas para que llenases de sangre mi jardín? ¡Amor!... Déjame ver tu rostro por un instante siquiera... ¡Ay! ¿Quién te dio muerte?... ¿Quién? (1016)

In recalling the traditional ballads, one especially notes Perlimplín's repeated exclamation "¡Se mueren de amor los ramos!" (1011, 1012), repeated after each stanza of the song in the garden. Here one may be reminded of repeated outbursts such as "¡Ay de mi Alhama!" uttered by the Moorish king of Granada in the well-known "Romance de la conquista de Alhama." Although the traditional *romance* does not make its presence felt as emphatically in *Perlimplín* as it did in *Mariana Pineda*, it nevertheless does insinuate itself into the text and thereby contributes to our perceiving a dramatic ebb and flow in this work.

    Thus, in *Perlimplín*, the boundaries between narrative line, allusive and evocative imagery, songs that frame action and motifs that constitute thematic material become less distinct than in *El maleficio de la mariposa* and *Mariana Pineda*. There is more evidence in *Perlimplín* that the dramatist is moving towards theater that combines Symbolist and

The Dynamics of the Imagery in the Theater of Federico Garcia Lorca

Modernista techniques with the use of song that was prevalent in the drama of the Golden Age, as well as with techniques employed by the *juglares* to infuse poetry with drama. Phrases such as "la noche canta desnuda sobre los puentes de marzo" and "jazminero flotante y sin raíces" not only coexist with prosaic statements such as "He aprendido muchas cosas, y sobre todo puedo imaginarlas" and "Pero ya estoy fuera del mundo y de la moral ridícula de las gentes" but also commingle with them in expressions such as "Cinco frías camelias de madrugada se han abierto en las paredes de la alcoba." The imagery is basically directed towards the outer-inner, body-soul continuity through images that express the idea that Belisa embodies the exterior, erotic world ("Entre mis muslos cerrados, / nada como un pez el sol") and Perlimplín the inner world of the imagination ("Ahora cierro los ojos y . . . veo lo que quiero" [1009]). But Lorca also taps the dramatic potential of the basic imagery continuity. Through elements of song and the traditional *romances*, the metaphorical language is given the opportunity to "move" with the narrative through various dramatic contexts; and the tension between the body and the soul as expressed in the outer-inner metaphorical continuity is linked to stages in Perlimplín's development from a man unmoved by the physical aspects of love to one so wounded by Belisa that he sacrifices himself to make her aware of the deeper significance of love. This is what Lorca's imagery accomplishes when words from Belisa's song in the prologue ("Agua tibia entre los juncos, / amor") come back to haunt an anguished Perlimplín in another song in Act III: "Por las orillas del río / se está la noche mojando. / Y en los pechos de Belisa / se mueren de amor los ramos."

What emerges in this play which occupies a place in the middle period of the development of Lorquian poetic drama is a combination of poetic techniques that produces imagery which permeates the text yet flows more continuously with the narrative. The final result is 1) a view of two worlds as expressed by Perlimplín: "Yo soy mi alma y tú [Belisa] eres tu cuerpo" (1017) and 2) an awareness of the fusion of both worlds as expressed by Marcolfa (1018) in an image that alludes to the fundamental inner-outer continuity in the metaphorical language of this drama: "Belisa, ya eres otra mujer. Estás vestida por la gloriosa sangre de mi señor."

Notes

1. "Don Perlimplin: Lorca's Theater-Poetry," *Kenyon Review*, 17, No. 3 (Summer 1955), pp.337-348.

2. W.B. Yeats, *The Shadowy Waters*, in *The Collected Plays of W.B. Yeats*, Revised Edition (New York: Macmillan, 1953), p.102.

3. Lope de Vega, *Peribáñez y el Comendador de Ocaña*, in *Comedias*, Vol. II, ed. Luis Guarner (Barcelona: Editorial Iberia, 1955), p.54.

4. "Ariettes oubliées" IX, *Romances sans paroles* in *Oeuvres poétiques complètes*, ed. Jacques Borel (Paris: Éditions Gallimard, 1962), p. 196.

5. *La ermita, la fuente y el río*, in *En Flandes se ha puesto el sol / La ermita, la fuente y el río* (Madrid: Castalia, 1996), p.262.

6. "Canción de una gentil dama y un rústico pastor," in *Flor nueva de romances que recogió de la tradición antigua y moderna R. Menéndez Pidal*, pp.283-284.

Chapter 6
Bodas de sangre

With *Bodas de sangre*, completed in 1932, the direction taken by Lorquian imagery becomes more apparent. As we have already observed, *El maleficio de la mariposa* and *Mariana Pineda* showed a strong affinity for Symbolist and Modernista theater, and *Amor de don Perlimplín con Belisa en su jardín* joins *Mariana Pineda* in admitting, adapting and expanding elements of the traditional Spanish *romance* and songs, a prevalent aspect of Golden Age theater. In *Bodas de sangre*, poetic imagery becomes more integrated into the dramatic context of the play and thus leads Lorca's theater more directly towards the complete fusion of poetry and drama.

Writing about the strategy of Lorca's dramatic works between 1930 and 1936, Andrew A. Anderson maintains that the playwright intended his so-called rural trilogy to establish a "power base" so that he might be able to return to his more experimental or avant-garde plays (*El público, Así que pasen cinco años* and the incomplete *Comedia sin título*) and thereby impose the kind of theater he believed appropriate for his time.[1] If one applies Anderson's assertion to the imagery in Lorca's theater, it can be said that Lorca's strategy was not to abandon temporarily the imagistic style of his earlier plays but rather to incorporate it into a more cohesive presentation of poetry and drama. Therefore, *Bodas de sangre* (and *La casa de Bernarda Alba* which we will discuss in the final chapter) simply continues the development of Lorca's poetic drama.

Bodas de sangre dramatizes the idea that fate and honor drive love and grief into extreme isolation and finally to tragedy. It is our intention to demonstrate that Lorca expresses this action through metaphorical language that is more in harmony with the human dimension of the characters and their conflicts than was the case in *El maleficio de la mariposa, Mariana Pineda* and *Perlimplín*. The poetic imagery in *Bodas de sangre* retains the

128   *The Dynamics of the Imagery in the Theater
of Federico Garcia Lorca*

highly evocative quality of the earlier plays and also allies itself with elements of thematic and symbolic material. However, the dramatic potential of the imagery is more fully realized at this stage of the development of Lorca's poetic theater—a period in which the playwright was very active in La Barraca's presentations of Golden Age dramas.

As the tragedy of *Bodas de sangre* unfolds, one can trace imagery continuities that express the withdrawal of Leonardo and La Novia into the darkness of love and La Madre into the isolation of deep-rooted anguish and grief. Images of blades, blood, horses, flowers, heat, light and darkness permeate the text and interact to express the all-consuming nature of pent up passion and the obstacles that prevent its consummation. Rather than remaining static symbols of various components of the conflict (revenge, youth, passion, death, etc.), these images frequently adapt themselves to dramatic contexts, assuming different values and interacting to form a network of imagery with "nerve endings" that are sensitive to changes in elements of the human drama.

Bodas de sangre is a complex poetic drama which contains a confluence of the methods for integrating poetry and drama used earlier by Lorca. The ominous atmosphere created by the interplay between light and darkness in Act III recalls "atmospheric" environments in Symbolist plays by Maeterlinck and Yeats. An image such as "mis cenizas / de soñolientos metales / buscan la cresta del fuego" has a strong affinity with Symbolist lyrics. Moreover, there are scenes in *Bodas de sangre* that have an accelerating motion which reminds one of the sweep of a *romance*. Also the use of songs that frame and foreshadow events suggest scenes containing *coplas* in the plays of Lope de Vega. Archetypal symbols, expanded metaphors and the almost liturgical tone at the conclusion of the play provide echoes of the theater of Calderón. In short, *Bodas de sangre* has what Anderson calls Lorca's intent to place the contemporary Spanish theater in direct contact with its origin and "true" tradition" (217). Nevertheless, in Lorca's theater, archetypal symbols are linked to the human emotional conflict. The songs contain images related to the unfolding events as well as allusions and evocations of feelings and thoughts emanating from imagery continuities. Ballad effects become a poetic technique for maintaining the flow of the narrative line and providing a setting for fleeting images that can help send the imagination into flight. In other words, *Bodas de sangre* maintains the drama *continuously* at a human level while sustaining evocative poetic imagery through which characters express themselves.

The Dynamics of the Imagery in the Theater   129
of Federico Garcia Lorca

In our analysis of the dynamics of the imagery in *Bodas de sangre*, we will first direct our attention to the principal imagery continuities and then examine Lorca's use of elements of songs and *romances*.

One of the most obvious indicators of the manner in which Lorca imbues dramatic contexts with metaphorical language related to thematic material appears in the image of blades—"navajas"—introduced in the opening moments of the drama. A blade, we quickly learn, was the instrument of death for the father and brother of El Novio. It makes its presence felt throughout the play and becomes part of a fate motif associated with the eventual death of El Novio. But while repeated references and allusions to "la navaja" gradually evoke the presence of death, the image serves dramatic contexts as well. For example, in the opening scene, "la navaja" is the focal point of a natural exchange of dialogue between El Novio and La Madre. "Comeré uvas. Dame la navaja," says El Novio casually to his mother (1172).[2] The playwright has thus introduced a knife into a natural context that links the young man, his mother and the cutting instrument. This provides the mother with an opportunity to place the knife in the wider context of death: "La navaja, la navaja . . . Malditas sean todas y el bribón que las inventó . . . Y las escopetas, y las pistolas, y el cuchillo más pequeño, y hasta las azadas y los bieldos de la era" (1172). As La Madre continues, the playwright tightens the association between the cutting blade and the young man to whom the lines are addressed: "Todo lo que puede cortar el cuerpo de un hombre. Un hombre hermoso, con su flor en la boca que sale a las viñas" (1173). An even more foreboding link between El Novio and "la navaja" is present in the mother's wish not to go to the vineyards with her son, for she has already taken that fatal route with her husband ("Tu padre sí que me llevaba" [1174]).

The "voice" warning of instruments that cut men in the flower of their youth is heard throughout the first scene of Act I, punctuating the scene with a more immediate reference to danger in a cutting instrument. In this instance (also an unforced element of conversation), La Vecina says that a youth was severely cut by a machine ("Hace dos días trajeron al hijo de mi vecina con los dos brazos cortados por máquina" [1179]). Shortly thereafter, she recalls the blade image in the word "segadores" when she comments upon the heat: "Iban negros los chiquillos que llevan el agua a los segadores" (1183). We also note that by closing the scene with the dominating image of blades lingering in the mind of the reader, Lorca has given the text a transition leading directly into the next dramatic context—i.e., the cradle song that opens the second scene ("El agua era negra / . . . / que el caballo no quiere beber /. . . / dentro de los ojos / un puñal de plata" [1184]). Thus, we begin to follow the "movement" of the blade image as if it were acting out a role in a drama rather than serving merely as a static symbol of death.

The knife imagery is kept alive in Act II again in natural-sounding conversation. At this point in the drama, a knife image links Leonardo with the fate of the family of El Novio and La Madre when the latter tells El Padre that Leonardo "sigue en toda la mala ralea [de su familia], manejadores de cuchillos" (1227). This baleful image then proceeds to maintain its momentum later in the act by insinuating itself into the wedding festivities through a subtle allusion to sharp points when two girls argue over who was given the first pin ("alfiler") by the bride.

After creating a feeling of increasing tension and danger, the blade image participates more directly in the action at the beginning of Act III in the conversation of woodcutters whose blades are engaged in a hunt for trees to cut down—a hunt that reflects that of El Novio in search of Leonardo and La Novia. The association between blades and the fate of the principal characters is intensified when the moon and death in the form of a beggar allude to the action of the daggers that Leonardo and El Novio have poised for each other:

> Luna: La luna deja un cuchillo
> abandonado en el aire,
> que siendo acecho de plomo
> quiere ser dolor de sangre. (1249)

> Luna: El aire va llegando duro, con doble filo.
> Mendiga: Ilumina el chaleco y aparta los botones,
> que después las navajas ya saben el
> camino. (1251)

After sending out its warning and fulfilling its predictions with the death of El Novio and Leonardo, the image of a knife, appearing as early as the beginning of Act I, adapts itself to another context when it is used to express grief in the final scene. The knife that La Madre said killed her husband and elder son and which she feared held danger for El Novio has indeed killed two more young men and also found its way into her own heart:

Vecinas: con un cuchillo,
con un cuchillito,
en un día señaldo, entre las dos y las tres,
se mataron los dos hombres del amor.
Con un cuchillo,
con un cuchillito
que apenas cabe en la mano,
pero que penetra fino
por las carnes asombradas
y que se para en el sitio
donde tiembla enmarañada
la oscura raíz del grito. (1271-1272)

Thus, Lorca has taken an image and moved it through the drama, adapting it to changing contexts while maintaining its evocative quality. One might say that because of the dynamics of the image, the foreboding knife of the opening scene has penetrated the lives of two more young men of ill-fated families and pierced the heart of the women who survive with grief.

The flower imagery in *Bodas de sangre*, unlike the blade imagery, "represents" more than it "acts." Flowers in this play symbolize life, youth and beauty—"Un hombre hermoso, con su flor en la boca" (1172-1173)— and when placed in a context of damaged beauty, they become linked to the blade imagery and further intensify the evocation of death:

Primero, tu padre, que me olía a clavel
y lo disfruté tres años escasos.
Luego, tu hermano. ¿Y es justo y
puede ser que una cosa pequeña
como una pistola o una navaja
pueda acabar con un hombre, que es un toro? (1173)

Mis Muertos . . . dos hombres que eran
dos geranios (1173)

y una planta que se llama Júpiter, que da
flores encarnadas, y se secó (1195)

flores rotas los ojos (1266)

Sobre la flor del oro, sucia arena. (1266)

Mira que mi cuello es blando; te costará
menos trabajo que segar una dalia de tu huerto. (1270)

Although the foregoing passages can be compared to Maeterlinck's frequent references to forests, blindness, grottos, wells and crypts to create a suffocating atmosphere in *Pelléas et Mélisande*, or to Valéry's images of devouring in "La Jeune Parque," we see Lorca's images not as static evocations but rather as increments in the continuities of the metaphorical language expressing what is happening or what has happened. For example, by linking "geranios muertos" with "planta que se secó," "flores rotas" and "Sobre la flor del oro, sucia arena," we have an imagistic sequence that joins the blade imagery in expressing thoughts concerning death's insidious pursuit of men in their prime. In effect, here too Lorca establishes what Brower calls "felt qualities"[3] which, in various contexts, help put us in touch with the powerful forces that the principal characters feel control their movements and from which they try to escape.

To the extent that *Bodas de sangre* contains allusive and often fragmented images whose aggregate effect creates a mood, evokes a feeling or the presence of an abstraction such as death, one can say that Lorca, at this stage in his dramatic output, retains an affinity with Symbolism. In addition, expanded metaphors, symbolic language and themes such as honor, love, death and fate still recall the theater of the Golden Age (especially Calderón). However, Lorca now integrates to such a high degree specific dramatic contexts with Symbolist and Golden Age techniques for presenting images that he establishes an individual style as a playwright developing the coalescence of poetry and drama. In this regard, the light-darkness imagery in *Bodas de sangre*—especially as it pertains to the moon—is most helpful in indicating that Lorca does not abandon Symbolist and Golden Age techniques of handling images but rather transforms them into an important ingredient of poetic drama with the stamp of originality.

The presence of moonlight, shadows and darkness in Act II shows Lorca still working off the Symbolist poets and playwrights, who frequently use the light of the moon as a foreboding witness to human events or as an element of imagery that creates a mood congenial to the evocation of human feelings or emotions. In the mysterious atmosphere created by the "vivo resplandor azul" of the moon in *Bodas de sangre*, we can "see" a moon like "la lune triste et beau" in Verlaine's "Clair de Lune;" and the intermittent moonlight and cries of anguish uttered by La Novia and Leonardo bring to mind a scene like the one in which Blanca, a protagonist of Martínez Sierra's *Cuento de labios en flor*, says her tears shine with the light of the moon.[4]

The moon that pursues Leonardo and La Novia, however, is more than an evocative component of a scene charged with a sense of impending danger. Lorca's moon is an active participant in the drama, assuming the role of fate and acting as the handmaiden of a beggar woman who symbolizes death. We pause to observe, therefore, that in this sense, the moon in *Bodas de sangre* is an archetypal symbol like Night in Maeterlinck's *The Blue Bird* and Light and Darkness in Calderón's *auto*, *La vida es sueño*. Lorca's Mendiga entreats the moon: "¡De prisa! Mucha luz. ¿Me has oído? / ¡No pueden escaparse!" (1252). Maeterlinck's Night, in the form of a very old woman, entreats Tyltyl to abandon the search for the Blue Bird and not tempt fate by opening the great middle door leading to the abyss from which there is no escape.[5] As we shall see, however, Lorca's moon does not act primarily as Light and Darkness but rather fulfills the active role of Lorca's imagery in theater by participating in a human drama.

As we approach Lorca's more dynamic use of the moon as a component of the metaphorical language than was the case with the dramatists and poets cited above, we will again compare Lorca to his predecessors in order to show how he uses techniques associated with them but at the same time creates the image of a moon that appears (and disappears) in the context of a human drama unfolding in the night. In *Bodas de sangre*, two lovers seek the cover of darkness in order to escape the watchful eye of the families that pursue them. To enter their own world of love, they must elude the path illuminated by the lethal rays of the moon. In an expanded metaphor, the light of the moon becomes an instrument of death aimed at lovers who need darkness in order to escape from their pursuers. Because the action of the characters is, to a degree, conditioned by the presence or absence of moonlight, the playwright takes the opportunity to present the metaphor with symbolist (and almost surrealist) images and still maintains the narrative line of the human tragedy. This is accomplished through the Symbolist style of layered images that evoke the presence of death and by an expanded metaphor personifying the moon in a style reminiscent of Calderón. But Lorca takes these techniques further by combining them to produce poetry that contains key imagery continuities (blades, blood, light, heat) which express the action of the drama.

As if it were a mood poem, Lorca uses the soliloquy of the moon to evoke the feeling of a cold metallic light casting an eerie spell on the forest. In a series of images—"alba fingida en las hojas," " . . . un cuchillo / abandonado en el aire, / que siendo acecho de plomo / quiere ser dolor de sangre;" "¡Tengo frío! Mis cenizas / de soñolientos metales / buscan la cresta del fuego" (1249)—Lorca calls on nature, the senses, synesthesia and the allusive properties of words to shape a moon whose sensuous light carries with it a sense of doom. Thus we observe that although *Bodas de sangre* creates an environment and characters quite different from *El maleficio de la mariposa*, *Mariana Pineda* and *Perlimplín*, it does not relinquish Symbolist and Modernista characteristics of the imagery in those earlier plays. These lines which begin the soliloquy of the moon belong to the tradition of Verlaine, Darío and Marquina:

> Cisne redondo en el río,
> ojo de las catedrales,
> alba fingida en las hojas
> soy... (1249)

In addition to layering images to make visible an other-worldly place to which Leonardo and La Novia have fled, the playwright uses the moon image to create an expanded metaphor in the style of Calderón. But as we shall see, Lorca leads this poetic element in the direction of the on-going action. First, from Calderón we have the following example from Act II of *El alcalde de Zalamea*. In a lengthy poetic passage in which El Capitán describes the anguish and joy of love, Calderón expands an answer to a rather prosaic question into a composition of similes and metaphors that serves the dramatic moment by heightening its emotional content:

Sargento:	¿Para qué intentas que una mujer en un día te escuche y te favorezca?
Capitán:	En un día el sol alumbra y falta; en un día se trueca un reino todo; en un día es edificio una peña; en un día una batalla pérdida y victoria ostenta; en un día tiene el mar tranquilidad y tormenta; en un día nace un hombre y muere; luego pudiera en un día ver mi amor sombra y luz como planeta, pena y dicha como imperio, gente y brutos como selva,

paz y tranquilidad como mar,
triunfo y ruina como guerra,
vida y muerte como dueño
de sentidos y potencias;
y habiendo tenido edad
en un día su violencia
de hacerme tan desdichado,
¿por qué, por qué no pudiera
tener edad en un día
de hacerme dichoso?[6]

With its extensive parallel construction, the response of El Capitán serves the dramatist by highlighting this portion of the action with a "tour de force" speech. Similarly, the verses that describe the moon as an instrument of death in *Bodas de sangre* constitute an expanded metaphor injected into the action of a drama. But the passage serves the dramatist not only by making the presence of the moon palpable as a cold body desiring warm blood ("Tengo frío . . . Pues esta noche tendrán / mis mejillas roja sangre" [1249]) but also by maintaining the momentum of the fatal hunt in which the principal characters are involved. Like the woodcutters with their axes in search of trees to cut down, the moon is engaged in a search that will lead to death. This is precisely what is happening to the protagonists at this point in the drama. In the soliloquy of the moon, death, like El Novio, is actively seeking the blood of someone's heart. The hunt at the human level is still in progress, and the counterpoint between the light of the moon as death ("¡No haya sombra ni emboscada, / que no puedan escaparse!" [1250]) and darkness as a shield for the lovers ("¡Ay luna mala! / Deja para el amor la oscura rama" [1248]) has the effect of increasing the dramatic tension. Thus, an extensive and highly evocative poetic passage expresses what is happening in the human drama.

In addition to "narrating" what is happening at that point in the drama, the soliloquy of the moon places elements of the basic imagery continuities near the climactic moment of the play. Many phrases uttered by the moon reverberate with earlier segments of the imagery through which the conflict is being expressed. In phrases like "un cuchillo abandonado en el aire," "dolor de sangre," "la cresta del fuego," "no podrán escaparse," "un corazón para mí," "Yo haré lucir al caballo / una fiebre de diamante," one "hears" the images of blades, a horse, light, darkness and heat that have been following the protagonists through the drama. Thus, in Act III of *Bodas de sangre*, with the soliloquy of the moon as a focal point, Lorca has taken his imagery in the theater beyond Symbolism and Calderón by focusing on the relationship between metaphysical language and human drama and by sustaining continuities in the poetic language through interlocking images.

The blood imagery in *Bodas de sangre* is particularly revealing with respect to Lorca's use of a symbol tied to natural dramatic dialogue. In this regard, a comparison between Lorca and Calderón will help to put the former's achievement in perspective, for Lorca expands a metaphorical process employed by Calderón through what García-Posada refers to as "la polivalencia textual del símbolo."[7] When one compares the use of the word "sangre" in Calderón's *El médico de su honra* with that of *Bodas de sangre*, it becomes apparent that both dramatists use "sangre" as an archetypal symbol for death and family bonds (and, by extension, honor). Further, both playwrights place the symbol in appropriately relevant dramatic contexts. However, in Calderón's play, the symbol remains at an elevated level, working in the reader's mind as a philosophical abstraction that makes appearances in heightened dramatic moments. Lorca, on the other hand, taps the "polivalente" potential of the symbol. For example, by including sexual connotations in the word "sangre," the playwright gives the image the potential to follow certain aspects of the human drama as it develops while still intensifying the ability of the word to evoke the presence of death and family honor which close in upon and isolate the characters caught in their web.

El médico de su honra has as its central metaphor a husband acting as a surgeon to cure his wounded honor by bleeding his wife to death. Act III has two concentrated passages in which blood imagery is first rooted in a dramatic context and then radiates outward towards the general context relating to the key metaphor. In the first instance, Don Gutierre secretly witnesses a scene between the king, Don Pedro, and his brother, El Infante Don Enrique. When the king asks Don Enrique to identify the dagger he lost, he uses "sangre" in reference to family honor:

Rey: ¿Y no sabéis
                dónde la daga perdiste?
Don Enrique: No, señor.
Rey: Yo sí, pues fué
                adonde fuera posible
                mancharse con sangre vuestra.[8]

Then when Don Enrique accidentally cuts Don Pedro's hand with the dagger and draws blood, the image of "sangre" reaches out from its obvious contextual meaning to include: 1) the on-going feud between the brothers ("¿Desta manera / tu acero en mi sangre tiñes?") and 2) a premonition of death ("¡Oh, qué aprensión insufrible! / Bañado me vi en mi sangre, / muerto estuve." [211]). But Calderón's use of the radiating image does not stay here. When Don Gutierre comes out from hiding after witnessing this scene, he makes a comment that includes the word "sangre" as a link between the scene he has just witnessed and the fate of his wife with himself as the "surgeon": "Muera Mencía, su sangre / bañe el pecho, donde asiste" (211). Calderón has thus placed "sangre" in a dramatic context in addition to using the image to remind the reader of the feud between the two brothers, to anticipate a future event (i.e., the historical killing of Don Pedro by Don Enrique) and to keep alive the key metaphor of the husband as surgeon of his honor, articulated during the climactic action of the drama (i.e., Doña Mencía's death by blood-letting):

> Doña Mencía: ¿Qué fiera mano, que sangriento acero,
> en mi pecho ejecutas? . . .
> . . . .
> . . . ¿No estaba agora
> Gutierre aquí? ¿No vía (¿quién lo ignora?)
> que, en mi sangre bañada,
> moría en rubias ondas anegada? (213)
> . . . .
> Don Gutierre: Médico soy de mi honor,
> la vida pretendo darle
> con una sangría; que todos
> curan a costa de sangre. (215)

Although Calderón does expand the dramatic implications of the image of blood by giving it multiple values, Don Gutierre's pronouncement— "Médico soy de mi honor"—has the effect of returning the image to the single dominating metaphor specifically articulated by the protagonist. One could say that the dramatic impact of the image of blood has been overwhelmed by its association with a social-moral premise that governs the play.

Like Calderón, Lorca implants images in dramatic contexts, but the power of Lorca's imagery derives more from the cumulative effect of all the values given to an image in varying segments of dialogue at a very human level rather than from conscious social, moral or philosophical pronouncements. Lorca himself wrote: "La imaginación fija y da vida clara a fragmentos de la realidad donde se mueve el hombre."[9]

The first indication that "sangre," one of the key images in this play, is associated with death appears in the title. Although one may argue that "blood" here could connote something other than death ("bonds of blood," for example), its proximity to a word ("bodas") so heavily charged with the idea of joy tends to make the title an oxymoron. This first ominous impression of "sangre" is confirmed almost immediately in Act I when La Madre laments the death of two men in her family, and it is reconfirmed as she withdraws deeper into a world of solitary grief and acceptance of a fate that finally claims her other son. "Sangre" also follows El Novio and Leonardo as they move directly into the path of death. Further, the blood imagery moves on other levels and follows various stages of the evolving human relationships. "Sangre" is used to express family bonds and family honor which draw into their orbit El Novio, Leonardo and La Novia as inheritors of the reputation of their families; and it also represents the passion that leads Leonardo and La Novia towards an imagined state of bliss described by a woodcutter in these words near the beginning of Act III: "Pero ya habrán mezclado sus sangres y serán como dos cántaros vacíos, como dos arroyos secos" [1247]).

This "polivalencia" of an image is of great importance to Lorquian imagery, for it provides the playwright with many opportunities to set the image in varying dramatic contexts without interrupting the flow of action that can result even momentarily if the image is locked in a statement that "announces" its symbolic connotations. Early in Act I, La Madre reminds her son that he comes from a strong blood line ("Tu padre sí que me llevaba. Eso es de buena casta. Sangre. Tu abuelo dejó a un hijo en cada esquina. Eso me gusta. Los hombres, hombres; el trigo, trigo" [1174]). In Act II, she sets her son's blood line in opposition to Leonardo's ("¿Qué sangre va a tener? La de toda su familia. Mana de su bisabuelo, que empezó matando, y sigue en toda la mala ralea, manejadores de cuchillos y gente de falsa sonrisa" [1227]). At the conclusion of Act II, the playwright intensifies the death-family connotations of "sangre" when La Madre rallies the wedding guests to pursue the fleeing lovers: "Ha llegado otra vez la hora de la sangre. Dos bandos. Tú con el tuyo y yo con el mío" (1244). At this critical moment in the action, the dramatist calls upon metaphorical language to express what is happening. Having already invested the word "sangre" with images of death and family lineage, its use in this instance fuses 1) the mother's obsession with death 2) family enmities 3) family pride and 4) the immediate action. By sustaining the presence of a key image through interrelated but varying dramatic contexts, the playwright gives the metaphorical language power to express felt qualities as well as overt actions without interrupting the human drama in order to "proclaim" what is happening. This is our reason for saying that Lorca goes beyond Calderón.

Even when "sangre" acquires more than one symbolic value, Lorca controls its association with death by reinforcing it with the blade imagery, thereby bringing its cumulative force to bear on passages in which it occurs. For example, when Leonardo angrily says to La Novia "No quiero hablar, porque soy hombre de sangre, y no quiero que todos estos cerros oigan mis voces" (1213), one "hears" allusions to family blood, personal pride and lurking danger as well. "La polivalencia del símbolo" has infused this brief passage with added meaning that helps shape Leonardo's character in our mind.

As the three young principal characters become more enmeshed in the net that fate (death) has laid in their path, the poet-playwright increases the use of blood imagery and links its various symbolic components. In the cradle song of the second scene of Act I, we hear "La sangre corría / más fuerte que el agua" (1184)—words imbued with a faint allusion to blood as a symbol of family ties and as a portent of dire happenings. From the context of this *nana* with its black water, the image of blood moves to another stage in the developing relationship among the characters when La Criada sings a wedding song containing these lines: "Galana, / galana de la tierra, mira cómo el agua pasa /. . . / Porque el novio es un palomo / con todo el pecho de brasa / y espera el campo el rumor / de la sangre derramada" (1226). These lines, although charged with sexual connotations, faintly echo the *nana* ("Bajaban al río. / La sangre corría / más fuerte que el agua") and anticipate these words spoken soon after by La Madre referring to her dead son:

> Por eso es tan terrible ver la sangre de una derramada por el suelo. Una fuente que corre un minuto y a nosotros nos ha costado años. Cuando yo llegué a ver a mi hijo, estaba tumbado en mitad de la calle. Me mojé las manos de sangre y me las lamí con la lengua. Porque era mía. Tú no sabes lo que es eso. En una custodia de cristal y topacios pondría yo la tierra empapada por ella. (1228-1229)

A parent-child relationship, life, love and death fuse in the image of blood which retains qualities of an archetypal symbol but becomes "humanized" in the context of this passage that probes the depths of a mother's loss. Through blood imagery, Lorca has linked the wedding, the tragic events that preceded it and the sense of danger that has been hovering over the characters, so that when La Madre screams at the close of Act II "Ha llegado otra vez la hora de la sangre" (1244), we feel the enormous weight of her outburst.

As the drama reaches another level in Act III with the flight of Leonardo and La Novia, the tempo of the blood imagery increases. The moon begins this movement by anticipating the discovery of the lovers: "un cuchillo . . . quiere ser dolor de sangre;" "Pues esta noche tendrán / mis mejillas roja sangre;" "para que esta noche tengan / mis mejillas dulce sangre;" "Que la sangre / me ponga entre los dedos su delicado silbo" (1249, 1250, 1251). Then a woodcutter foresees tragedy—"¡No abras el chorro de la sangre!" (1255)—and finally Leonardo, in effect acting out what was narrated in the *nana* ("El agua era negra," "dentro de los ojos un puñal de plata") tells La Novia: "Pero [yo] montaba a caballo / y el caballo iba a tu puerta. / Con alfileres de plata / mi sangre se puso negra" (1258). The fact that death is approaching Leonardo and that he feels helpless in controlling his destiny is being expressed in the accelerated use of the image of blood in varying contexts that avoid the feeling that "sangre" is acting as an archetypal symbol at a distance from the human drama. By fusing the images of "un puñal de plata" and "alfileres de plata" through what Lorca called a "salto ecuestre" in our imagination, the sense of tragedy that pervaded the cradle song is linked to the human passion in the on-going action.

Having already orchestrated the images of blood through multiple values and resonances appearing in contexts that touch and intermingle with the lives of the principal characters, Lorca then uses "sangre" to powerful effect in representing the final stage of the human conflict—the death of Leonardo and El Novio. In the final scene, the thin red line of a skein of yarn evokes an image of trickling blood (with the girls winding the yarn evoking the Fates) that underscores what one of the girls reveals: "Amante sin habla. / Novio carmesí" (1263). Blood has been spilled, and the "thin slow stream" first reaches La Novia (" . . . la novia vuelve / teñida en sangre falda y cabellera" [1266]) and then makes its way towards La Madre ("Vuestras lágrimas son lágrimas de los ojos nada más, y las más... serán más ardientes que la sangre" [1267]). "Sangre," therefore, has become more than a symbol of death. It is a cohesive imagery continuity linking the fate of one character to that of another and eventually expressing the idea that the only possible escape a character might have wished for existed only in his or her imagination. This is the result of family bonds, overwhelming passion and tragedy in the past—expressed in the blood imagery—joining forces to prevent a solution without violence.

To conclude this lengthy analysis of the blood imagery in *Bodas de sangre*, we can turn to Lorca's text for a summary of how the playwright makes this metaphorical continuity expressive of the human conflict. In the succinct lines spoken by the woodcutters in Act III, what is ostensibly a narrative similar to that of a Greek chorus becomes the story of a fleshed-out drama, because the blood imagery during the course of the play has dove-tailed with the narrative line of the human drama:

Leñador 1°: Se estaban engañando uno a otro y al fin la sangre pudo más.
Leñador 3°: ¡La sangre!
Leñador 1°: Hay que seguir el camino de la sangre.
Leñador 2°: Pero la sangre que ve la luz se la bebe la tierra.
Leñador 1°: ¿Y qué? Vale más ser muerto desangrado que vivo con ella podrida. (1246)

Before turning our attention away from the final act of the play in order to scrutinize another key imagery continuity, we again refer to Calderón to show how Lorca places an individual stamp on an affinity with classical Spanish literature. This time Calderón's *auto sacramental La vida es sueño* provides a model for a method Lorca uses to infuse a specific dramatic context with continuities in the metaphorical language. If one speaks in terms of the imagery in Lorca's play, it can be said that at the conclusion of the drama, the fire of passion has been extinguished in a dark river like the one in the *nana*, and that tragedy, so powerfully present in the subtext in images of "navajas" and "sangre," assumes the form of ritual in the litany intoned by the women in the final scene. La Madre leads the chant:

Madre: Es lo mismo.
La cruz, la cruz.
Mujeres: Dulces clavos,
dulce cruz,
dulce nombre
de Jesús.
Novia: Que la cruz ampare a muertos y vivos.

Madre: Vecinas: con un cuchillito,
con un cuchillito,
. . . . .
con un cuchillo,
con un cuchillito
que apenas cabe en la mano,
pero que penetra fino
por las carnes asombradas
y que se para en el sitio
donde tiembla enmarañada
la oscura raíz del grito.
Novia: Y esto es un cuchillo,
un cuchillito
que apenas cabe en la mano
. . . . .
Madre: Y apenas cabe en la mano,
pero que penetra frío . . . (1271-1272)

These passages with their liturgical overtones are not unlike the refrains chanted in Calderón's *auto*, such as when Poder declares "Sufra, llore, gima y sienta / cuánto un pecado le muda, / al ver de un instante a otro / que el que en su primera cuna / durmió en brazos de la Gracia, / despierta en los de la Culpa;" and then the Four Elements, carrying El Hombre away to his prison, repeat "Sufra, llore, gima, sienta."[10] Lorca, like Calderón, has his characters chant thematic material (in this instance, the fate motif); but he enriches the texture of the metaphorical language by including imagery continuities set in motion early in the play. The blade imagery from Act I that was set in the context of death (the death of the father and brother of El Novio) and foreboding (the fear of La Madre that the same fate will befall el Novio) reappears at the end of the drama to confirm La Madre's earlier fears by expressing what is actually in progress: i.e., a dirge lamenting the fact that a blade has indeed fulfilled its destiny and found the heart of two more victims—El Novio who is actually slain and La Madre who remains behind to grieve. By reshaping imagery from Act II ("Tengo en mi pecho un grito siempre puesto de pie a quien tengo que castigar y meter entre los mantos" [1227]) to fit it into the context of Act III ("un cuchillo . . . que se para en el sitio / donde tiembla enmarañada / la oscura raíz del grito" [1272]), the dramatist makes of the metaphorical language a continuous expression of what is happening en la drama.

The Dynamics of the Imagery in the Theater of Federico Garcia Lorca

In his detailed analysis of the oft-requested image of a horse in *Bodas de sangre*, Villegas sums up Lorca's use of symbols by saying that the value of a symbol lies in the place it occupies in the cosmos of the particular literary work.[11] Indeed, the image of a horse in *Bodas de sangre* provides another important dynamic imagery continuity and acts as a catalyst for an expanded metaphor that eventually expresses Leonardo's and La Novia's attempted flight out of reality into an isolated world controlled by death; and it is in this context that the Golden Age technique of including *romances* and elements of song serves especially well Lorca's purpose of uniting poetry and drama.

The horse that eventually carries Leonardo and La Novia into a dreamlike world first makes its appearance in the tranquil setting of a *nana* that is a microcosm of Leonardo's actions in the larger human drama. The horse that is first the central image in a cradle song becomes associated with Leonardo and follows him on a course guided by destiny. In the *nana* we hear, "Nana, niño, nana / del caballo grande / que no quiso el agua;" "el caballo no quiere beber;" "el caballo se pone a llorar" (1184). The rider of this horse is Leonardo, and the *nana* tells his story. Like the horse in the *nana* ("A los montes duros / solo relinchaba / con el río muerto / sobre la garganta" [1185]), Leonardo tries to distance himself from La Novia, but the passion seething within him ("No quiso tocar / la orilla mojada, / su belfo caliente / con moscas de plata [1185]), will not permit it. The cradle song emits restraint and foreboding ("¡No vengas! Detente, / cierra la ventana con rama de sueños / y sueño de ramas" [1185]); but like Leonardo, the rider of the horse in the *nana* is carried headlong to a fateful rendezvous with dark waters in a dream-like world ("Las patas heridas, / las crines heladas, / dentro de los ojos / un puñal de plata. / Bajaban al río. / ¡Ay, cómo bajaban! [1184]). Finally, the horse drinks the black water ("Duérmete, clavel, / que el caballo se pone a beber" [1193]).

After presenting this poetic rendition of an expanded horse-rider metaphor, Lorca proceeds to involve it dynamically in specific dramatic contexts. In Act III Leonardo himself echoes the foreboding, dark world of the cradle song when he justifies his action to La Novia by saying "Y cuando te vi de lejos / me eché en los ojos arena. / Pero montaba a caballo / y el caballo iba a tu puerta. / Con alfileres de plata / mi sangre se puso negra" (1257-1258). By recalling lines from the *nana* ("No quiso tocar / la orilla mojada, su belfo caliente / con moscas de plata" [1185]; "¡Ay, caballo grande, / que no quiso el agua!" [1193]), the playwright has used a continuity in the imagery to express what is happening (i.e., an explanation of why Leonardo, despite himself, has left everyone behind and escaped with La Novia into a dream-like world fraught with danger). When the *nana* is interrupted by Leonardo's arrival, the horse-rider imagery yields another example of the close identification between metaphorical language and drama:

Mujer: ... ¿Fuiste a casa del herrador?
Leonardo: De allí vengo. ¿Querrás creer? Llevo más de dos meses poniendo herraduras nuevas al caballo y siempre se le caen. Por lo visto se las arranca con las piedras.
. . . . .
Mujer: Ayer me dijeron las vecinas que te habían visto al límite de los llanos.
. . . . .
... el caballo estaba reventado de sudor.
. . . . .
Suegra: Pero ¿quién da esas carreras al caballo? Está abajo, tendido, con los ojos desorbitados, como si llegara del fin del mundo. (1187, 1188, 1189)

Hearing this exchange of dialogue, we recall elements of the *nana*: "las patas heridas," "La sangre corría" / más fuerte que el agua," "su belfo caliente / con moscas de plata." Similarly, at the conclusion of Act I, a phrase from the *nana* ("el caballo se pone a beber") reverberates in the dialogue whose subtext tells us that Leonardo has altered his relationship with La Novia by placing himself in close proximity to her:

Criada: ¿Sentiste anoche un caballo?
. . . . .
Novia: Sería un caballo suelto de la manada.
Criada: No. Llevaba jinete. (1204)

Even in apparently casual utterances, the horse image alludes to Leonardo's relationship to both La Novia and La Mujer. For example, before the wedding festivities, fragments of the dialogue read as follows:

Leonardo: Por eso vengo.
Criada: ¿Y tu mujer?
Leonardo: Yo vine a caballo. Ella se acerca por el camino.
Criada: ¿No te has encontrado a nadie?
Leonardo: Los pasé con el caballo.
Criada: Vas a matar al animal con tanta carrera. (1210-1211)

Mujer: Vamos.
Leonardo: ¿Adónde?
Mujer: A la iglesia. Pero no vas en el caballo. Vienes conmigo.
Leonardo: ¿En el carro?
Mujer: ¿Hay otra cosa?
Leonardo: Yo no soy hombre para ir en carro. (1223-1224)

The image of the horse in the *nana* that foreshadowed the flight of Leonardo and La Novia ("Bajaban al río / ¡Ay, cómo bajaban!" [1184]) actually enters the dialogue during their escape and thus lends the same sense of inevitability and unreality to their action that was present during the movements of the horse in the *nana*:

> Es que no le encuentro y el caballo no
> está tampoco en el establo. (1239)

> ¡Han huido! ¡Han huido! Ella y Leonardo.
> En el caballo. Van abrazados, como una
> exhalación. (1243)

Leñador 3°: ¿Crees que ellos lograrán romper el cerco?
Leñador 2°: Es difícil. Hay cuchillos y escopetas a diez leguas a la redonda.
Leñador 3°: El lleva buen caballo.
Leñador 2°: Pero lleva una mujer. (1247-1248)

Because the playwright has established a close association between the image of the horse and events in the human drama, the importance of the image's relationship to the natural flow of dialogue cannot be overstated. By adapting the image to varying contexts, Lorca maintains the movement of the dramatic line as well as the dynamic quality of the poetic language. This is precisely what occurs when Lorca uses the image of the horse to reveal the active participation of La Novia in taking the step towards escape that leads her and Leonardo into an isolated space where love and death are present:

Leonardo: ¿Quién le puso
         al caballo bridas nuevas?
Novia: Yo misma. Verdad.
Leonardo: ¿Y qué manos
         me calzaron las espuelas?
Novia: Estas manos que son tuyas ... (1257)

Finally with respect to "caballo," we note that the image of the ill-fated horse is embedded in the action at the point in the drama in which the idea that the lovers' escape into isolation means that a ride towards death becomes an almost certainty:

> Mozo 1°: Creo que se han ido por otra vereda.
> Novio: No. Yo sentí hace un momento el galope.
> Mozo 1°: Sería otro caballo.
> Novio: (Dramático) Oye. No hay más que un caballo en el mundo, y es éste. ¿Te has enterado? Si me sigues, sígueme sin hablar.
> Mozo 1°: Es que yo quisiera . . .
> Novio: Calla. Estoy seguro de encontrármelos aquí. ¿Ves este brazo? Pues no es mi brazo. Es el brazo de mi hermano y el de mi padre y el de toda mi familia que está muerta. (1252)

To follow the image of the horse through *Bodas de sangre* is to follow Leonardo on a tragic course to "el río negro" of the *nana*. This symbiotic relationship between imagery and drama is another indication that in his later plays, Lorca takes the metaphorical language further in the direction of what Brower called linked stages in presenting human relationships[12] and what Knight referred to as the situation in which poetry becomes actively engaged in directing the plot and action.[13]

One of the most important features of *Bodas de sangre* that places Lorquian imagery further along the trajectory towards uniting poetry and drama is the use of elements of *romances* and songs. Although *Mariana Pineda* was framed by a *romance* as well as underpinned at various points by *romances* whose imagery reflected Mariana as a protagonist who consciously slips into legend, and although *Perlimplín* used elements of song to frame various stages of Perlimplín's withdrawal into his imagination, their placement in relation to the action of the drama made them stand out more in relief rather than as elements integral to the drama—this despite their being linked in varying degrees to thematic and dramatic contexts. Because the songs bearing imagery continuities in *Bodas de sangre* emerge very naturally in the context of the drama, the narrative line of the human conflict remains undisturbed throughout. Lorca has infused the songs with images that make us feel the presence of forces such as family honor, passion and fate—forces so strong that they make two lovers finally attempt an escape into the night. Further, Lorca has given *Bodas de sangre* an underlying poetic movement akin to that of a traditional Spanish ballad and thus invested the dialogue with a sweeping intensity that parallels the increasing force of destiny that pursues Leonardo and La Novia.

Since Lorca was very active in La Barraca's performances of Golden Age plays during the period represented by *Bodas de sangre*—plays that included *Fuenteovejuna*, *El caballero de Olmedo* and *El burlador de Sevilla*—it is not surprising that he would incorporate elements of song into his rural drama. However, at this stage in his development of poetic drama, Lorca places this technique more at the service of the metaphorical language as it relates to dramatic contexts than was evidenced in his earlier plays.

For the most outstanding example in *Bodas de sangre* of the use of the narrative properties of a song to link poetic imagery with dramatic contexts, we again direct our attention to the *nana* that frames the second scene of Act I. Although this cradle song essentially forebodes and foreshadows events in the manner of Lope's celebrated song in *El caballero de Olmedo*, it is not a static comment on the characters and their actions (the situation that inheres in the songs of *Peribáñez*, for example). As the cradle song narrates a lugubrious scenario with a horse as protagonist, it establishes a relationship with the dynamics of the imagery of this play. Allusive and evocative images express the tension and violence that hover over the characters as well as the dream-like quality of the actual flight of Leonardo and La Novia in Act III. Whereas Lope's song in *El caballero de Olmedo* carries a straightforward narrative—"Que de noche le mataron / al caballero, / la gala de Medina, / la flor de Olmedo"[14]—Lorca's song bears images (flowers, a horse, blades, water, blood) that become continuities in the language used to present the drama.

Under closer scrutiny, the *nana* demonstrates that in addition to its highly evocative imagery, it has the quality of narrative poetry that helps to relate it to the human drama in which it occurs. First, as a cradle song, it sets a domestic scene ("Nana, niño, nana") which is, in fact, the one in progress between two women and a child. Then the song, in effect, relates the present state of affairs between Leonardo and La Novia ("el caballo no quiere beber," "el caballo se pone a llorar"). Lines in the song ("Las patas heridas / las crines heladas;" "su belfo caliente") anticipate Leonardo's arrival and the questions he is asked concerning his horse ("Pero, ¿quién da esas carreras al caballo? Está abajo, tendido, con los ojos desorbitados, como si llegara del fin del mundo" [1189]). The song also looks ahead with foreboding to events that assume a dream-like quality in Act III ("¡No vengas! Detente, / cierra la ventana / con rama de sueños / y sueño de ramas"). Through a shift in the tense of the verbs from the present to the past, the *nana* narrates the outcome of the drama ("El agua era negra;" "no quiso el agua;" "Bajaban al río;" "La sangre corría"). Because this narrative is also imbued with images related to those introduced earlier in the play to evoke a brooding atmosphere and a sense of fate (blades and blood, for example), one can say that Lorca has found in poetry with narrative qualities a way to keep the dramatic pulse of a play alive while presenting at the same time fragmented images that help make "visible" the emotional content of the drama.

Through a similar analysis, the wedding song sung by La Criada early in Act II 1) reflects the action of the drama at that point and 2) resonates with imagery that has already been expressing the fate awaiting lovers who seek escape from societal constraints that have kept them apart. Lorca's special use of a wedding song—an element common to many Golden Age plays—can be placed in relief by contrasting it with an example from Lope de Vega. In the opening scene of *Peribáñez*, musicians sing:

> Dente parabienes
> el mayo garrido,
> los alegres campos,
> las fuentes y ríos.
> Alcen las cabezas
> los verdes alisos,
> y con frutos nuevos
> almendros floridos.
> Echen las mañanas,
> después del rocio,
> en espadas verdes
> guarnición de lirios.
> . . . . .
> Y a los nuevos desposados
> eche Dios su bendición;
> parabién les den los prados
> pues hoy para en uno son.[15]

This song is appropriately placed during a festive occasion and thus fulfills its immediate purpose—that of expressing joy. The song, through its irony, also relates to the total text. But in *Bodas de sangre*, the song sung by La Criada functions at a different level, because it is integrated into both the dramatic and the metaphorical structure of the play. This song which beseeches the rivers to bear away the wedding crown occurs almost immediately after La Novia throws her orange-blossom crown to the ground and shortly after a conversation between La Novia and La Criada in which heat imagery shifts from references to the night to sexual implications ("No se puede estar ahí dentro, del calor;" "En estas tierras no refresca ni al amanecer" [1206]; "Una boda, ¿qué es? Una boda es esto y nada más. ¿Son los dulces? ¿Son los ramos de flores? No. Es una cama relumbrante y un hombre y una mujer" [1207]). The water imagery in the wedding song counterbalances the references to heat in the tense dialogue between La Novia and La Criada, and the wedding crown in the song counterbalances the negative context in which the crown was placed prior to the song. Thus, the wedding song becomes linked to the immediate dramatic context through subliminal connections between key words in the metaphorical language. As a result, the ominous aspects of the scene subtly filter into the song (and hence, the wedding). Similarly, when we hear "¡Que los ríos del mundo / lleven tu corona!", we "hear" echoes from the Act I *nana* with its black waters. Indeed, the rivers of both songs, flowing through a verdant landscape, have similar settings. "El ramo verde" and "la rama de los laureles" of the wedding song evoke the image of the river of the cradle song flowing "dentro de las ramas . . . por su verde sala;" and when the images of the waters of both songs are juxtaposed, the intermingling of the black water of the river in the *nana* with the water of the wedding song reinforces the gloom that permeates the scene of the approaching wedding. Lorca's song thus reaches into the dynamics of the metaphorical language of the play in addition to being a natural, human touch as La Criada anticipates the wedding.

Through a similar process of linking images, a wedding song in the second scene of Act II unleashes voices that warn of impending dangers as the principal characters are drawn into a vortex from which their only escape is death. The scene begins in a natural manner with La Criada again singing of the approaching wedding, but the subtext of her song is fraught with a feeling of imminent doom. She begins the song with an image of water turning a wheel, as if the wedding were in the hands of fate ("Giraba, / giraba la rueda / y el agua pasaba / porque llega la boda" [1225]). Then the song anticipates the movements of the cold moon in Act III:"que se aparten las ramas / y la luna se adorne / por su blanca baranda / . . . / que relumbre la escarcha" (1225-1226). Further, the song immerses blood and heat imagery deeper into the text by fusing sexual images related to marriage with the ominous overtones emitted earlier by other images (especially those related to blood). "Nunca salgas de tu casa," sings La Criada, "porque el novio es un palomo / con todo el pecho de brasa / y espera el campo el rumor / de la sangre derramada" (1226). Since the playwright has already set in motion a "rumor de sangre derramada," especially in the *nana*, many words in the wedding song ("ramas," "luna," "escarcha," "amargas," "brasa," "rumor," "sangre") assume darker colorations and accumulate to produce a resonance with earlier warnings of an unlucky fate hovering over the bridal couple. Again Lorca, in the tradition of Lope de Vega, has introduced a song into a drama as an authentic touch of rustic local color; but he has also infused that song with elements of the metaphorical language expressing the tension already created in the drama up to that point.

Images in the second wedding song also sustain continuities in the metaphorical language by reappearing in altered form in the context of events in Act III. When the moon in Act III shouts "¡No haya sombra ni emboscada, / que no puedan escaparse!" and then directly addresses "las ramas" saying "No quiero sombras. Mis rayos / han de entrar en todas partes" (1250), we recall La Criada singing "porque llega la boda, / que se aparten las ramas / y la luna se adorne / por su blanca baranda" (1225-1226). When the moon declares "¡Vengo helada / por paredes y cristales! / . . . / Pero me lleva la nieve / sobre su espalda de jaspe" (1249), we "hear" an echo from the wedding song ("porque llega la boda, / que relumbre la escarcha" [1226]); and when the moon says "para que esta noche tengan / mis mejillas dulce sangre" (1250), the wedding song again reverberates beneath the text ("y espera el campo el rumor / de la sangre derramada" [1226]). Also in Act III when Leonardo and La Novia are alone and he tells her "Clavos de luna nos funden / mi cintura y tus caderas" (1260), in effect he is reshaping the sexual imagery of the Act II wedding song ("Porque el novio es un palomo / con todo el pecho de brasa / y espera el campo el rumor / de la sangre derramada [1226]) and subtly reinforcing the blade imagery and the subtextual negative connotation of the phrase "la sangre derramada" sung earlier by La Criada. Thus, with a song strategically placed in the text, a complex and dynamic interaction of images has permitted metaphorical continuities to keep pace with the human drama. Indeed, the wedding song provides an outstanding example of poetic drama that Lorca has been developing since its rudimentary inception in *El maleficio de la mariposa*.

Even as the swift, fluid dialogue of *Bodas de sangre* reminds us of the fast-paced conversational exchanges in the plays of Lope de Vega, we are aware of how far *Bodas de sangre* has brought Lorca along the route to developing poetic theater. This is especially evident with regard to an affinity with the traditional *romance*. In their ability to condense a narrative and thereby provide a text with a feeling of movement, *romances* like "Los siete infantes de Lara"[16] and those about the Cid[17] offer outstanding examples.

The dialogue and action in *Bodas de sangre* keep pace with the mounting tension created by uncontrollable emotional and societal forces that prompt Leonardo and La Novia to seek escape and El Novio to preserve the honor of his family—forces which the protagonists describe thus: "Pero montaba a caballo / y el caballo iba a tu puerta . . . / Que yo no tengo la culpa, / que la culpa es de la tierra / y de ese olor que te sale / de los pechos y las trenzas" (1258); "¡Tu hijo era mi fin y yo no lo he engañado, pero el brazo del otro me arrastró como un golpe de mar, como la cabezada de un mulo, y me hubiera arrastrado siempre, siempre, siempre, aunque hubiera sido vieja y todos los hijos de tu hijo me hubiesen agarrado de los cabellos!" (1269). Even in these essentially narrative passages, we note a characteristic of the ballad in the repetition of words, giving the narrative a poetic ebb and flow; and through images such as those of "caballo" and "mar," the dramatist has kept alive elements of the metaphorical language within a predominantly narrative setting.

The concentrated narrative technique of *romances* underlies various scenes of *Bodas de sangre* that have rapid, condensed dialogue and a swift sequence of events. Evidence of the rhythm of narrative poetry emerges very early in this play. In Act I, Scene I, there is an insistent, almost urgent apprehension and a succinct divulging of the tragic past of the family of El Novio and his intention to marry. Scene 3 quickly presents the meeting of La Madre with La Novia and her father, terse exchanges pertaining to the formalities attendant upon the proposed marriage, arrangements for the wedding and the departure of El Novio and his mother.

Lorca employs the insistent rhythm of narrative poetry at two crucial points in the drama, and in both instances, the image of the horse is the dominant component of the language in the subtext expressing the passionate attraction that Leonardo and La Novia have for each other. First, in the dramatic conclusion to Act I, when a horse (with Leonardo as its rider) quickly makes an appearance at the house of La Novia, the dialogue assumes a pace that is consonant with the action being portrayed:

Criada: ¿Sentiste anoche un caballo?

Novia:	¿A qué hora?
Criada:	A las tres.
Novia:	Sería un caballo suelto de la manada.
Criada:	No. Llevaba jinete.
Novia:	¿Por qué lo sabes?
Criada:	Porque lo vi. Estuvo parado en tu ventana. Me chocó mucho.
Novia:	¿No sería mi novio? Algunas veces ha pasado a esas horas.
Criada:	No.
Novia:	¿Tú le viste?
Criada:	Sí.
Novia:	¿Quién era?
Criada:	Era Leonardo.
Novia:	(Fuerte) ¡Mentira! ¡Mentira! ¿A qué viene aquí?
Criada:	Vino.
Novia:	¡Cállate! ¡Maldita sea tu lengua!
	(Se siente el ruido de un caballo.)
Criada:	(En la ventana) Mira, asómate. ¿Era?
Novia:	¡Era!
	(Telón rápido) (1204-1205)

One can also sense the rhythm of a *romance* in the staccato dialogue in Act II when events culminate in the discovery that La Novia and Leonardo have fled from the wedding festivities. Again the dramatist places the image of a horse in a dramatic context that not only keeps the action moving but also continues the capability of the metaphorical language to fulfill its potential to express the tension mounting in the drama. When Leonardo's wife cannot find her husband, she quickly mentions the absence of his horse ("Es que no le encuentro y el caballo no está tampoco en el establo" [1239]) whereupon El Novio responds: "Debe estar dándole una carrera." Even in this brief exchange we can "hear" the anguished horse of the *nana* and the unbridled, frenetic gallop of Leonardo's horse racing through Scenes 2 and 3 of Act I. The pace quickens until Leonardo's wife shouts "¡Han huido! ¡Han huido! Ella y Leonardo. En el caballo" (1243), thereby bringing earlier images of the panting horse associated with Leonardo into the dramatic reality of the scene in progress. The horse now bears Leonardo and La Novia headlong towards their destiny—a destiny depicted in the imagery as one splattered with blood. "Ha llegado otra vez la hora de la sangre," shrieks La Madre as the curtain quickly falls on Act II. With the speed of a *romance*, Lorca has: 1) maintained the narrative line, 2) increased dramatic tension, and 3) retained continuities in the imagery.

Images that have been acquiring a dynamic quality by interacting with the drama through the methods we have been describing have their most telling effect in the final pages of the play. Components of the imagery that have been accompanying the characters as fate leads them to total isolation either through death or grief coalesce to such a degree that the actual announcement of the death of Leonardo and El Novio sounds almost casual and superfluous. The metaphorical language that has been preparing us for the reality of the death of Leonardo and El Novio continues to "narrate" the events of the tragedy. Flower imagery (including an allusion to "la navaja") joins images of the cold moon in relating the death of the two young men: "Flores rotas los ojos, y sus dientes dos puñados de nieve endurecida" (1266); "Sobre la flor del oro, sucia arena" (1266); "Pero mi hijo es ya un brazado de flores secas" (1267).

With the death of Leonardo and El Novio, actions retreat into images of silence and the hermetically sealed world of poetry:

Clavaremos las ventanas
Y vengan lluvias y noches
sobre las hierbas amargas. (1264)

. . . Sobre la cama
pon una cruz de ceniza
donde estuvo su almohada. (1265)

Yo los vi; pronto llegan dos torrentes
quietos al fin entre las piedras grandes. (1266)

When La Madre laments "Mi hijo es ya una voz oscura detrás de los montes," the voice of the poetry in both the *nana* ("A los montes duros / solo relinchaba / con el río muerto / sobre la garganta") and the soliloquy of the moon (" . . . Mis rayos / han de entrar en todas partes, / y haya en los troncos oscuros / un rumor de claridades") now retreats into the heart of the person who grieves. This withdrawal is completed by La Madre who, at the conclusion of the drama, retreats not only into the world enclosed by the thick walls she mentioned in Act I, Scene 3 ("una pared de dos varas de ancho para todo lo demás" [1200]) but also into the world of the mind, tranquilized by poetic images which give her the power to express the desolation felt by a grieving mother:

Yo haré con mi sueño una fría paloma
de marfil que lleve camelias de escarcha

sobre el camposanto. (1267)

Like a metaphor and its "forma y radio de acción" described by Lorca in "La imagen poética de don Luis de Góngora," the lament of La Madre encircles other more distant images of cold silence and the world of dreams: "¡Ay dolor de nieve, / caballo del alba!" (1185); "¡No vengas! Detente, / cierra la ventana / con rama de sueños / y sueño de ramas" (1185); "Pero me lleva la nieve / sobre su espalda de jaspe" (1249). Echoes from the text unite with the lament of La Madre to evoke the "presence" of a complete withdrawal into the silence of grief. By setting our imagination in motion, the accumulating poetic images associated with coldness and desolation make overwhelming grief "visible."

The greatest confluence of images that have been gathering to express the tragedy of *Bodas de sangre* comes in the final emotional outburst by La Novia. Due to its poetic content, its compressed form and its narrative quality, one might say that La Novia is reciting a *romance* composed of images explicitly and implicitly related to blood, blades, water, heat, coldness, darkness and flowers—images that shape the language used to express the drama. La Novia now brings into focus how she has been affected by "el agua negra" of the river where "la sangre corría más fuerte que el agua":

> Yo era una mujer quemada, llena de llagas por dentro y por fuera, y tu hijo era un poquito de agua de la que yo esperaba hijos, tierra, salud; pero el otro era un río oscuro, lleno de ramas, que acercaba a mí el rumor de sus juncos y su cantar entre dientes. Y yo corría con tu hijo que era como un niñito de agua, frío, y el otro me mandaba cientos de pájaros que me impedían el andar y que dejaban escarcha sobre mis heridas de pobre mujer marchita, de muchacha acariciada por el fuego . . . (1269)

Finally, to summarize how *Bodas de sangre* has taken Lorca's use of poetry in the theater considerably further along its trajectory towards the fusion of poetry and drama, we refer again to images of blood—this time in the concentrated context of the beginning of the second scene of Act II. Here, elements of the metaphorical language demonstrate that they have increasingly become a function of specific dramatic contexts. Like the light-darkness opposition in *El maleficio de la mariposa*, the images of blood in *Mariana Pineda* and the inner-outer counterpoint in *Perlimplín*, "sangre" in this sequence in the dialogue of *Bodas de sangre* generates a force that expresses not only thematic content of the drama but also has the power to evoke the presence of danger and death. In Act II, Scene 2, "sangre" relates essentially to the overwhelming influence of family honor and blood ties in determining the fate of individuals in this play who desire to escape their oppressive reality and who finally retreat into a world of isolation doomed by forces beyond their control. In addition, "sangre" emits overtones from meaning and emotional content with which it has been previously infused.

The second scene of Act II opens with La Criada singing a wedding song that is appropriate to preparations being made for the arrival of wedding guests. Yet in this song which alludes to the sexual aspect of marriage ("y espera el campo el rumor / de la sangre derramada"), we "hear" in the subtext earlier references to blades and spilt blood which repeatedly reminded us of the death of the father and the brother of El Novio. The song also anticipates a sequence of dialogue that immediately follows it. This occurs when La Criada mentions the fact that Leonardo and his wife were the first guests to arrive, prompting El Padre to refer to Leonardo by saying "no tiene buena sangre" (1227). Because of its proximity to the wedding song, the connotation of blood relationship in the word "sangre" fuses with the image of a sexual relationship as well as the brooding overtones inherent in "la sangre derramada" of the wedding song. The image of blood, therefore: 1) helps to express what is transpiring in the drama; i.e., the fate of Leonardo is becoming more involved with that of La Novia, 2) keeps the relationship between La Novia and El Novio active in the reader's mind, and 3) carries forward a foreboding reminder of family enmities that resulted in bloodshed earlier. Further, immediately after El Padre mentions "sangre," La Madre seizes upon the word—"¿Qué sangre va a tener? La de toda su familia . . . manejadores de cuchillos" (1227), thereby reminding those present of past grievous events involving Leonardo's family while confirming the present assessment of Leonardo's character. Having linked the past tragic event, the wedding song and the current dialogue through the image of blood, Lorca not only solidifies this relationship but also expresses the innermost thoughts of La Madre by almost immediately by recalling the image: "Por eso es tan terrible ver la sangre de una derramada por el suelo" (1228). Finally in this sequence that encapsulates the dynamic use of imagery, a highly evocative image associated with blood fits naturally into the dramatic context, because the overtones emitted earlier by the image have made us receptive to its "sound": "Me mojé las manos de sangre," says La Madre, "y me las lamí con la lengua. Porque era mía. . . . En una custodia de cristal y topacios pondría yo la tierra empapada por ella" (1229). In other words, Lorca has succeeded in embedding what we may call a symbolist image (very reminiscent of these words from Marquina: "...Morir, / y, muerta, hacer de mis huesos / y el paño de mi mortaja / el relicario y la caja / para conservar tus besos!"[18]) into a dramatic context without disrupting the flow of natural dialogue. On the contrary, the image enhances the dialogue, because the playwright has already invested its nucleus ("sangre") with emotional and thematic content.

The above analysis of a portion of Act II helps us demonstrate that Lorca has taken an archetypal symbol such as one would expect to find in the *autos sacramentales* of Calderón and has given it human settings in which it expands its capability to express what is happening. Moreover, by "layering" baleful images like those associated with blood, the playwright has employed a characteristic of Symbolist theater in the tradition of Maeterlinck. But he has placed this stylistic device at the service of drama. By giving components of the imagery multiple values, the playwright has given images the capability of flowing in and out of dramatic contexts.

In *Bodas de sangre*, Lorca increases his use of techniques for crafting a drama that were prevalent in Golden Age theater; namely, the inclusion of songs (especially as evidenced in the theater of Lope de Vega) and symbolic language in expanded metaphorical contexts (recalling the theater of Calderón). *Bodas de sangre* also recalls the traditional *romance* in the sweep of its dialogue and compact narrative style; and in imagery imbued with the power to give flight to the imagination—a quality most appropriate to a drama where characters imagine an escape from reality, this play demonstrates an affinity with the Symbolists. However, what is most important to our study of the development of Lorquian poetic drama is the evidence that the poetic language in this play is more closely tied to the human drama than was the case in the contrasting examples drawn from Golden Age and Symbolist theater. When, for example, the image of a knife appears at the conclusion of the play ("Y apenas cabe en la mano, / pero que penetra frío / por las carnes asombradas / y allí se para, en el sitio / donde tiembla enmarañada / la oscura raíz del grito" [1272]), it not only helps to express the tragedy that occurred and the emotion felt by the character speaking the lines but also lingers in our imagination as an evocation of dramatic contexts with which it was intimately associated.

Notes

1. "The Strategy of Garcia Lorca's Dramatic Composition 1930-36," *Romance Quarterly*, 33 (1986), 212, 216-218.

2. All page numbers within parentheses that refer to *Bodas de sangre* are from the following text: Federico García Lorca, *Bodas de sangre*, in *Obras completas*, ed. Arturo del Hoyo, 12th ed. (Madrid: Aguilar, 1966), pp.1171-1272.

3. In writing of *The Tempest*, Brower says: "The images that recur in Prospero's speech take us back to felt qualities embedded in particular dramatic contexts." (*The Fields of Light* [New York: Oxford Univ. Press, 1962], p.120).

4. *Cuento de labios en flor*, in *Teatro de ensueño* (Yonkers-on-Hudson, N.Y.: World, 1917), p.62.

5. *The Blue Bird*, trans. Alexander Teixeira Mattos (New York: Dodd, Mead and Co., 1965), pp.114-115.

6. *El alcalde de Zalamea*, in *Obras completas*, I, ed. Luis Astrana Marín (Madrid: Aguilar, 1951), p.534.

7. *Lorca: interpretación de "Poeta en Nueva York"*, (Madrid: Akal Editor, 1981), p.108.

8. Calderón, *Obras completas*, I, ed. Luis Astrana Marín (Madrid: Aguilar, 1951), p.211.

9. "Imaginación, inspiración, evasión," in *Obras completas*, ed. Arturo del Hoyo, 12th ed. (Madrid: Aguilar, 1966), p.86.

10. *La vida es sueño: drama y auto sacramental*, ed. José María Valverde (Barcelona: Planeta, 1981), p.162.

11. "El leitmotiv del caballo en *Bodas de sangre*," *Hispanófila*, No. 29 (Jan. 1967), 34.

12. *The Fields of Light* (New York: Oxford Univ. Press, 1962), p.96.

13. *The Shakespearian Tempest*, 3rd ed. (London: Methuen, 1960), p.267.

14. *El caballero de Olmedo*, ed. Francisco Rico, 6th ed. (Madrid: Ediciones Cátedra, 1985), p.197.

15. *Peribáñez y el Comendador de Ocaña*, in *Comedias*, Vol. II, ed. Luis Guarner (Barcelona: Editorial Iberia, 1955), pp.10-11.

16.   Ya se salen de Castilla
castellanos con gran saña,
van a combatir los muros
de la vieja Calatrava;
derribaron tres pedazos
por partes de Guadiana;
por uno entran los cristianos,
por dos los moros escapan . . .

"Ya se salen de Castilla . . .", Historia de los siete infantes de Lara, in *Flor nueva de romances que recogió de la tradicion antigua y moderna R. Menéndez Pidal*, pp.127-128.

17. Estas palabras diciendo
contra el moro arremetía;
encontróle con la lanza,
en el suelo le derriba,
cortárale la cabeza
y colgóla de la silla.
"Por el val de las Estacas...", Sexto romance del Cid, in *Flor nueva de romances que recogió de la tradicíon antigua y moderna R. Menéndez Pidal*, pp.175-176.

18. *La ermita, la fuente y el río*, in *En Flandes se ha puesto el sol / La ermita, la fuente y el río* (Madrid: Castalia, 1996), p.230.

Chapter 7
Doña Rosita la soltera

Doña Rosita la soltera o el lenguaje de las flores which was completed twenty years after *El maleficio de la mariposa* and one year before Lorca's death provides the reader with an opportunity to reflect upon the degree to which Lorca, in his last plays, still uses the Symbolist techniques that prevailed early in the development of his theater and combines them with those he employed to bring metaphorical language to dramatic life in his later plays.

Doña Rosita is basically the dramatization of a single metaphor—"la rosa mutabile"—embodied in a protagonist who experiences a spiritual death after seeking escape from reality by nourishing an illusion and sustaining her life with memories. What is especially significant for this study of the trajectory of the development of Lorquian poetic drama is the fact that the central metaphor of a rose that blossoms, withers and dies in one day is played out in dialogue and actions expressed through the language suggested by the metaphor itself. The alternative phrase in the title—"el lenguaje de las flores"—calls attention to the fundamental role of the poetic language in this drama and thus prompts us to recall and reaffirm, with respect to Lorca's theater, Brower's statement that "we cannot feel the peculiar quality of what is taking place or grasp its meaning apart from the metaphorical language through which it is being expressed."[1] In this sense, *Doña Rosita* is not different from *Bodas de sangre* which preceded it, and *La casa de Bernarda Alba* which followed. Although *Doña Rosita* looks back to the Symbolist and Modernista characteristics of his early plays, we observe that when placed on the trajectory of the development of the playwright's imagery, this play is another step towards solidifying the union of poetry and drama.

Doña Rosita is a mood play in the spirit of Maeterlinck's Symbolist theater. It accumulates images that evoke the feelings, thoughts and emotions which help to give shape to Rosita's illusion that the passage of time has been arrested. Yet there is dramatic movement in what is essentially a play that looks inward towards a state of mind rather than outward. An important reason for this feeling of movement is that the dramatist has been refining techniques for giving images a milieu conducive to their interacting with what is happening in the evolving human relationships. Like *Mariana Pineda*, *Doña Rosita* gives the appearance of a long *romance* with frames for various stages in the life of its protagonist. In addition to infusing Rosita's story with a sense of being frozen in time, like an oft-told tale, Lorca again draws on characteristics of the Golden Age theater by using songs (recalling especially the "glosa lopesca") and expanding metaphors (reminding one particularly of Góngora and Calderón) —techniques that he has been developing up to this point for the purpose of expressing drama through dialogue steeped in poetic imagery. However, the metaphorical continuities in *Doña Rosita* generate language that further demonstrates the dramatic possibilities of imagery in Lorca's theater.

In *Doña Rosita*, Lorca strengthens techniques for creating poetic drama by giving poetry more amplitude in its symbiotic relationship with drama. The metaphorical language of this play works on three interrelated levels as the narrative line of Rosita's life moves forward. Lorca's language of flowers 1) functions at a narrative-thematic level to tell Rosita's story and place it in a generalized sentimental-social context 2) contains images which evoke the emotions of the protagonist as well as the emotional climate created by those who surround her and 3) implants imagery in dramatic contexts that express various stages in the course of Rosita's life that takes her from being a young woman filled with love and hope to a spinster overcome by disillusion and despair. Most significant to a study of the development of Lorca's poetic theater is the total effect of the poetry in presenting a drama of a woman who embodies the "rosa mutabile" which, when cut, is quickly overcome and destroyed by time. Applying various aspects of the rose metaphor to story, mood and drama, one can say that Lorca's play is not simply the tale of a woman who withers like a flower but the re-creation of the feelings of an individual and a setting that coalesce to represent the personal drama of a woman whose life is made bearable by her imagination; by her holding onto an illusion as time inexorably slips by. And it is through the imagery that the reader visualizes Rosita's personal drama.

The Dynamics of the Imagery in the Theater 161
of Federico Garcia Lorca

In order to observe Lorca's multiple uses of the central metaphor, we must bear in mind the lines delivered by El Tío in Act I when he reads a description of the "rosa mutabile." Since this is the controlling metaphor, we quote it in its entirety:

> Cuando se abre en la manaña,
> roja como sangre está.
> El rocío no la toca
> porque se teme quemar.
> Abierta en el mediodía
> es dura como el coral.
> El sol se asoma a los vidrios
> para verla relumbrar.
> Cuando en las ramas empiezan
> los pájaros a cantar
> y se desmaya la tarde
> en las violetas del mar,
> se pone blanca, con blanco
> de una mejilla de sal.
> Y cuando toca la noche
> blanco cuerno de metal
> y las estrellas avanzan
> mientras los aires se van,
> en la raya de lo oscuro,
> se comienza a deshojar. (1356-1357)

The complexity of Lorca's use of flower imagery in *Doña Rosita* emerges when we examine how the imagery functions at the narrative level and then proceeds to explore its evocative and dramatic nature. Also, if we compare and contrast Lorca's use of imagery pertaining to theme and narrative line with examples from Lope de Vega and Calderón, it becomes apparent that Lorca's key metaphor assumes variations that make it appear less as a "conscious" insertion in the drama, less "elevated" in style, and more a natural component of the dialogue than was the case with Lorca's predecessors.

At the very outset, Rosita's name sets the course of the protagonist in the direction of the "rosa mutabile." Like the rose that opens in the morning, acquires strength and full bloom at noon, then turns white and begins to die at nightfall, Rosita will be "cultivated" by "gardeners" (particularly her aunt, her uncle and the cousin whom she loves) whose nurturing leads her to be "cut," separated from the "garden" and eventually left to sustain her weakening spirit with the illusion that her fiance will return.

Like Lope in *El caballero de Olmedo* and Calderón in *El médico de su honra*, Lorca plants numerous indicators of the controlling metaphor in his text. But unlike his predecessors, Lorca does not explicitly state the character-metaphor relationship. *Doña Rosita* does not use its metaphor merely to illustrate or heighten the basic dramatic conflict, but, rather, sets the metaphor in action. In other words, the metaphor—although stated first in its entirety—unfolds along with the human relationships, giving them means of expression and direction in their development.

When Lope's Alonso says ". . . no puedo / vivir sin Inés, de Olmedo / a Medina vengo y voy, / porque Inés mi dueño es / para vivir o morir,"[2] he is stating the "Olmedo-muerte," "Medina-vida" polarity. Similarly, when Calderón's protagonist declares "Médico soy de mi honor, / la vida pretendo darle / con una sangría: que todos curan a costa de sangre,"[3] one "hears" narrative or thematic material consciously pronounced. Whereas when Rosita tells the man she loves "Una noche . . . vi bajar dos querubines / a una rosa enamorada; / ella se puso encarnada / siendo blanco su color / . . . / Así yo . . . / daba al aire mis afanes / y mi blancura a la fuente" (1371), we "hear" feelings of a human being first and then the thematic material emanating from the subtext. We listen to a woman expressing her love and then associate her words with the theme of a woman who becomes a languishing white rose in a society which nurtures the idea that the hope or illusion of marriage for an aging, unmarried woman is her only source of strength for bearing an unhappy life. In other words, the flower imagery not only is related to the theme of the play but is a natural, unforced component of the dialogue as well. This situation is similar to what Knight calls poetic actualization in speaking of *The Tempest*.[4] Although Rosita's words quoted above allude to the key metaphor, they express one stage in the unfolding human drama; i.e., Rosita's expressing her love directly to the man who eventually causes her despair.

With respect to the narrative line, *Doña Rosita* can be compared to *El maleficio de la mariposa*, *Mariana Pineda*, *Perlimplín*, and, to a lesser degree, *Bodas de sangre*. In each play, imagination impels a protagonist to recede further into the mind to create a reality that motivates his or her life. Rosita, by "freezing" the memory of her happiness when she fervently believed the promise of marriage, makes an impossible life bearable until she becomes overwhelmed by sadness when totally resigned to her fate as "una soltera." What Lorca has done in this play is to create a "tour de force" with respect to the function of imagery continuities as we have been examining them in selected plays; for he has used one continuity (a language of flowers) to tell Rosita's story, evoke feelings experienced by the protagonist and control the direction of the dialogue. In this play, one "hears" flower imagery telling what happens to the withering virgin whose hope for marriage vanishes and leaves her to the ridicule of the word "solterona."

We pause here to note that the story as outlined and the key flower image show an affinity with Modernista theater (Marquina's Deseada, for example, is also deeply affected by time, hope and disillusionment). Rosita, however, is more than a character limned through metaphorical language suggesting comparisons. She sets a metaphor in motion, for she is the *enactment* of "la rosa mutabile."

The very first words in *Doña Rosita*—"¿Y mis semillas?"—relate to the narrative line. Significantly, these words are spoken by Rosita's uncle, the head of the household who is later referred to explicitly as "un cultivador de rosas" (1376). While El Tío looks for seeds, he continues what appears to be an innocuous spat with La Tía and El Ama, saying "Es necesario que cuidéis las flores . . . Lo digo por todos" (1352). However, these lines have a subtext that defines La Tía as "una cultivadora de flores," a fact that she confirms in Act II in a retort to her husband: "En vez de hacer encajes, podo las plantas. ¿Qué haces tú por mí?" (1386). It is she, of course, who "prunes" Rosita by convincing her nephew to leave the cousin he loves in order to return home to his parents in South America. The language associated with flowers is carried even further into the narrative aspect of the drama when La Tía, in her endeavor to convince her nephew to leave, entreats him by saying: "Aquí no eres más que un paseante de los jardinillos, y allí serás un labrador" (1362)—a remark that is both natural to the context and indicative of the fleeting nature of the physical presence of El Sobrino in Rosita's life. There is even an echo of the image of a cut flower and an allusion to the motif of "freezing" a happy memory in this comment by El Ana: "No sé quién me gusta más, si el novio o ella. . . . Un par de primos para ponerlos en un vasar de azúcar, y si se murieran, ¡Dios los libre!, embalsamarlos y meterlos en un nicho de cristales y de nieve" (1359). Thus, the metaphorical language of the key metaphor touches each character who participates in the actualization of that metaphor, and it continually appears in conversational contexts that keep the dialogue of the human drama flowing naturally.

At many points in the dialogue, references to flowers narrate what is actually happening to Rosita, the personification of a "rosa mutabile" cultivated in Granada. At the beginning of Act I, El Tío reproaches his wife by saying "Ayer me encontré las semillas de dalias pisoteadas por el suelo" (1352). When El Ama answers an accusation of not having shown respect for the flowers, she adds, "A mí las flores huelen a niño muerto, o a profesión de monja, o a altar de iglesia. A cosas tristes. Donde esté una naranja o un buen membrillo, que se quiten las rosas del mundo" (1352). In phrases such as these, we perceive a developing subtext related to the ill fate accorded to a flower, or a character's insensitivity towards the life of a flower. Therefore, at the metaphorical level, we "hear" what, in fact, happens to Rosita in her earlier years. She, a "flower" capable of heartfelt love, experiences pain ("y en mi corazón sentí / agujas estremecidas / que me están abriendo heridas / rojas como el alhelí" [1372]).

Later, in Act II, Rosita tells her uncle on her saint's day "voy a cortar unas rosas" (1387)—a statement whose subtext communicates an almost subconscious decision to state the growing realization that she is a "rosa mutabile" which, once cut, begins to die. Also in Act II, when Solterona 3ª sings a song that contains the words "gimen las flores cortadas" (1404), she is, in effect, singing about Rosita.

In all the passages cited above, we are being given information about the fate of a "solterona" in Rosita's society, yet there is no obvious declaration of a theme. Rather, thematic material emerges from an accumulation of images conveying the personal drama. This is a process that becomes a characteristic of Lorquian poetic drama, in contrast to Calderónian drama, for example, in which a character like Segismundo articulates a philosophical statement.[5] Although Calderón, like Lorca, manipulates key imagery continuities (like the "hombre-bestia" polarity in *La vida es sueño*), the imagery essentially remains illustrative of thematic material. As we shall see in closer examination of *Doña Rosita*, Lorca's poetry expresses thematic material in a series of cumulative and related images that tend to rest comfortably in ordinary-sounding discourse, even when the dialogue is highly charged with poetry as it is in the scene between Rosita and El Primo in Act I.

Moreover, when thematic material in this play appears to surface in the form of a statement with social implications rather than emanating from a series of linked images, the immediate dramatic context remains consciously in the mind of the reader. For example, after stating "A mí las flores me huelen a niño muerto," El Ama elaborates upon this sentiment by adding what is, in effect, a declaration of how she feels about gardens with "rosas": "Donde esté una naranja o un buen membrillo, que se quiten las rosas del mundo. . . . ¡Qué ganas tengo de ver plantados en este jardín un peral, un cerezo, un caqui!" (1352-1353). Although we may read "solteronas" for "rosas" in the subtext, our reaction is momentary, because the subtextual reading is overridden by the quality of reality inherent in the context in which it occurs (i.e., an argument about the proper maintenance of flowers). In a similar example, when El Tío is still fuming over the disregard others show for his plants, he expresses himself in language that resonates with the central metaphor while still maintaining the flow of the argument in which he is engaged: "Bien está que se pisen las semillas, pero no es tolerable que esté con las hojitas tronchadas la planta de rosal que más quiero" (1355).

The ability of the metaphorical language to make its presence felt in natural-sounding discourse without disrupting it nor interrupting the dramatic line with direct social commentary can also be observed in two significant passages from late in the play. When La Tía, in a pique of anger over her husband's having mortgaged their house, shouts: "¡Viejo tonto! Pusilánime para los negocios. ¡Chalado de las rosas!" (1427), at the narrative level she has linked her husband to the plight of "la rosa." But the image in "chalado de las rosas" is an invective that appears natural to this context, following as it does the preparatory phrase "pusilánime para los negocios" and given the fact that El Tío was in fact a cultivator of roses. Finally, when Rosita's aunt contemplates the ravages of time on the house they are about to leave, she speaks about the flower garden in a remark that the reader perceives first as a comment upon the immediate situation and then as a generalized statement about the "rosa" that falls prey to the natural elements of its environment. "Como siga este viento," she declares, "no va a quedar una rosa viva. Los cipreses de la glorieta casi tocan las paredes de mi cuarto. Parece como si alguien quisiera poner el jardín feo para que no tuviésemos pena de dejarlo" (1436-1437). The metaphorical language can be placed in the context of social commentary about "rosas" like Rosita, but the playwright has not obscured the narrative line of this particular drama, nor has he lost sight of the controlling "rosa mutabile" metaphor.

In addition to using language associated with flowers to convey Rosita's story and to make a "statement" about aging, unmarried women, Lorca infuses the flower imagery with the spirit of Symbolism that was especially evident in his earliest plays. By adapting Symbolist characteristics to a play that dramatizes the story of a woman who places in a time capsule the hope for marriage she had in the bloom of her life, the dramatist is able to penetrate the spiritual death of this woman. Through a gradual accretion of images, Rosita, resigning herself to the fact that marriage is out of reach, becomes the red rose that turns white and dies as nightfall overtakes the light of day.

Because of the sadness that befalls her love, Rosita's story has a tone and spirit that bring to mind feelings expressed by Verlaine as well as by Maeterlinck's Mélisande, Marquina's Deseada and Lorca's own Mariana Pineda. Although these women inhabit different dramatic contexts, they, like Rosita, look inward and perceive their condition in terms rich in poetic imagery. They live in overwhelming sadness, articulated thus by Rosita in Act III:

> Me he acostumbrado a vivir muchos años fuera de mí, pensando en cosas que estaban muy lejos, y ahora que estas cosas ya no existen sigo dando vueltas por un sitio frío, buscando una salida que no he de encontrar nunca. . . . Todo está acabado . . . y, sin embargo, con toda la ilusión perdida, me acuesto, y me levanto con el más terrible de los sentimientos, que es el sentimiento de tener la esperanza muerta. Quiero huir, quiero no ver, quiero quedarme serena, vacía . . . Lo que tengo por dentro lo guardo para mí sola. (1428, 1429, 1430)

While one is reading *Doña Rosita*, a "feeling" emerges from beneath the sentiments conveying the emotional state of the protagonist and gradually acquires a presence. The total effect of the flower imagery in fragments of the text or in more extended passages creates a quality that is "felt;" something that makes the reader sense what a character is feeling. This process of layering images is very similar to that used by Lorca in the light-darkness continuity which follows Curianito through *El maleficio de la mariposa*, the rain-tears imagery associated with Mariana Pineda and the images of heat that evoke tension in *Bodas de sangre*. However, in *Doña Rosita*, as in *Bodas de sangre*, and to a far greater degree than in *El maleficio de la mariposa*, *Mariana Pineda* and *Perlimplín*, the imagery which the poet metes out in increments to evoke abstract qualities (sadness, hurt and love) also provides components of dialogue flowing naturally in a very personal human setting.

Flower imagery in the ardent farewell between El Primo and Rosita at the close of Act I not only expresses love (thus serving the immediate dramatic context comprised of the only meeting in the play between the two young people in love) but also tinges it with sadness by linking it to the "rosa mutabile" image delivered earlier by El Tío. When Rosita asks "¿Por qué tus manos tejieron, / sobre mi cabeza, flores?" (1370), the playwright begins to infuse the dialogue between the two lovers with language pertaining to flowers. By responding "no es de hielo mi desvío, / que, aunque atraviese la mar, / el agua me ha de prestar / nardos de espuma y sosiego / para contener mi fuego / cuando me vaya a quemar" (1371), El Primo echoes a line from the passage which stated the "rosa mutabile" metaphor: "El rocío no la toca / porque se teme quemar" (1356). Rosita then inverts the metaphor ("Cuando ... se desmaya la tarde ... se pone blanca") when she alludes to herself by saying "Una noche, adormilada / en mi balcón de jazmines, / vi bajar dos querubines / a una rosa enamorada; / ella se puso encarnada / siendo blanco su color" (1371). One can say that this inversion carries within it a foreshadowing of Rosita's future as a "rosa blanca" yearning for a love that would, in effect, transform her into a "rosa encarnada." Thus far in our analysis of the imagery in this scene, we observe that the rose metaphor has sent out from its nucleus what Lorca called "una redonda perspectiva en torno de él." According to Lorca, "El núcleo se abre como una flor que nos sorprende por lo desconocida, pero en el radio de luz que lo rodea hallamos el nombre de la flor y conocemos su perfume."[6] The rose metaphor not only provides Rosita with language to express her love at this point in the drama but reaches deeper into the protagonist's inner being as she continues speaking: "pero, como tierna flor, / sus pétalos encendidos / se fueron cayendo heridos / por el beso del amor" (1371)—lines which resonate with "en la raya de lo oscuro / se comienza a deshojar" from the rose metaphor. Thus, in all these utterances spoken by Rosita as if she were in a dream, the flower imagery 1) expresses her love 2) recalls elements of the central metaphor 3) demonstrates the power of her imagination and 4) foreshadows the overwhelming unhappiness that awaits her in the future.

The narrative capability of images is in further evidence as the language of the "rosa mutabile" continues to permeate the farewell between Rosita and El Primo while undergoing subtle changes that allude to the fact that the man Rosita loves will not return to marry her. The language is dramatically believable in the context of a declaration of love, but it also exudes a sadness that anticipates Rosita's future. When she says "y en mi corazón sentí / agujas estremecidas / que me están abriendo heridas / rojas como el alhelí" (1372), she evokes these lines from the "rosa mutabile" passage: "Cuando se abre en la mañana, / roja como sangre está." When El Primo tells her "Cuando mi caballo lento / coma tallos con rocío . . . / y la escarcha deje en mí / alfileres de lucero, / te digo, porque te quiero, / que me moriré por ti" (1372), he evokes these lines from the passage of the key metaphor: "el rocío no la toca," "[y] cuando toca la noche / blanco cuerno de metal / y las estrellas avanzan;" thereby establishing a counterpoint in the metaphorical language (especially through the word "rocío") which expresses what occurs in the human drama when El Primo actually pledges his love but never fulfills his promise. Also, lines from the "rosa mutabile" passage stir beneath the text when Rosita declares "Yo ansío verte llegar / una tarde por Granada / con toda la luz salada / por la nostalgia del mar" (1372-1373), recalling "Y se desmaya la tarde / en las violetas del mar, / se pone blanca, con blanco / de una mejilla de sal" (1357). Lorca has thus infused the lovers' farewell with images that resonate with elements of the flower metaphor that contain a sense of unease. "En la mañana roja como sangre está" from the rose image becomes "heridas rojas" in the farewell; "el rocío no la toca" has a counterpart "la escarcha deje en mí alfileres de lucero," and "las violetas del mar" is reshaped into "la nostalgia del mar."

In the farewell scene as we have examined it above, Lorca has placed the rose image at the service of a dramatic context, but he has also tapped its ability to generate more images which, when linked one to the other, penetrate deeper into the core of the emotional content of the drama. One could say that Lorca has taken an image in the spirit of Mallarmé's "De roses tarissant tout parfum au soleil"[7] or Verlaine's "Des mots anciens comme un bouquet de fleurs fanées"[8] and given it the power to help narrate a story. In *Doña Rosita*, Lorca has thus retained qualities of Symbolism that were particularly evident in his earliest plays and used them to help unite poetry and drama. If, for example, one compares Rosita's question "¿Por qué tus manos tejieron, / sobre mi cabeza, flores?" with this line spoken by Rosa María in Martínez Sierra's symbolist *Pastoral*—"Y voy junto a él quitando las espinas de su paso y cortando las flores para su frente"[9]—it becomes apparent that there is an affinity between the imagery in both passages; but what is static and descriptive in *Pastoral* becomes an image active in the dynamics of the dramatic structure of *Doña Rosita*; for Rosita's question is a natural part of dialogue between two young people in love—a dialogue that is shaped by flower imagery.

While carrying the narrative line forward, Lorca invests the language of flowers with the power to make Rosita's sadness and hurt palpable. A partial inventory of flower images alluding to sadness or hurt yields the following: "semillas de dalias pisoteadas por el suelo," "las flores me huelen a niño muerto," "en la raya de lo oscuro, / se comienza a deshojar," "las telas no sólo sirven para hacer flores, sino para empapar lágrimas," "pero como tierna flor, / sus pétalos encendidos / se fueron cayendo heridos / por el beso del amor," "y en mi corazón sentí / agujas estremecidas / que me están abriendo heridas / rojas como el alhelí," "[la rosa"] se deshojó suspirando / por los cristales del alba," "Sobre tu largo cabello / gimen las flores cortadas." Each phrase is one of many layers of imagery which, when "peeled away," expose the core of the profound sorrow Rosita experiences—an emotional condition articulated at the surface level of the text by El Ama in Act III when she tells La Tía: "Pero esto de mi Rosita es lo peor. Es querer y no encontrar el cuerpo; es llorar y no saber por quién se llora, es suspirar por alguien que uno sabe que no se merece los suspiros" (1416).

The process whereby Lorca creates an awareness of the sad fate and the hurt felt by the protagonist while maintaining the dramatic line becomes even more apparent when we review the inventory of images cited above by placing them in the context in which they appear. El Tío says "Ayer me encontré semillas de dalias pisoteadas por el suelo" (1352) when he shows his anger towards his wife and housekeeper for not taking better care of his flowers. The housekeeper says "A mí las flores me huelen a niño muerto" (1352)—another allusion to a "wasted life" as well as to aversion—while registering a complaint at being surrounded by so many flores. "En la raya de lo oscuro, / se comienza a deshojar" (1357) refers directly to the "rosa mutabile" which El Tío is actively cultivating. When La Tía tries to convince her nephew to depart for a visit to his aging father, she uses a flower image to tell him that Rosita will simply become aware that life is not all happiness ("las telas no sólo sirven para hacer flores sino para empapar lágrimas" [1362]). Rosita, when left alone with the man she loves just before he tells her that he is going away, voices an apprehension she feels by relating that one night she imagined that petals of a tender flower "se fueron cayendo heridos / por el beso del amor" (1371) and by saying that when she saw El Primo she felt "agujas estremecidas / que me están abriendo heridas / rojas como el alhelí" (1372). In the context of a song sung by Rosita and three "solteronas," these lines appear: "se deshojó suspirando / por los cristales del alba;" "Sobre tu largo cabello / gimen las flores cortadas" (1404). In other words, allusions to sadness and pain are embedded in the flower imagery used to convey the thoughts of the head of a household to his housekeeper, an aunt to her nephew and a young woman to the man she loves. As one image follows another in changing dramatic contexts, our mental picture of the situation in which the woman who embodies the rose metaphor finds herself becomes clearer and our sense of the feelings she experiences more palpable. This process also takes place when we read *Pelléas et Mélisande*, but unlike Maeterlinck, Lorca does not present a series of tableaux to establish a mood. Lorca has found a way to evoke a prevailing tone or allude to thoughts or emotions felt by the protagonist as time slips by without halting the action that takes place in her household. Poetic images do not intrude upon "natural" conversation but rather imbue it with felt qualities pertaining to thought, mood or emotion. Through metaphorical language with the ability to flow with the dramatic line, Lorca accomplishes what Knight calls "the task of marrying movement and action to design"[10] and what Brower refers to as an "arc of metaphor"[11] relating to gradual dramatic movement.

In furthering our analysis of Lorca's control over dramatic movement, we note that *Doña Rosita*, like its predecessors, contains evidence of poetic techniques common to the traditional Spanish *romance*. This is an important factor in linking images to the dramatic line and for setting in relief various stages in the changing dramatic circumstances. A significant element in this regard is the ability of the *romance* to leave many details to the imagination of the reader as the narrative line moves swiftly within a condensed "poetic space" controlled by the *juglar*. An especially good example is the ballad entitled "Romance del conde Arnaldos." The Count in this *romance* is on the seashore. He hears a song from a mysterious galley. The sailor who sings the song tells the count that he will repeat the song for him only if he accompanies him in his galley on the sea. Although this *romance* stirs our imagination with respect to time ("la mañana de San Juan"), action ("que a la tierra quiere llegar") and description ("Las velas traía de seda"), it strongly retains its narrative quality and our awareness of the "presence" of a narrator ("¡Quién hubiese tal ventura —sobre las aguas de mar;" "Allí fabló el conde Arnaldos,—bien oiréis lo que dirá").[12]

In *Doña Rosita*, Lorca does for a drama what the *juglar* did for "Romance del conde Arnaldos." He 1) maintains a narrative line 2) has characters commenting on the action (giving the reader a sense of listening to someone narrating a tale) and 3) provides the imagination with opportunities to expand and flesh out the mood and spirit of the work. The fact that this play, completed one year before Lorca's death, has a strong affinity with the *romances* can perhaps be explained by the fact that this drama was conceived in 1924, the same year that Lorca began to write *Romancero gitano*.[13] However, a more compelling reason lies in the fact that as early as *Mariana Pineda*, the traditional ballads provided Lorca with a means for making poetic imagery an integral part of communicating human drama.

In addition to providing the language of love, sadness and hurt that evokes emotions experienced by Rosita, flower imagery supplies a narrative expressing Rosita's story in three acts which, because of the way they are framed, give the appearance of being segments of a long *romance*. Before Rosita appears in Act I, there is what one might call a prologue. Immediately after the curtain rises, El Tío asks "¿Y mis semillas?" (1351), initiating an argument and making "semillas" a catalyst for placing images of flowers in a negative context ("Ayer me encontré las semillas de dalias pisoteadas por el suelo [1352]; "A mí las flores me huelen a niño muerto, o a profesión de monja, o a altar de iglesia. A cosas tristes" [1352]). Thus, the metaphorical language begins to anticipate the ill-fated Rosita who is the seed that becomes a youthful blossom destined to die after being cut from the garden. After this brief "introduction," the flower metaphor is set in motion on the human level when Rosita enters, "vestida de rosa."

The image of a seed being deprived of a natural life is then recalled and expanded to set the stage for the social context of this unfolding "ballad." The head of the household remarks: "Bien está que se pisen las semillas, pero no es tolerable que esté con las hojitas tronchadas la planta de rosal que más quiero" (1355), whereupon we "listen" to dialogue with a subtext that seems to ask who is responsible for the action that leads to a flower's being trampled upon:

Tío: Yo me pregunto: ¿quién volcó la maceta?
Ama: A mí no me mire usted.
Tío: ¿He sido yo? (1356)

It is at this point—with a bit of tension growing in a context associated with flowers—that the playwright introduces the *romance* of the "rosa mutabile," the guiding metaphor for the entire drama as well as the frame for Act I. Then after indicating that the blossom of this special rose lasts only one day, El Tío remarks: "Uno. Pero yo ese día lo pienso pasar al lado para ver cómo se pone blanca" (1357)—a comment similar to one a *juglar* might make telling us that we are going to see the "rosa mutabile" actualized. Thus, the playwright has extended the rose metaphor into the early stages of the human drama as it begins to unfold.

In our examination of the language associated with flowers used in such a way that it seems to be composing a *romance*, the first direct contact between flower imagery and a specific reference to Rosita comes when La Tía urges her nephew to leave for America despite his inclination to stay with the woman he loves. If one recalls "semillas pisoteadas" from an earlier scene and the housekeeper's denial that she was the one responsible for overturning a flower pot ("¿Quién volcó la maceta?"), what the aunt now tells her nephew has the effect of delineating her role in the social milieu that affects Rosita's future. "Soy yo," says La Tía, "la que te tiene que obligar a que tomes el vapor. . . . De tu prima no quiero acordarme. . . . Ahora se enterará de que las telas no sólo sirven para hacer flores, sino para empapar lágrimas" (1362). Now that the die has been cast and the nephew decides to take the trip that will separate him from Rosita, the link between flowers and sadness in the metaphorical language, strengthened by the proximity of "hacer flores" and "empapar lágrimas," prepares us for the next segment of what we might call this extended *romance*: i.e., the dialogue of the farewell between Rosita and the man she loves. First, El Ama voices a feeling of foreboding:

> Por el ajonjolí,
> por las tres santas preguntas
> y la flor de la canela,
> tenga malas noches
> y malas sementeras.
> Por el pozo de San Nicolás
> se le vuelva veneno la sal. (1364)

Shortly thereafter, Rosita adds an ominous note in the midst of a *romance* she recites teasing three *manolas* about their coquettishness and the suitors that pursue them:

> ¿Adónde irán las manolas
> mientras sufren en la umbría
> el surtidor y la rosa? (1367)

The "romance de las manolas" appears to serve two purposes: 1) to entrench Granada as the setting, and 2) to underscore, through irony, the fact that sadness awaits Rosita because her relationship with El Primo has been altered by his decision to leave. We note that again the rose image is implanted in another context, adding another "layer" to the sadness evoked by the metaphorical language. A further note regarding the effect and the placement of this *romance* is that it reminds us of the *romance* of the bullfight in Ronda in *Mariana Pineda*. In both instances, the ballads are essentially static with respect to the dramatic line of the play; yet as interludes, they both allude to, and therefore aid in heightening the plight of the protagonist. Flower images have, in effect, set the stage for Rosita herself to use this metaphorical continuity to express the love she feels—a love that the reader already senses is tinged with sadness.

The fact that the *romance* of the "rosa mutabile" frames Act I is confirmed by the farewell between Rosita and El Primo. In this scene, the language related to flowers gives the first act a cohesiveness by recounting events and anticipating Rosita's withdrawal into illusion in order to transcend her bitter disappointment. With flower imagery, Rosita first asks why she has been placed in her present situation (¿Por qué tus manos tejieron, / sobre mi cabeza, flores?" (1370). Then in what might be considered a *glosa* of the *romance* of the rose, she says "Vi bajar dos querubines / a una rosa enamorada; / ella se puso encarnada / siendo blanco su color: / pero, como tierna flor, / sus pétalos encendidos / se fueron cayendo heridos / por el beso del amor" (1371). Although the playwright has inverted the colors of the rose to accommodate the change in context, in effect he sustains the "presence" of the *romance* of the "rosa mutabile" in which we heard "se pone blanca" in place of "se puso encarnada." The ability of the imagery associated with flowers to allude to a relationship between pain and love continues when Rosita draws an echo from the *romance* of the three *manolas* ("mientras sufren en la umbría / el surtidor y la rosa") when she says "Así yo, primo inocente, en mi jardín de arrayanes / daba al aire mis afanes y mi blancura a la fuente" (1371). One could say at this point in the drama that Rosita, like Mariana Pineda before her, acts as a *juglar* telling her own story in narrative poetry.

Flower imagery suffuses *Doña Rosita* to such a degree that when El Primo tells Rosita "He de volver, prima mía, / para llevarte a mi lado / en barco de oro cuajado / con las velas de alegría" (1372), Rosita's response, resonating with the language of flowers, appears very natural: "Pero el veneno que vierte / amor, sobre el alma sola, / tejerá con tierra y ola / el vestido de mi muerte" (1372). The phrase "el veneno que vierte amor" subtly recalls "sus pétalos encendidos / se fueron cayendo heridos / por el beso de amor"—an image she used moments earlier; and through the word "tejer," the death of Rosita's spirit is linked with love, because the word was heard moments earlier in a flower image in the context of love ("¿Por qué tus manos tejieron, / sobre mi cabeza, flores?" [1370]).

The *romance* of the "rosa mutabile" does, in fact, frame the action of Act I when Rosita picks up the book of roses at the conclusion of the act and reads the *romance*. This action not only underscores the unfolding dramatization of the *romance* but also provides a poetic setting consonant with the imaginative world of illusion that Rosita begins to create when the man she loves leaves her. We have already observed in earlier plays by Lorca the dramatist's use of narrative poetry to conclude a scene, notably Perlimplín's lament at the end of Act I and the *nana* at the end of the second scene of Act I of *Bodas de sangre*. Indeed, both of these examples and Rosita's reading at the close of Act I bear a striking resemblance in their tone of despair. Perlimplín laments: "que vengo mal herido / herido de amor huido" (1000). Leonardo's wife sings "Duérmete, rosal, / que el caballo se pone a llorar" (1194), and Rosita reads "en la raya de lo oscuro / se comienza a deshojar" (1374). However, in *Doña Rosita* Lorca has integrated the metaphorical language with dramatic contexts to a higher degree of concentration in one act than in the earlier plays. In Act I, flower imagery, in addition to supplying the central metaphor for Rosita's story and a frame for the action, provides language for 1) a prologue to the drama 2) the revelation of relationships among the characters 3) the foreshadowing of events and 4) the expression of love and farewell between Rosita and El Primo. This is accomplished by rooting the imagery in natural dialogue spoken in a believable domestic setting—an accomplishment that stands out even more in relief if one turns to Calderón for contrast and comparison.

For an example from *El médico de su honra*, we cite fire imagery which Calderón associates with love ("una llama en noche oscura / arde hermosa, luce pura, / cuyos rayos, cuyo aliento / dulce ilumina del viento la esfera; / . . . / una dama me alumbraba; / pero era una llama aquélla, / que eclipsas divina y bella / siendo de luces crisol").[14] Although images of fire supply Calderón with a language to express love, they remain at the level of simile; of illustration. They do not work in the way Lorca presents imagery; i.e., dynamically in tandem with dramatic contexts.

El médico de su honra does demonstrate, however, Calderón's use of an imagery continuity to reflect the *changing* conditions of the unfolding action—a process that Lorca refines in his middle and later plays by investing images with dynamism. Doña Mencía, fearing her husband will discover the presence of Don Enrique, purposefully snuffs out a candle.

Shortly thereafter, her husband expresses his suspicions by exclaiming: "¡Oh ciego abismo / del alma!" (201). The darkness that Doña Mencía caused by putting out the candle gradually makes its presence "felt" while Don Gutierre continues to brood and eventually signals his wife's death with a similar action ("Mato la luz, y llego, [Apaga la luz.] sin luz y sin razón, dos veces ciego; / pues bien encubrir puedo / el metal de la voz, hablando quedo. / ¡Mencía!" [207]). It is this correlation between imagery and drama that Lorca develops as a fundamental characteristic of poetic drama. At the stage in his career represented by *Doña Rosita*, we see a dramatist whose poetry possesses what Knight (speaking of Shakespeare) termed an energy that is dynamic and evolving; a natural coalescence of movement and solidity;[15] and what Brower called the participation of imagery in the linked stages in the presentation of human relationships.[16]

In Act II of *Doña Rosita*, there is an increase in the tempo of the rhythm established between references to flowers and dramatic contexts. It is in this act that we learn that Rosita is a woman who willfully holds onto her illusion of marriage and closes her eyes to the passing of time. When her uncle asks her what she intends to do with the scissors in her hand, Rosita, as if realizing that once the rose has been cut immediate decline is inevitable, replies by saying "Voy a cortar unas rosas" (1387); and she continues to express her present intention thus: "Quiero poner en las jardineras y en el florero de la entrada" (1388). As if responding to the subtext of Rosita's remarks, El Ama says "Pues para lo único que sirven las rosas es para adornar las habitaciones" (1388). Again, a reference to flowers is actively engaged in setting the scene of another phase of this long "narrative poem." But the playwright does not stop here. Rather, he moves the action in this scene forward by means of the metaphorical language which now becomes extraordinarily condensed in its capacity to narrate. This occurs when La Tía, the prime mover in severing Rosita's attachment to El Primo, tells Rosita "Anda, corta las flores" (1388) almost immediately after Rosita, expecting a letter from El Primo, asks if the mail has arrived. By almost juxtaposing the image of a flower being cut with Rosita's asking if a letter has arrived from her cousin. The dramatist has used the image of a flower to anticipate Rosita's break with the past which she is unwilling to acknowledge. As this scene continues, Rosita reiterates her determination to follow the course she has set for herself, expressing her feelings through the flower continuity that tells her story: "¡Pero, tía! Tengo las raíces muy hondas, muy bien hincadas en mi sentimiento" (1389). In this brief exchange among the three women, the playwright has managed to keep a domestic scene in motion while conveying, through allusions to the rose metaphor, Rosita's situation vis à vis her cousin who is absent but whose "presence" in the text is indicated by Rosita's asking repeatedly if the mail has arrived.

With the anticipation of the arrival of an important letter from El Primo still in the reader's mind, Lorca introduces into this act a song that serves as the centerpiece for the act, just as the *romance* of "la rosa mutabile" did for Act I. Moreover, this song assumes the appearance of a *glosa* on the ballad of the rose. Again one notes the affinity with the *glosa lopesca* (notably exemplified in Acts II and III of *El caballero de Olmedo*) as one clue to Lorca's techniques for integrating poetry and drama. First this song is a means for recalling the ballad of the rose and for reinforcing the fact that Rosita has resolved to hold onto an illusion which, in effect, will make her a "rosa mutabile." The song begins by telling us that there is a language of flowers ("Mil flores dicen mil cosas / para mil enamoradas" (1403) and that the narrator wishes to listen to it ("Madre, llévame a los campos / . . . / a ver abrirse las flores / cuando se mecen las ramas"). Then as the song proceeds, we can "hear" a *glosa* of the ballad of the rose:

Song	*"Romance" of the "rosa mutabile"*
Abierta estaba la rosa	Cuando se abre en la mañana,
con la luz de la mañana;	roja como sangre está.
tan roja de sangre tierna	
que el rocío se alejaba	El rocío no la toca
tan caliente sobre el tallo,	porque se teme quemar.
que la brisa se quemaba	
pero la tarde llegaba,	Cuando en las ramas empiezan
y un rumor de nieve triste	los pájaros a cantar
le fue pesando las ramas	y se desmaya la tarde
cuando la sombra volvía	en las violetas del mar,
. . . . . .	se pone blanca . . .
se puso transida y blanca	
y cuando la noche, grande	y cuando toca la noche
cuerno de metal sonaba	blanco cuerno de metal
. . . . . .	. . . . . .
se deshojó suspirando	se comienza a deshojar
por los cristales del alba.	(1356-1357)
(1403-1404)	

The Dynamics of the Imagery in the Theater   177
of Federico Garcia Lorca

In effect, what we are listening to in this song sung during the visit of three *solteronas* is Rosita's story. Further, the song evokes the presence of El Primo who at this point in the drama is uppermost in Rosita's thoughts. Lorca accomplishes this evocation by embedding in the song the language of love and sadness used by Rosita and El Primo in their farewell scene in Act I:

Song
y la fuente está contando
lo que el ruiseñor se calla
(1403)

Farewell
¡Qué luto de ruiseñores
dejas a mi juventud . . .
(1371)

tan caliente sobre el tallo,
que la brisa se quemaba
. . . . . .

el agua me ha de prestar
nardos de espuma y sosiego
para contener mi fuego
cuando me vaya a quemar (1371)

dice el jazmín: "Seré fiel"
(1403)

jazminero desangrado (1373)

y un rumor de nieve triste
le fue pesando las ramas
(1404)

¡Ay prima, tesoro mío!
ruiseñor en la nevada
(1371)
no es de hielo mi desvío
(1371)

As the above comparisons demonstrate, the allusive words in the song recall the key metaphor and the lovers' farewell; and they do so at a time when Rosita is showing apprehension concerning her future and determination to let her imagination take hold after fifteen years have elapsed since the departure of the man she loves. In other words, metaphorical language resonates with dramatic context.

As in earlier plays, Lorca's use of a *glosa* invites comparison with the *glosa lopesca*. For example, in Act III of *El caballero de Olmedo*, the Olmedo-Medina, muerte-vida axes, so often present in the text, reappear when Alonso tells Inés how much he regrets leaving her in order to return to Olmedo:

Yo lo siento, y voy a Olmedo,
dejando el alma en Medina:
no sé cómo parto y quedo;

amor la ausencia imagina:
los celos, señora, el miedo;
así parto muerto y vivo,
que vida y muerte recibo.
Mas ¿qué te puedo decir,
cuando estoy para partir,
"puesto ya el pie en el estribo?"[17]

The melancholy and foreboding that Lope's protagonist expresses as he bids Inés farewell is not unlike the hopelessness that seeps into Rosita's life at the time her *glosa* is sung. Nevertheless, a reader who senses declamation in Lope's lines may be inclined to speak of a "felt quality" in Lorca's verses. This may be explained by saying that Lorca diverges from Lope by frequently infusing the developing narrative line with imagery whose power of allusion and evocation, rather than statement, give substance to a feeling. In Act II of *Doña Rosita*, one *feels* the presence of memory and illusion which become more real for Rosita as time slips by.

As Act II draws to a close, references to flowers continue to shape the language expressing the course of the drama. After Rosita reaffirms her belief that her cousin will return even though she has been discouraged to marry him by proxy, her uncle enters with a rose in hand, saying: "Lo he oído todo, y casi sin darme cuenta he cortado la única rosa mudable que tenía en mi invernadero. Todavía estaba roja . . ." (1410). In the subtext we read that Rosita, like the rose cut almost unwittingly by her uncle, still has the color of life and hope. But when her uncle expands the metaphor by saying "Si hubiera tardado dos horas más en cortarla te la hubiese dado blanca" (1411), we realize the toll that time has already exacted from Rosita. The rose is still red, but its withering approaches like the afternoon light that descends upon the "rosa mutabile." Again we note in this play, as did Brower in *The Tempest*, that what we feel is happening cannot be separated from the metaphorical language through which it is expressed.

In Act III, the language related to flowers completes its task of serving as the means of expressing Rosita's transformation from a young woman in love with hopes of marriage into a middle-aged woman with lost illusions, an empty future and the label of "solterona." A feeling of emptiness, of total withering, permeates the final act by means of flower imagery that begins to infiltrate the dialogue as El Ama, La Tía and Rosita prepare to vacate their home for new lodgings. When La Tía tells El Ama that she was "quitando las últimas macetas del invernadero" (1412), the "listener" of the language of flowers "hears" that Rosita, the last "flower" of the household, is about to leave a home that saw her hopes for love disappear. The effects of time are also elicited by the housekeeper through an allusion to the rose metaphor when she tries to bolster her mistress's spirit ("¡Que nos espere muchos años todavía cortando rosas!" [1413]), drawing this response from La Tía: "Estoy muy viejecita." Again one visualizes the flower that turns white as night approaches. In other words, one "feels" in the imagery what is happening to Rosita.

Beneath the whimsical dialogue between El Ama and La Tía in Act III, one hears the flower imagery talking about total withering or death: "¿Al infierno yo? . . . No, señora, no. Yo entro en el cielo a la fuerza. . . . Con usted. . . . En medio de las dos, en un columpio de jazmines y matas de romero, Rosita meciéndose, y detrás su marido cubierto de rosas, como salió en su caja de esta habitación . . . y detrás el Señor tirándonos rosas" (1425). Again roses are associated with (and thus express) the inevitable passage of time. Even with respect to the new house, one notes a sense of inevitability through a reference to flowers. This occurs in an allusion to confinement that one felt Rosita experienced in the old house. "La nueva casa," says La Tía, "no es esto. Pero tiene buenas vistas y un patinillo con dos higueras donde se pueden tener flores" (1418).

What we have been calling Rosita's *romance* of the "rosa mutabile" begins to draw to a close when time has caught up with Rosita. Although she knew that the man she loved married another woman, Rosita held onto an illusion—"una ilusión llena de sollozos"—until others began to discover the truth and to talk behind her back. Now a ridiculed "solterona," Rosita expresses her present situation with a flower image that evokes, and therefore sustains, the presence of the image of the cut rose: "Yo, lo mismo que antes, cortando el mismo clavel, viendo las mismas nubes" (1428). Rosita has reached the final stage of the "rosa mutabile," realizing that the preservation of a love in bloom was only an illusion and that loneliness and isolation are her fate. In a succinct exchange of dialogue in which the underlying rose image fuses with the dramatic context, Lorca sums up what happened to the bloom of life that Rosita held in her imagination:

Muchacho: ¡Qué jardín más precioso tienen ustedes!
Rosita: ¡Teníamos!
Tía: Ven y corta unas flores (1434)

The subtext is saturated with allusions to the flourishing garden of Act I, Rosita's recognition that blossoms have disappeared and a sense that nothing really has changed—that the younger generation will continue to "cut" flowers. This brief, yet richly textured allusion to the rose metaphor leads directly to the appearance of a *glosa* of the *romance* of the rose which Lorca again employs as a frame for the action in the long "narrative poem" that is Rosita's story. The placement of the *romance* at this point in the drama underpins the idea that Rosita has imagined a world in which she could escape from the grasp of time ("Me he acostumbrado a vivir muchos años fuera de mí, pensando en cosas que estaban muy lejos" [1428]) and expresses her utter disillusion after she consciously pronounces her name, associating it with the rose metaphor:

¡Anda con Dios, hijo! (Salen. La tarde está cayendo.)
¡Doña Rosita! ¡Doña Rosita!
　Cuando se abre en la mañana
　roja como sangre está.
　La tarde la pone blanca
　con blanco de espuma y sal.
　Y cuando llega la noche
　se comienza a deshojar. (1435)

By consciously glossing the *romance* of the "rosa mutabile" and shortly thereafter concluding the drama by repeating the final two lines of this *glosa*, Rosita places herself out of time by "leaving" the human drama and "entering" the *romance* sung in a language associated with flowers.

The striking similarity between the conclusion of *Doña Rosita* and that of *Mariana Pineda* with respect to a *romance* that frames the drama can perhaps be explained by a fact that we have already indicated; i.e., Lorca began writing *Romancero gitano* and conceived the idea of *Doña Rosita* in the same year (1924), and then completed *Mariana Pineda* at the beginning of the following year. However, if one bears in mind that *Doña Rosita* was completed ten years after *Mariana Pineda*, and after *Perlimplín* and *Bodas de sangre*, what then emerges is the difference in the manner in which Lorca uses ballads with respect to drama. In *Doña Rosita*, Lorca refines the use of a *romance* as a means of sustaining continuities in the metaphorical language which *expresses* interaction among the characters, whereas in *Mariana Pineda*, the *romance* serves more as a vehicle for conveying images that *describe* the protagonist at various stages in the conflict she experiences. By drawing on a variety of techniques to help images intensify their resonance with evolving human relationships, *Doña Rosita* occupies a position distinctly further along the trajectory of Lorca's use of imagery in the theater than *Mariana Pineda*. Poetry that primarily supported the dramatic line has become poetry that cannot be separated from the unfolding action it expresses.

Because *Doña Rosita* concentrates on a single metaphorical continuity (a language of flowers) and on a specific image ("la rosa mutabile"), this play can be considered a paradigm of how Lorca implants poetry in dramatic contexts so cleverly that it is difficult to feel what is happening apart from the poetic language spoken by the characters.

At its most obvious level, the imagery related to flowers forms the basis of a central metaphor (the "rosa mutabile") for a woman who undergoes a transformation similar to that of the rose. A young woman blooming with love becomes a mature woman holding onto the illusion that her love will be fulfilled, until she is overcome by time and the realization that like the rose, the red blossom has turned white and is beginning to shed its petals. At another metaphorical level, the flower metaphor expands and becomes engaged in the narration of various stages of Rosita's story. Through language related to flowers, Act I: 1) contains a prologue ("¿Y mis semillas?"; "Es necesario que cuidéis las flores;" "A mí las flores me huelen a niño muerto"), 2) establishes character relationships ("Aquí no eres más que un paseante de los jardinillos"), 3) foreshadows events ("Ahora se enterará de que las telas no sólo sirven para hacer flores, sino para empapar lágrimas"), and 4) expresses love between Rosita and El Primo ("¿Por qué tus manos tejieron / sobre mi cabeza, flores?") as well as their sad farewell and his promise to return ("y en mi corazón sentí / agujas estremecidas / que me están abriendo heridas / rojas como el alhelí;" "Por los diamantes de Dios / y el clavel de su costado, / juro que vendré a tu lado").

References to flowers in Act II 1) express the beginning of Rosita's decline ("Voy a cortar unas rosas") 2) show her determination ("Tengo las raíces muy hondas, muy bien hincadas en mi sentimiento" 3) reveal the presence of her hopes as time passes ("Abierta estaba la rosa / con la luz de la mañana") 4) express her sadness ("gimen las flores cortadas") and 5) anticipate the condition of her life in Act III ("Si hubiera tardado dos horas más en cortarla te la [rosa] hubiese dado blanca").

In Act III, language related to flowers 1) strikes a note of desolation ("Quitando las últimas macetas del invernadero") 2) indicates the effect of time on Rosita ("yo, lo mismo que antes, cortando el mismo clavel") and 3) expresses her realization of the loss of any hope for marriage and her future as a "solterona" ("Y cuando llega la noche / se comienza a deshojar").

Thus, the imagery of this play narrates Rosita's story, provides language for the dialogue through which the characters interact and evokes and expresses feelings of love and sadness. In *Doña Rosita*, as earlier in *Bodas de sangre*, Lorca develops the dynamics of images to a high degree and thus avoids giving them the appearance of a distinct "superstructure" of metaphorical language that tends to have a life outside the drama (as evidenced especially in Calderonian imagery with cosmic or moral implications). Moreover, the ability of a Lorquian image to adapt itself to its dramatic surroundings gives it more flexibility than if it were assigned a single symbolic value (a situation that prevailed in passages cited from Lope de Vega).

With respect to the human quality of Lorca's imagery, we are again reminded of the playwright's words stating that poetic imagination always works upon real situations.[18] *Doña Rosita*, the dramatization of a flower hurt by time and people close to it, recalls for us these words from the dramatist: "El poeta dramático no debe olvidar, si quiere salvarse del olvido, los campos de rosas, mojados por el amanecer, donde sufren los labradores, y ese palomo, herido por un cazador misterioso, que agoniza entre los juncos sin que nadie escuche su gemido."[19]

Finally, as one reviews *Doña Rosita* with respect to its position on the trajectory traced by the development of Lorca's imagery in the theater, it becomes apparent that Lorca has not totally abandoned the Symbolist-Modernista spirit. *Doña Rosita*, like Lorca's earliest plays, creates a mood and evokes feelings of melancholy and sadness. But Lorca now accomplishes this through dialogue that unites poetry and drama. This leads us to conclude that in *Doña Rosita*, Lorca has retained the power of poetry to stir the imagination while supplying the language for the dramatization of Rosita's life as a "soltera."

Notes

1. *The Fields of Light* (New York: Oxford Univ. Press, 1962), p.119.

2. *El caballero de Olmedo*, ed. Francisco Rico, 6th ed. (Madrid: Ediciones Cátedra, 1985), p.146.

3. *El médico de su honra*, in *Obras completas*, I, ed. Luis Astrana Marín (Madrid: Aguilar, 1951), p.215.

4. *The Shakespearian Tempest*, 3rd ed. (London: Methuen, 1960), p.257.

   In Knight's words, "the poetic faculty itself is personified, takes action in a drama whose events are but expanded poetic imagery."

5. At the conclusion of Act II of *La vida es sueño,* Segismundo says, in part, "que el vivir sólo es soñar; / y la experienca me enseña / que el hombre que vive sueña / lo que es hasta despertar."
(Pedro Calderón de la Barca, *La vida es sueño,* ed. Evangelina Rodríguez Cuadros, 8ª ed. Colección Austral [Madrid: Espasa-Calpe, 1987], p.131.)

6. "La imagen poética de don Luis de Góngora," in *Obras completas,* p.68.

7. "L'après-midi d'un faune," in *Selected Poems by Stéphane Mallarmé,* trans. C.F. MacIntyre (Berkeley: Univ. of California Press, 1957), p.50.

8. "Kaléidoscope," in *Oeuvres poétiques complètes,* ed. Jacques Borel (Paris: Éditions Gallimard, 1962), p.321.

9. *Pastoral,* in *Teatro de ensueño* (Madrid: Renacimiento, S.A., 1911), p.69.

10. *Poets of Action* (London: Methuen, 1967), p.23.

11. *The Fields of Light,* p.108.

12. "Romance del conde Arnaldos," in *Representative Spanish Authors,* Walter T. Pattison, Vol. I (New York: Oxford Univ. Press, 1954), p.48.

13. Arturo del Hoyo, ed., *Obras completas de Federico García Lorca,* 12th ed. (Madrid: Aguilar, 1966), p.1903.

14. Calderón, in *Obras completas,* p.193.

15. *Poets of Action,* p.23.

16. *The Fields of Light,* p.96.

17. Lope de Vega, pp.190-191.

18. "Imaginación, inspiración, evasión," in *Obras completas,* p.86.

19. Charla sobre teatro," in *Obras completas,* p.150.

Chapter 8
La casa de Bernarda Alba

In his article entitled "Apuntes sobre el teatro de García Lorca," Lázaro Carreter maintains that *La casa de Bernarda Alba* is Lorca's most realistic and least poetic play.[1] However, if one follows the development of the role of imagery in Lorquian drama as we have done, from its earliest stages in *El maleficio de la mariposa*, *La casa de Bernarda Alba* emerges as one of Lorca's most poetic plays, because its imagery continuities are perfectly in tune with the dramatic reality through which the characters move.

The women who inhabit Bernarda Alba's house live in a world isolated from the life of the community that surrounds them. Their house is submerged in silence, heat and solitude to such an extent that escape from Bernarda's domination becomes the focus of the dramatic conflict and a special obsession of Adela's, Bernarda's youngest daughter. In this play, Lorca penetrates the inner emotional reality of human relationships and exposes it to view through images associated primarily with interminable heat without relief, and water and fresh air that promise relief but fail to give it. Further, as the desire to escape is enacted in this drama, the reader becomes even more attuned to the emotional reality of Bernarda's house through the pervasive presence of images of imprisonment (stasis) and regeneration as well as silence and outbreaks. In other words, the poetry in *La casa de Bernarda Alba* resides in the metaphorical language which expresses a reality that is more "felt" than "seen." In this way, the dramatist brings to life what Christoph Eich calls Adela's "intensity," which leads to her being consumed by the fire that burns within her,[2] and what Francisco Ruiz Ramón refers to as the negation of reality that inheres in Bernarda's instinct for power.[3] In this play, drama is enhanced by a poetic or inner reality that deepens our understanding of what is taking place by radiating through the action—a situation alluded to by

André Belamich in speaking of images associated with heat: "Ce n'est pas en dessinant les flammes, mais en les faisant brûler dans sa dernière oeuvre que Lorca rejoint dans la realité sa poésie la plus profonde."[4]

The idea that *La casa de Bernarda Alba* offers the unified vision of an action occurring more in an emotional space than in conventional exterior reality becomes clearer if we ask questions like the following: Granted the context of a rural, tradition-bound and very strict household, how "real" is a woman, the mother of five daughters, who is as relentlessly brutal as Bernarda both in direct actions and in the judgment of her by her servants and daughters? How "real" is a situation in which this woman, Bernarda, herself married twice, keeps five daughters, ranging in age from twenty to thirty-nine years, imprisoned in her house with virtually no contact with men nor with the community in general? How "real" is the situation, as La Ponica intimates, where no one has entered Bernarda's house since the death or her father; or where two hundred women (according to the stage directions) file through the house after the funeral of Bernarda's husband; or where the house itself will be sealed off by eight years of mourning; or that an off-stage incident as violent as the stoning of the daughter of La Librada (by the townspeople) is never mentioned again? How "real" are the events that conclude the drama, where only seconds separate a gunshot putting a man to flight and a young woman's resulting suicide by hanging? Even allowing for the conventionality of theater, it appears that answers to these questions lead us to conclude that *La casa de Bernarda Alba*, far from being Lorca's most realistic play, is rather an enactment of human relationships in a hermetically sealed world that comes to life through its metaphorical language.

Although we, the readers of this play, can visualize "real" women, the house they inhabit, their actions as well as those they describe, our most powerful image of Bernarda's house comes from what Brower calls "felt qualities" firmly planted in specific dramatic contexts."[5] Through key imagery continuities, Lorca creates increasing emotional tension and a sense of desperate desire to escape a sexually repressive social environment. Through imagery, Lorca illuminates the conflict of the play, permitting us to feel the state of mind that makes Bernarda's house a prison from which death is the only escape. This is the context in which we would place the declaration by Francis Fergusson that in a poem, play or novel, an artist presents a vision that is ordered; and its meaning lies in the work as a whole rather than in its component parts.[6] In *La casa de Bernarda Alba*, Lorca has created an ordered vision of a house whose ultimate dramatic reality is not in the immediate action and circumstances but rather in a more general destructive emotional climate that produces sexual tensions and frustration. And although we "see" what the characters do and "hear" what they say, we feel the power of their conflict through the metaphorical language of the dialogue.

La casa de Bernarda Alba is the culmination of the development of the dynamics of Lorquian imagery that began with *El maleficio de la mariposa*. To the degree that *La casa de Bernarda Alba* creates an atmosphere, makes feelings "visible" and evokes the presence of something incorporeal such as silence, this play, like Lorca's earlier dramatic works, reveals an affinity with Symbolist theater and Symbolist poetry. Also, the use of images which set one's imagination in motion by radiating outward from their nucleus recalls Lorca's analysis of metaphor in "La imagen poética de don Luis de Góngora" as well as expanded metaphors in plays by Calderón. What is more, the use of song and the ebb and flow of rapidly moving dialogue remind one of the theater of Lope de Vega and the traditional Spanish *romance*. Nevertheless, it is very difficult to isolate similarities between *La casa de Bernarda Alba* and works by authors who preceded Lorca. In this play, poetry is fused with drama to such an extent that it is easier to speak more in terms of "felt qualities" in dramatic settings rather than point to techniques that moved Lorquian imagery along a path from its Symbolist beginnings to complete poetic drama.

Bernarda is a jailor; her house is a prison, and her captives yearn for freedom. Adela and María Josefa, the youngest and the oldest inhabitants of the house of Bernarda Alba, embody the theme of escape from the domination of a woman who creates and controls a repressive environment. Escape, therefore, is the over-arching metaphor implicit in the key images. To follow the imagery continuities in *La casa de Bernarda Alba* is to follow the course of the increasing tension that leads Adela to tragedy as she attempts to pierce the silence and isolation imposed on the house by Bernarda.

In *La casa de Bernarda Alba*, one can identify at least three fundamental continuities in the network of dramatically involved metaphorical components that interrelate with each other in the dramatization of escape from confinement. They are: 1) heat-relief, 2) imprisonment (stasis)-regeneration, and 3) silence-outburst. Although each one carries symbolic value (silence, for example, symbolizes Bernarda's domination and unwillingness to listen to anything that might penetrate the facade she has erected for her house), their ability to generate what Lorca called "radios de acción"[7] gives them the power to acquire multiple values as one component of the imagery fuses with another. This results in permeating the text with imagery that is dynamic enough to help shape dialogue at various stages in the development of the drama. As the playwright increases the appearances of images of heat and thirst, the emotions that motivate the actions of characters become more palpable to the reader. As the thought of solitude gnaws more insistently at the heart of Bernarda's daughters, isolation from the company of men creeps more deliberately into their lives; and as verbal demands for silence proliferate with each emotional outburst, silence itself begins to overtake Bernarda's house. While images of heat become associated with Bernarda's demands for silence and images of water allude to relief as well as drowning, Bernarda's house becomes more isolated from natural human contact and offers death and madness as the only forms of escape. In other words, as the reader follows the course of the key imagery continuities, he is also following the course of a conflict that causes a grandmother to escape deeper into her imagination, a mother to demand further isolation for her family, and a daughter to turn to death as an escape from "imprisonment."

We shall now follow the course of basic imagery continuities through which the playwright dramatizes the frustration felt by women dominated by the will of Bernarda.

The heat and water continuities in *La casa de Bernarda Alba* work together to enhance the movement of characters from sexual tension to a possibility of relief to an ultimate frustration and submission to authority. The dynamics of the imagery parallel the action of the drama. First, heat imagery in a natural setting is the nucleus from which a metaphorical heat emanates. The action takes place during an unusually hot summer. "Cae el sol como plomo," says one of the mourners early in Act I (1446). "Hace años no he conocido calor igual," adds another mourner (1446) just before a stage direction indicates "Se abanican todas." Next, the word "heat" acquires a metaphorical value associated with sexual tension that will produce the major conflict in the play. Early in Act I, La Poncia, referring to Bernarda, mutters beneath her breath "¡Sarmentosa por calentura de varón!" (1448)—a remark that comes just before the choral responses of the women mourning the death of Bernarda's second husband. Here the dramatist implants a key word in the text without disturbing the flow of natural dialogue. Like a "radio de acción" emanating from the nucleus formed by the summer heat, the sexual connotations of heat begin to insinuate themselves into the text. The "polivalencia" of the image makes it receptive to a counterpoint with "water" and "air" which the playwright also infuses with multiple meanings, first associated with the summer heat and then with relief from tension. "Heat," therefore, is set on the course to fulfilling its dramatic potential.

The first encounter between Bernarda and Adela, her most rebellious daughter, takes place in the context of heat when Bernarda rejects the colorful fan Adela offers her ("¿Es éste el abanico que se da a una viuda?" [1451]). This seemingly minor incident nevertheless causes a ripple in the heat-relief continuity that gathers momentum when Martirio says "Yo no tengo calor," to which Bernarda responds "En ocho años que dure el luto no ha de entrar en esta casa el viento de la calle" (1451). The subtextual connotation of the deprivation of "el viento de la calle" is reinforced if one thinks of "el viento" as the men already "entering" the house through the animated conversation of the women. La Poncia tells Bernarda that Augustias was eavesdropping on the conversation of the male guests. The men's sexual relations with Paca la Roseta are revealed, and Martirio tells Amelia about the sexual escapades of Adelaida's father. Lorca thus sets images of heat and relief in motion like "radios de acción" that will pervade the metaphorical language of the play.

At the beginning of Act II, Lorca rapidly expands and intensifies the use of the image of heat as it applies to the heat of summer as well as to the ripples of sexual tension emitted in Act I. Angustias pointedly declares: "Afortunadamente, pronto voy a salir de este infierno" (1472), linking in the reader's mind the heat that penetrates the house with a hellish situation associated with imprisonment and a natural desire for escape. Then in rapid succession, all three connotations of heat—summer, sex and confinement—fuse in a rush of comments whose subtext communicates the mounting frustration Bernarda's daughters feel in being kept isolated in their house:

Amelia: (A La Poncia.)
Abre la puerta del patio a ver si nos entra un poco de fresco.
(La Criada lo hace.)
Martirio: Esta noche pasada no me podía quedar dormida por el calor.
Amelia: Yo tampoco.
Magdalena: Yo me levanté a refrescarme. Había un nublo negro de tormenta y hasta cayeron alguans gotas.
La Poncia: Era la una de la madrugada y subía fuego de la tierra. (1473)

The Dynamics of the Imagery in the Theater of Federico Garcia Lorca

In these brief exchanges, the playwright has rooted metaphorical language pertaining to heat in a context of increasing physical and emotional unease, and he climaxes this increasing tension with the phrase "subía fuego de la tierra" which recalls the image of "infierno" used earlier by Angustias in referring to the emotional climate in the house.

Further appearances of the heat-relief continuity intensify the feeling that sexual matters are at the heart of much of the tension in Bernarda's house. La Poncia, in response to a request to speak about her first meeting with her husband, comments: "Me corría el sudor por todo el cuerpo" (1476). Adela intensifies the image of heat when she rejects La Poncia's admonition not to interdict Angustias's relationship with Pepe: "Es inútil tu consejo. Ya es tarde. No por encima de ti, que eres una criada; por encima de mi madre saltaría para apagarme este fuego que tengo levantado por piernas y boca" (1482).

Heat becomes the focus of the language Bernarda's daughters use to express thoughts concerning men. "¡Y no les importa el calor!" (1486), says Amelia referring to the harvesters whose song attracts the attention of Bernarda's daughters. And as if Adela were attending to the subtext of Amelia's remark, she makes this comment that expresses the sense of escape from isolation and the sexual connotations of the heat-relief continuity: "Me gustaría segar para ir y venir. Así se olvida lo que nos muerde" (1487). Because of the accumulated references to "calor," one can "feel" the dramatic impact of the phrase "lo que nos muerde." In other words, it is impossible to separate what is happening to Adela and her sisters from the language they use.

Images of heat that have become increasingly linked to a growing sense of wanting to escape are joined by more allusions to the mounting tension expressed through the heat-relief continuity. In the chorus of the harvesters we hear "Abrir puertas y ventanas / las que vivís en el pueblo" (1487), and in a more concrete allusion to a desire to escape sexual repression Martirio says "Me sienta mal el calor. . . . Estoy deseando que llegue noviembre, los días de lluvias, la escarcha, todo lo que no sea este verano interminable" (1488).

After increasing our awareness through two acts of the importance of "heat" to our "feeling" the tensions experienced by Bernarda's daughters, the effect of the heat imagery acquires its full impact in Act III. The sexual implication of "heat" becomes mores explicit at the beginning of Act III when a confined stud horse kicks the walls of the stable in an attempt to free itself. This incident pertaining to confinement, sexual tension and relief and even potential danger resonates with events taking place in Bernarda's house and becomes linked to the domestic scene through a fusion of the multiple values of "heat." Bernarda's order that the fillies be isolated and the stud horse let out is immediately followed by Adela's getting up from the table to obtain a drink of water and then shortly thereafter expressing a desire for relief from the heat ("Voy a llegarme hasta el portón para estirar las piernas y tomar un poco de fresco" [1512]). Again the metaphorical language associated with an abatement of the heat makes us aware of Adela's desire to escape. Adela herself confirms this by specifically mentioning the stud horse: "El caballo garañón estaba en el centro del corral ¡blanco! Doble de grande, llenando todo lo oscuro" (1515). The image of the horse that wants freedom pervades this segment of the drama and echoes thoughts spoken by the characters. The tempo of the reappearance of the heat-relief continuity increases even more when Adela exclaims "¡Qué noche más hermosa! Me gustaría quedarme hasta muy tarde para disfrutar el fresco del campo" (1517) and later in this exchange of dialogue:

La Poncia:	¿No te habías acostado?
Adela:	Voy a beber agua. (Bebe en un vaso de la mesa.)
La Poncia:	Yo te suponía dormida.
Adela:	Me despertó la sed. (1522)

While we "listen" to Adela seeking water and fresh air as relief from the actual heat, we are reminded of the restless stud horse noisily indicating that it wants release from confinement and is finally let out of the stable.

The confluence of images associated with a confined stud horse, temporary escape and refreshment, and Adela's imaginative reflections on the night air subtly underscore the metaphorical relationship between María Josefa and Adela. Like Adela, María Josefa wants to escape—a situation that was indicated in the opening moments of the play when the grandmother, locked in her room, shouts for release. One could say that for Adela, María Josefa is a visible reminder of the firm grip Bernarda has on the fate of two generations of her family. Thus, in Act III, when Adela seeks relief in the night air, the subtext not only echoes María Josefa's predicament but also sets the stage for her final appearance:

Martirio: Abuela, ¿dónde va usted?
María Josefa: ¿Vas a abrirme la puerta? ¿Quién eres tú?
Martirio: ¿Cómo está aquí?

María Josefa:	Me escapé. . . . (1524)
María Josefa:	Yo tengo que marcharme, . . . ¿Me acompañarás tú a salir al campo? Yo quiero campo. Yo quiero casas, pero casas abiertas . . . (1525)

Again María Josefa, the oldest inhabitant of the house, echoes Adela, the youngest; and at this point the symbiotic relationship between the two women is strengthened by elements linked in the metaphorical language. The image of the open countryside, "seen" first in the song of the harvesters ("Abrir puertas y ventanas") and later in Adela's musings ("Me gustaría quedarme . . . para disfrutar el fresco del campo"), has now surfaced more emphatically in words spoken by María Josefa whom we know to be forcibly confined in Bernarda's house ("Yo quiero campo"). The playwright has made the heat-relief continuity such an important component of the drama that its elements interact like characters. As one increases its dominance, the other demands relief; just as when Bernarda presses for silence and confinement while María Josefa seeks escape, echoing Adela's desire to flee from the increasing emotional heat. This interplay between metaphorical language and action creates a situation in which we "feel the peculiar quality of what is taking place," as Brower says of *The Tempest*.

The heat-relief continuity also supplies the context for an analysis of Lorca's use of song in his final play. Through strategic placement, brief songs bearing elements of the metaphorical language blend with the action to such an extent that they appear to be part of the ongoing dialogue. Even the childlike ditties of María Josefa contain phrases pertaining to what is happening in the drama. For example, in Act III, María Josefa appears just after La Poncia has bemoaned the fact that the tense situation in Bernarda's house has developed to a breaking point and after Adela has left the heat of her room in order to drink some water. The dialogue, just before María Josefa's entrance, reads, in part:

La Poncia:	Las cosas se han puesto ya demasiado maduras. Adela está decidida a lo que sea y las demás vigilan sin descanso.
	Son mujeres sin hombre, nada más.
Adela:	Voy a beber agua. (Bebe en un vaso de la mesa.)
La Poncia:	Yo te suponía dormida.

Criada: Los perros están como locos.
La Poncia: No nos van a dejar dormir. (1521-1523)

It is at this point in the mounting tension that Lorca places the element of song. María Josefa enters singing to an ewe cradled in her arms:

Ovejita, niño mío,
vámonos a la orilla del mar.
La hormiguita estará en su puerta,
yo te daré la teta y el pan.
. . . . . .
Vamos a los ramos del portal de Belén.
. . . . . .
Ni tú ni yo queremos dormir;
la puerta sola se abrirá
y en la playa nos meteremos
en una choza de coral. (1523)

At its basic level, this is a *nana*—a relationship between a mother and child which we sense the daughters of Bernarda will not experience. Moreover, with its images of wakefulness, unease, relief and escape, this *nana* resonates with the preceding dialogue (through its references to water, doors and sleep). And by reaching back to the conclusion of Act I by recalling María Josefa's cry ("¡A casarme a la orilla del mar, a la orilla del mar!"), this song also helps us penetrate the underlying "reason" for the comments and activities of the other women (i.e., the growing frustration, especially of Adela, in having no prospect of marrying). The placement of the song, therefore, serves the role of the metaphorical language in the presentation of drama. In effect, the song expresses the prevailing situation in Bernarda's house.

The song of the harvesters is placed in Act II in a natural context that fits into the dramatic structure of the action in Bernarda's house. Shortly before the song is heard, La Poncia had confronted Adela with the latter's relationship with Pepe el Romano; and immediately before we hear the words of the song, La Poncia tells Bernarda's daughters that on the previous night fifteen harvesters received the sexual favors of one woman in the olive grove. Thus, the air in Bernarda's house is charged with the topic of sexual matters at the moment the song is heard. Through allusions to heat and relief that speak directly of the tensions developing in the house, the song has the effect at this point in the drama of admitting the "presence" of men ("el viento de la calle") into Bernarda's house:

Coro: Ya salen los segadores
en busca de las espigas;
se llevan los corazones
de las muchachas que miran.
. . . . . .
Abrir puertas y ventanas
las que vivís en el pueblo,
el segador pide rosas
para adornar su sombrero. (1486, 1487)

In addition to singing about relationships between the sexes, the harvesters—in lines such as "salen los segadores," "en busca de las espigas," "abrir puertas y ventanas"—are singing about the struggle between isolation and escape that is taking place in Bernarda's house. In other words, the harvesters, in the heat of the day, project images that resonate with and expand those pertaining to the increasing heat, the persistent demand for silence and the closing of doors and windows in Bernarda's house. The harvester's song is, therefore, a catalyst for further interaction between the metaphorical language and the developing dramatic tension. Thus, when Martirio repeats the refrain of the song and then says "Me sienta mal el calor. . . . Estoy deseando que llegue noviembre, los días de lluvias, la escarcha, todo lo que no sea este verano interminable" (1488), the song conveys a deepening sense of the mounting tension.

Along with the heat-relief continuity, frequent allusions to stasis or imprisonment counterpoised by references to the natural flow of generations also focus on the desire to escape confinement. By increasing the reader's awareness of the extreme isolation from social contact experienced by Bernarda's family and counterbalancing it with relief implied in references to the sexual relationship between men and women, the playwright underscores the frustration felt by the women who seek escape from Bernarda's prison. Like Curianito, Mariana Pineda, Don Perlimplín, Leonardo, La Novia and Doña Rosita, Adela and María Josefa withdraw into themselves and become enclosed in a solitary emotional space. Still, in this, Lorca's final play, a continual ebb and flow of images alluding to a desire for escape evokes the *feeling* of isolation to a higher degree than do his previous plays.

At the beginning of Act I, we read a stage direction that sets in motion the continuity of solitude: "Al levantarse el telón está la escena sola" (1439). Talk of loneliness and imprisonment interrupts the silence when the maid, speaking about Magdalena's reaction to her father's death, says

"Es la que se queda más sola" (1440) and when La Poncia, referring to María Josefa's confinement, asks: "La vieja. ¿Está bien cerrada?" (1440). As Act I develops, we notice other allusions to stasis and confinement "Desde que murió el padre de Bernarda no ha vuelto a entrar las gentes bajo estos techos" (1442); "¡Ojalá tardéis muchos años en pasar el arco de mi puerta!" (1450); "Hacemos cuenta que hemos tapiado con ladrillos puertas y ventanas" (1451). Such statements enhance our awareness of extreme isolation bordering on unreality, with María Josefa's confinement its most visible dramatic expression.

Bearing in mind that María Josefa is a prisoner, the reader can bring the image of the grandmother's confinement to the dialogue at various stages in the developing drama. For example, when Magdalena says in Act I "Vengo de correr las cámaras. Por andar un poco. De ver los cuadros bordados de cañamazo de nuestra abuela, el perrito de lanas y el negro luchando con un león que tanto nos gustaba de niñas" (1461), one is reminded of María Josefa's present situation and "hears" her desire to escape even if the escape is only into memory. Also, in Adela's reaction to being told that she will become accustomed to the isolation imposed by the mourning period, one "hears" a young granddaughter desperately expressing a wish to avoid the same fate as her grandmother. As Act I draws to a close, Adela says "Pienso que este luto me ha cogido en la peor época de mi vida para pasarlo. . . . No me acostumbraré. Yo no puedo estar encerrada" (1466). The affinity between Adela and María Josefa is further strengthened shortly after Adela's outburst when María Josefa succeeds in escapando from her room. While carrying the dramatic line forward by the appearance of María Josefa, here Lorca also deepens our sense of the central conflict through textual echoes with Adela's expressions of frustration. In effect, María Josefa's words heighten the impact of Adela's earlier outburst by echoing her granddaughter's cries with words that radiate outward from a central image of the sea as escape:

Criada:	¡Se me escapó!
María Josefa:	Me escapé porque quiero casar, porque quiero casarme con un varón hermoso de la orilla del mar, ya que aquí los hombres huyen de las mujeres.
Bernarda:	¡Calle usted, madre!
María Josefa:	No, no me callo. No quiero ver a estas mujeres solteras rabiando por la boda, haciéndose polvo el corazón, y yo me quiero ir a mi pueblo. Bernarda, yo quiero un varón para casarme y para tener alegría.

The Dynamics of the Imagery in the Theater   195
of Federico Garcia Lorca

Bernarda: ¡Encerradla!
María Josefa: ¡Déjame salir, Bernarda! (La Criada coge a María
                Josefa.)
Bernarda: ¡Ayudarla vosotras! (Todas arrastran a la vieja.)
María Josefa: ¡Quiero irme de aquí! ¡Bernarda! ¡A casarme a la
                orilla del mar; a la orilla del mar! (1470-1471)

Although the reader visualizes a mad old woman pleading for something impossible, the virtual image is of Adela, a young woman beginning to be frustrated in her attempt to gain something logically possible. This is accomplished through textual similarities that juxtapose images of both women.

In Act II, more images pertaining to a desire to escape from Bernarda's house deepen our sense of the frustration felt by the women who are trapped. In the context of confinement, again we refer to the song of the harvesters. Immediately after La Poncia says "Ya me ha tocado en suerte este convento" (1484), the conversation shifts attention to the harvesters singing as they return from the fields. In both the song and the dialogue of the women listening to it, images related to freedom of movement coincide with a subtext of yearning for relief from the "heat" of the "convento":

Adela: ¡Ay, quién pudiera salir también a los campos!
     . . . . . .
La Poncia: No hay alegría como la de los campos en esta época.
     . . . . . .

Amelia: ¡Y no les importa el calor!
     . . . . . .
Adela: Me gustaría segar para ir y venir. . . .
     . . . . . .
Coro: Abrir puertas y ventanas
   las que vivís en el pueblo,
   el segador pide rosas
   para adornar su sombrero. (1485-1487)

Gradually, through many references to men and allusions to sexual activity, Lorca underscores frustration and a desire for release. This situation is stressed at the conclusion of Act II which, like the end of Act I, refers explicitly to a woman's attempt to circumvent constraints placed on her by others. At this moment in the drama, news reaches Bernarda's house that an unmarried woman who tried to conceal an illegitimate baby she has killed is being pursued by men bent on killing her. Adela shrieks: "¡Que la dejen escapar!" (1505), and Bernarda counters with "¡Matadla! ¡Matadla!" (1506). For the reader who has been "listening" to the metaphorical language, the "reality" of this scene shifts from the vivid description of the event happening offstage, to the daughter-mother, escape-control oppositions which have intensified to such a degree that they anticipate the unyielding position each woman will take in Act III.

By juxtaposing allusions to Bernarda's house as a prison with images related to the natural flow of generations, to liberation implied in regeneration, the playwright further heightens the heated frustration of women deprived of normal outlets for their desires. This is accomplished notably through water imagery. In addition to being an indicator of relief from the unbearable heat of the summer as well as an abatement for sexual tension, "water" emits a circle of meaning associated with love in marriage that is out of the reach of the daughters forced to lead a cloistered life in Bernarda's "convent."

At the close of Act I, María Josefa's distracted comments contain water imagery placed in the context of marriage. As we indicated earlier, María Josefa's words—"Me escapé porque me quiero casar, porque quiero casarme con un varón hermoso de la orilla del mar" (1470)—allude to Adela's desire to escape the "heat" in Bernarda's house. But by following the course of the metaphorical language, we perceive "la polivalencia textual del símbolo" in the image "casarme con un varón hermoso de la orilla del mar." In this phrase (uttered, significantly, by the oldest of three generations represented in Bernarda's house), we "hear," in the reference to marriage, a natural outlet for the repressed desires of Bernarda's daughters. But in the description of the man as "un varón hermoso de la orilla del mar," we sense that marriage can only be a dream for them. Thus, by expanding the metaphorical content of María Josefa's utterance, we "hear" 1) an allusion to marriage 2) imagination driven to an extreme and 3) futility, as well as the defiant attitude that Adela, the youngest member of the household, will assume later in the drama. Indeed, the connection between María Josefa and Adela becomes more evident at the beginning of Act II when talk about the unbearable heat and a desire for relief turns to Adela as the topic of conversation: "La envidia la come.... Se lo noto en los ojos. Se le está poniendo mirar de loca" (1478). Through the word "loca," we associate Adela with María Josefa at a point in the drama when there is more talk about the heat and about sexual matters (namely, when La Poncia talks about her relationship with her husband).

María Josefa's sea image, placed in the context of marriage and then assuming multiple connotative values, acquires even more force when it returns in a slightly altered form. The image adapts itself to a different dramatic context when La Poncia expresses her feeling concerning the dangerous tension in Bernarda's house. When La Poncia realizes that her efforts to warn Bernarda have been futile, she says "A mí me gustaría cruzar el mar y dejar esta casa de guerra" (1521). Hearing "cruzar el mar," we are reminded of the desperate desire of both the grandmother and her youngest granddaughter. Thus, by echoes of imagery in the flow of dialogue, the dramatist keeps the central conflict alive in the readers' minds even when the characters most affected by it are absent.

La Poncia's sea image occurs strategically in the drama, for it comes just before María Josefa makes her final appearance and before Adela's climactic confrontation with her mother. What García-Posada called "la polivalencia textual del símbolo" serves Lorca well at this crucial juncture in the action. When María Josefa enters singing a ditty beginning "Ovejita, niño mío, / vámonos a la orilla del mar" (1523), the word "mar" evokes important components of the human drama because of its association with key words such as "me escapé," "casarme," "varón" and "cruzar." In fact, María Josefa brings the water imagery close to the point of expressing the outcome of the conflict in the drama. "Vámonos a la orilla del mar" anticipates Adela's admission shortly thereafter—"El [Pepe] me lleva a los juncos de la orilla" (1528). Moreover, the express unreality of María Josefa's ditty ("y en la playa nos meteremos / en una choza de coral") underscores the idea that given the repressive emotional climate in which Adela lives, her desire to escape with a lover is to be frustrated.

Water imagery in the lines spoken by María Josefa in her final appearance strengthens the link between images related to regeneration and Bernarda's daughters by contrasting the expansive course of the generations with an allusion to the extreme isolation imposed on the daughters:

> . . . Como tengo el pelo blanco crees que no puedo tener crías y sí, crías y crías y crías. Este niño tendrá el pelo blanco y tendrá otro niño y éste otro, y todos con el pelo de nieve, seremos como las olas, una y otra y otra. Lluego nos sentaremos todos y tendremos el cabello blanco y seremos espuma. ¿Por qué aquí no hay espumas? (1524-1525)

Because of "la polivalencia del símbolo" ("espumas," in this instance), María Josefa's question ("¿Por qué aquí no hay espumas?") encapsules images of the whiteness of old age awaiting Bernarda's daughters and the sperm and regeneration that are absent from Bernarda's house. One could say that water imagery coming from María Josefa refers essentially to the continuance of life; but when it comes from Bernarda, it promises disaster. This is apparent when Lorca further expands water imagery as a means of expressing Bernarda's thoughts in the final moments of the drama. "Nos hundiremos todas en un mar de luto" (1532), says Bernarda, confirming earlier warnings of disaster conveyed through images associated with water ("[Martirio] Es un pozo de veneno. Ve que el Romano no es para ella y hundiría el mundo si estuviera en su mano [1521]; "La que tenga que ahogarse que se ahogue" [1528]; " . . . sin quererlo yo, a mí misma me ahoga" [1528]; "Hubiera volcado un río de sangre sobre su cabeza" [1531]).

The sea imagery we cited above in the passage spoken by María Josefa would seem to place Lorca's imagery in the tradition of Calderón's archetypal symbols as we observed them in commenting on Wilson's essay "The Four Elements in the Imagery of Calderón." However, Lorca's placement of the passage—i.e., after numerous and multi-faceted appearances of water imagery in other contexts—demonstrates how far Lorca has advanced. This is evident even in the short period of time that separates the completion of *Bodas de sangre*, *Doña Rosita* and *La casa de Bernarda Alba*. For example, although the moon and blood imagery of *Bodas de sangre* and the controlling "rosa mutabile" image of *Doña Rosita* are set in specific dramatic contexts, their effect lies mainly in their ability to make one feel the presence of an abstraction such as the concept of destiny. That is to say, although images of the moon, blood and the rose in the earlier plays are not static (primarily because they were able to assume *various* symbolic connotations), they nevertheless tend to evoke those specific connotations. Whereas in *La casa de Bernarda Alba*, Lorca has orchestrated the imagery continuities within dramatic contexts to such a high degree that while we receive images of heat and water, for example, our attention constantly remains focused on the unfolding drama; on the human conflict being acted out in Bernarda's house.

An element of fate hangs over Bernarda's house—a state of being that is strongly implied in such remarks as "Así pasó en casa de mi padre y en casa de mi abuelo" (1451); "Mi abuelo fue igual" (1452); "Pero las cosas se repiten. Y veo que todo es una terrible repetición. Y ella tiene el mismo sino de su madre y de su abuela" (1460); "¡Espejo de tus tías! (1469). But in the imagery used to describe this "cosmic" condition, Lorca sustains the human drama transpiring in a house individualized by its peculiar circumstances. When María Josefa says "seremos como las olas, una y otra y otra," her simile evolves naturally from the irony in her preceding words alluding to the sterility of life in Bernarda's house ("Como tengo el pelo blanco crees que no puedo tener crías, y sí, crías y crías y crías. Este niño tendrá el pelo blanco y tendrá otro niño y éste otro" [1524]).

The pervasive interplay between demands for silence and a desire for outburst also help make *La casa de Bernarda Alba* a dramatization of the desire to escape an oppressive reality. Silence in *La casa de Bernarda Alba* is either present, or, in its absence, demanded. As indicated in the playwright's opening stage directions—"Un gran silencio umbroso se extiende por la escena" (1439)—one of the first impressions we receive of Bernarda's house, and the one to which we return at the conclusion of the play, is that of silence. The word itself is introduced into the text by the character with whom it becomes closely associated ("¡Silencio!," demands Bernarda upon her first appearance. "Menos gritos y más obras" [1445]); and the play concludes with an emphatic reiteration of Bernarda's demand ("¿Me habéis oído? ¡Silencio, silencio, silencio he dicho! ¡Silencio!" [1532]). Further, the Bernarda-Adela conflict is expressed through a confrontation based on silence and outburst, making its presence felt even when María Josefa disturbs the household by escaping from her room and asking for her jewels and moire dress ("¡Calle usted, madre!" [1470], shouts Bernarda; to which María Josefa, responds: "No, no me callo"). Thus, through an exchange between a different mother and daughter, "silencio" articulates our perception of the growing tension in Bernarda's house and also prefigures a subsequent confrontation between a mother and daughter when Adela directly challenges Bernarda's authority. But it is silence as a character in the metaphorical language that attracts our attention in the study of imagery. The course of silence—when it is sustained, when it is broken, when it is demanded, when it is repelled—follows the course of the conflict.

Bernarda demands silence as a sign of her dominance. Adela and María Josefa seek to break silences and thereby signal their desire to escape. Silence and outbursts assume presences in the play. They appear and disappear in the context of conflictive moments. Sometimes they emanate from references to visible phenomena such as when Bernarda upbraids Angustias for having powdered her face on the day of her stepfather's funeral; when Adela is reprimanded for offering Bernarda a colorful fan at a time of mourning; or when Bernarda's daughters argue over the disappearance of a picture. But most often the silence-outburst continuity works at the subtextual level to enhance the drama. This is particularly evident in contexts pertaining to relationships between men and women. For example, when La Poncia tells Bernarda's daughters about her earliest relationship with her husband, Amelia interrupts: "Chisss... . ¡Que nos van a oír!" (1476). This call for silence has the effect of injecting Bernarda's presence into a light-hearted moment that momentarily breaks the gloom hovering over the house. Later, when La Poncia introduces the name of Pepe el Romano into her conversation with Adela, Bernarda's demand for silence makes its presence felt even more keenly in Adela's reaction ("¡Calla! . . . ¡Baja la voz!" [1480]) as well as in her emphatic "chitón" at the close of this sequence. Thus, even in Bernarda's absence, when the dialogue indicates that surface noises are to be driven away, one feels Bernarda controlling the action through an evocation of "¡Silencio!", her first utterance in the play.

The dynamics of the silence-outburst counterpoint are such that the level to which one is increased and the other decreased is an indication of the level of tension in the house at given moments in the drama. At the height of the argument over the disappearance of Angustias's picture of Pepe, Bernarda shouts: "¡Qué escándalo es este en mi casa y en el silencio del peso del calor!" (1492). Here we note that "silence," introduced in the context of the heat of summer, interlocks with the heat imagery to emit a ripple of sexual tension because of the nature of the argument among the daughters. Also, as the quarrel becomes more heated and Adela challenges Martirio's motive for taking the picture, the insistence upon holding one's tongue becomes more peremptory. "¡Calla," says Martirio to Adela, "y no me hagas hablar, que si hablo se van a juntar las paredes unas con otras de vergüenza!" (1494). By the forcefulness with which Martirio silences Adela, we can sense the extent to which Bernarda's demand for silence permeates the minds of her daughters. Further, by linking the silence-outburst continuity to the walls of the house, an image of shame insinuates itself into the mind of the reader and becomes more firmly entrenched when Bernarda reinforces a call for silence with another image suggesting isolation: "¡Silencio digo! . . . Pero todavía no soy anciana y tengo cinco cadenas para vosotras y esta casa levantada por mi padre para que ni las hierbas se enteren de mi desolación" (1495). The close association between "silencio," "calor," "paredes," and "desolación" increases our awareness of the power that "silencio" has for Bernarda and the intense desire for escape which it induces in her daughters. Bernarda herself alludes to this situation after the argument among her daughters when she tells La Poncia "Aquí no pasa nada. ¡Eso quisieras tú! Y si pasa algún día, estate segura que no traspasará las paredes" (1499). Here Bernarda "confirms" what the reader has come to feel: silence is Bernarda's strongest weapon for concealing the reality of any untoward occurrence.

The silence that the playwright decrees at the opening of Act II (as indicated in the stage direction "Al levantarse el telón hay un gran silencio" [1506]) relates directly to events in Act II and to what will occur in Act III. As we indicated above, at this point in the drama, Bernarda is determined to stifle any outburst that could be heard by the neighbors. Even in the momentary calm that has settled over the house at the beginning of Act III, Lorca does not let us forget the importance Bernarda placed on silence. This is evidenced first in the subtext of what Bernarda tells Angustias—". . . quiero buena fachada y armonía familiar" (1513)—and later more directly in a scene between Bernarda and La Poncia:

La Poncia: ¿Estás todavía aquí?
Bernarda: Disfrutando este silencio y sin lograr ver por parte alguna 'la cosa tan grande' que aquí pasa, según tú. (1518)

At the surface level in both instances there is a natural conversation, between mother and daughter and then between mistress and housekeeper; but both texts "say" that Bernarda is telling her listener that she relies on silence to control her household. One could say that at this moment in the drama, Bernarda is enjoying the company of silence as if it were a trusted companion helping her control the house. What is actually happening in the drama, therefore, is expressed through the silence-outburst continuity planted firmly in the dialogue.

Silence, with threats of having it disturbed and efforts to sustain it, has become so associated with Bernarda's position concerning the actions of her family that in effect it assumes the role of a character participating in human relationships. This is an aspect of the text that can be described in words similar to those used by Knight in speaking of the works of Shakespeare: i.e., the poetry becomes personified, expands and actively participates in shaping the events of the drama.[8] The Bernarda-silence motif is present to such an extent that it has become as "visible" as stillness or sadness in Maeterlinck's *Pelléas et Mélisande,* and Lorca does this while maintaining the dramatic pace. "¿Tú ves este silencio?", La Poncia asks Bernarda (1520). "Pues hay una tormenta en cada cuarto. El día que estallen nos barrerán a todos." The phrase "ves este silencio" is testimony to the "visibility" of "silencio" as the action unfolds. Lorca, like Maeterlinck, establishes a mood and evokes the presence of something intangible; but at this stage in the development of his craft, Lorca is able to take something like silence or its absence even further. He makes the metaphorical language expressive of a conflict becoming increasingly focused on Adela's outbursts pitted against her mother's insistence on silence; a conflict that reaches a climax conveyed first in terms of the sense of hearing ("Aquí se acabaron las voces de presidio" [1529]) and then in a direct action (indicated in a stage direction: "Adela arrebata un bastón a su madre y lo parte en dos" [1529]).

"Silence" as a means of establishing a mood or evoking a feeling has, of course, been used by other writers, not to mention Lorca himself. We recall Mariana Pineda's instinctive outburst in the presence of Fernando— "¡Qué silencio el de Granada! / Fija, detrás del balcón, hay puesta en mí una mirada (810)—and the absolute silence that closes the penultimate scene of *Bodas de sangre*, heightening the effect of the image of the beggar opening her cape in imitation of a bird of death. Silence plays a role in the fountain scene of Act II of *Pelléas et Mélisande* in which Mélisande says "Comme on est seul ici . . . On n'entend rien," and Pelléas responds "Il y a toujours un silence extraordinaire . . . On entendrait dormir l'eau . . ."[9] Mallarmé used "silence" to evoke a mood in "L'après-midi d'un faune"—"l'air assoupi de sommeils touffus;" "fier silence de midi."[10] One can also cite "silence" as a pervasive force in poems such as Rubén Darío's "Nocturno" ("Silencio de la noche, doloroso silencio / nocturno . . . ¿Por qué el alma tiembla de tal manera?")[11] or Valéry's "Le Cimetière marin" ("Ce toit tranquille, où marchent des colombes;" "Ô mon silence! . . . Édifice dans l'âme").[12] One also recalls the silence accompanying the fluttering of a butterfly when Juan Ramón Jiménez's Platero dies. In *La casa de Bernarda Alba*, however, images of silence and suppression of dissent interact with spontaneous outbursts and so express the ebb and flow of tension that erodes Bernarda's family. The completed dynamic interplay between silence and outbursts reflects the human drama which moves from repression to a desire to escape to a rebellion that leads eventually to further isolation and silence. This is a metaphorical process very similar to that which Brower applies to sequences of images in *The Tempest*, calling them arcs of metaphor perfectly related to dramatic movement.[13]

The dramatic impact felt by the reader of *La casa de Bernarda Alba* depends heavily on dialogue whose poetic nature consists primarily of imagery continuities that create a unified vision of an emotional climate within an enclosed space. As the heat of summer intensifies with a desire for relief, so does the emotional heat that seeks open doors and windows. Water provides not only immediate relief from the summer heat but also gradually becomes associated with liberation and a release of tension. Silence is demanded, broken and restored. The opposition between images of a cloistered house and the open countryside contribute to the feeling that an attempted escape from Bernarda's house can end only in tragedy. The metaphorical language in *La casa de Bernarda Alba* is so pervasive in the dialogue that one can say of this play that in it poetry and drama are one; that the imagery used to express the human relationships in the house of Bernarda Alba cannot be separated from the dramatic contexts in which the characters interact.

Notes

1. In *Federico García Lorca*, ed. Ildefonso-Manuel Gil (Madrid: Taurus, 1973), p.279.
2. *Federico García Lorca: poeta de intensidad*, 2nd ed. (Madrid: Editorial Gredos, 1970), pp.156-157.
3. *Historia del teatro español*, Vol. 2 (Madrid: Alianza Editorial, 1971), p.225.
4. *Lorca* (Paris: Éditions Gallimard, 1962), p.127.
5. *The Fields of Light* (New York: Oxford Univ. Press, 1962), p.120.
6. *The Human Image in Dramatic Literature* (New York: Doubleday Anchor, 1957), pp.xi-xii.
7. "La imagen poética de don Luis de Góngora," in *Obras completas*, ed. Arturo del Hoyo, 12th ed. (Madrid: Aguilar, 1966), p.68.
8. *The Shakesperian Tempest*, 3rd ed. (London: Methuen, 1960), p.257.
9. Maurice Maeterlinck, *Pelléas et Mélisande* (Paris: Fasquelle Editeurs, 1950), p.43.
10. "L'après-midi d'un faune," in *Selected Poems by Stéphane Mallarmé*, trans. C.F. MacIntyre (Berkeley, Univ. of California Press, 1957), pp.46,52.
11. "Nocturno," in *Antología / Rubén Darío*, p.157.
12. "Le Cimetière marin," in *Oeuvres*, Vol. I, ed. Jean Hytier (Paris: Éditions Gallimard, 1957), pp.147, 148.
13. *The Fields of Light*, p.108.

Conclusion

The dynamics of the imagery in the theater of Lorca follow a course of development that begin with his earliest plays. As we demonstrated with *La casa de Bernarda Alba*, the playwright finally accomplished such a high degree of fusion of metaphorical language and action that in his theater a new meaning is given to the expression poetic drama. Unlike Fergusson, who discusses Lorca's theater-poetry in terms of the overall conception of a play wherein a poetic effect is generated by transitions from one scene to another, we conclude that Lorca's poetic drama is the result of setting imagery continuities in dramatic contexts so that they enhance the dramatic movement of a play. We also conclude that Lorca's plays become less static as his career progresses; that the playwright never abandons lyrical elements from his earliest symbolist theater but rather places them more naturally in dramatic contexts; and that his control of metaphorical language helps the reader penetrate a character's feelings or an emotional climate without interrupting the flow of drama.

A large body of criticism pertaining to Lorquian imagery in the theater has focused on symbols as they relate to thematic oppositions, especially as between authority and individual liberty, and reality and fantasy. In our study, theme is important primarily as an organizer of imagery that fulfills its dramatic potential. In this context we have often noticed Lorca's use of the theme of the power of the imagination to lead characters to seek escape from confinement in their physical circumstances—a desire that leads Adela towards tragedy, Rosita further into illusion, Leonardo and La Novia into a dream-like world, Mariana Pineda into legend, and Perlimplín and Curianito deeper into imagination. Yet the focus of our attention has not been on thematic material but rather on the imagistic components of the plays and their role in the presentation of human drama. After closely examining the poetry in six plays by Lorca, spanning

The Dynamics of the Imagery in the Theater   205
of Federico Garcia Lorca

his dramatic output from his first play to his last completed work, we conclude that the course taken by a protagonist can be traced in images as poetic elements in sets of continuities that dramatize what is happening to that character. Lorquian imagery, therefore, goes beyond symbols and themes, because it is dynamic rather than static; it entertains a continuing symbiotic relationship with the unfolding drama.

As one follows continuities in the metaphorical language of *La casa de Bernarda Alba*, it becomes apparent that Lorca's affinities with past literary traditions and techniques have helped him accomplish this union of metaphorical language and drama. To fuse action and dialogue with the more inward situations of feeling that inhere in poetry, it seems to us that Lorca drew on the following resources: 1) the creation of layers of allusive and evocative images which characterized works by Symbolists and Modernistas such as Maeterlinck, Yeats, Verlaine, Marquina and Martínez Sierra, 2) the expansion of metaphor as demonstrated by Góngora and Calderón, 3) the use of songs, recalling especially the theater of Lope de Vega, as well as 4) lyric poetry and the traditional Spanish *romance*. By drawing on the resources of narrative poetry and the theater of the Golden Age, Lorca managed to grow beyond Symbolist theater; but he did not leave it completely behind. Instead, he found a way to mobilize continuities of metaphorical language without arresting the narrative line of his drama.

In his final play, *La casa de Bernarda Alba*, Lorca creates a tense atmosphere, evokes inner feelings and makes one sense the presence of isolation by permeating the text with a series of images associated with heat and silence. As one image follows another, we gradually approach a full realization of what a character is feeling. In other words, if we peel away the layers of related images, we expose the core of a feeling experienced by a character. This process can be traced back through images such as the flower that withers in *Doña Rosita*, blades and the moon that evoke the presence of death in *Bodas de sangre*; an inner-outer counterpoint in *Perlimplín*, the rain-tears continuity in *Mariana Pineda*, to images associated with dew, stars, flowers, light and darkness in *El maleficio de la mariposa*.

Looking back to *El maleficio de la mariposa*, we can observe that the spirit of Symbolism which pervades this play is absent from *La casa de Bernarda Alba*. Nevertheless, in Lorca's final drama there is the echo of a similarity between the way the playwright controls the heaven-earth continuity as it reflects the pull of reality on Curianito's imagination, and the manner in which Lorca orchestrates growing tensions in the house of Bernarda Alba. With each appearance of a heaven-earth opposition, we are reminded of a widening gap between Curianito's imagination and the reality that surrounds him. With each appearance of "heat" and "thirst" in *La casa de Bernarda Alba*, we are reminded of the mounting tension between Bernarda and her daughters.

Yet there is a fundamental difference between the plays: the images that evoke Curianito's idealized perception of love and beauty remain essentially static and descriptive, whereas in *La casa de Bernarda Alba*, an imagery continuity blends with thoughts and actions revealing changes in the developing human relationships. For example, as the heat of summer assumes the shape of the emotional heat of "un infierno" and then the sexual heat of "el caballo garañón," the characters move towards the breaking point in their conflictive situation. Thus Lorca goes well beyond Symbolism by leading imagery towards the fulfillment of its dramatic potential—leaving far behind the static presentation of tableaux in Maeterlinck's *Pelléas et Mélisande*. Whereas the accumulating images in the earlier plays may evoke an idea or frame an impression, in *La casa de Bernarda Alba*, Lorca has merged metaphorical language with the action. This began, of course, with his first play, but there we are treated only to brief glimpses of the technique of his dramatized imagery. By the time he came to write *La casa de Bernarda Alba*, long arcs of "dramatic" imagery criss-cross the whole play and flesh out the on-going human action.

By retracing the trajectory of Lorca's use of imagery in the theater, we conclude that the base of Lorca's poetic drama does not rest on dialogue interspersed with poetic elements nor on the mythical quality of the scenes, but rather on the control of metaphorical language within contexts of human drama.

In following the development of Lorca's dramatized imagery, we have observed the playwright's passing affinities with dramatists such as Maeterlinck, Yeats, Marquina, Martínez Sierra, Calderón and Lope de Vega; or with poets such as Góngora, Verlaine and Darío; not to mention the traditional Spanish *romance*. However, it is with originality that Lorca fuses poetic and dramatic techniques drawn from the past. This, in combination with his own poetic imagination, produces imagery continuities that express changing human relationships, thereby permitting us to call his theater poetic drama.

Biblgiography

Abel, Lionel. *Metatheater*. New York: Hill and Wang, 1964.

Alatorre, Margit Frenk. *Cancionero de romances viejos*. 2nd ed. México: Dirección General de Publicaciones, 1972.

Alborg, Juan Luis, Vol. I of *Historia de la literatura española*. 2nd ed. Madrid: Editorial Gredos, 1966.

Allen, Rupert C. *Psyche and Symbol in the Theater of Federico García Lorca*. Austin: Univ. of Texas Press, 1974.

___. *The Symbolic World of Federico García Lorca*. 1st ed. Albuquerque: Univ. of New Mexico Press, 1972.

Alonso, Amado. *Poesía y estilo de Pablo Neruda*. 3rd ed. Buenos Aires: Editorial Sudamericana, 1966.

Alonso, Dámaso. *Cuatro poetas españoles*. Madrid: Editorial Gredos, 1962.

___. Vol. I of *Góngora y el "Polifemo"*. 6th ed. Madrid: Editorial Gredos, 1974.

___. ed. *Soledades de Góngora*. Madrid: Revista de Occidente, 1927.

Anderson, Andrew A. "Some Shakespearean Reminiscences in García Lorca's Drama." *Comparative Literature Studies*, No. 2 Summer, 1985, 187-210.

___. "The Strategy of García Lorca's Dramatic Composition 1930-36." *Romance Quarterly*, 33 (1986), 211-224.

Anderson, Reed. *Federico García Lorca*. London: Macmillan, 1984.

Arias, Ricardo. *The Spanish Sacramental Plays*. Boston: Twayne, 1980.

Ayéndez Alder, Ruth. "Revisión crítica de *El maleficio de la mariposa*." *Hispanic Journal*, 6, No. 2 Spring, 1985, 149-163.

Babín, María Teresa. *Estudios lorquianos*. 1st ed. Barcelona: Colección Mente y Palabra, 1976.

___. "García Lorca, poeta del teatro." *Asomante*, 4, No. 2 (1948), 48-57.

Balakian, Anna. *The Symbolist Movement: A Critical Appraisal*. New York: New York Univ. Press, 1977.

Barnes, Robert. "The Fusion of Poetry and Drama in *Blood Wedding*." *Modern Drama*, 2, No. 4 (1960), 395-402.

Baudelaire, Charles. *Fleurs du Mal*. Paris: Éditions Gallimard et Librairie Générale Française, 1964.

___. *The Flowers of Evil*. Trans. Francis Duke, n.p.: Univ. of Virginia Press, 1961.

Bauer, Carlos, trans. *"The Public" and "Play Without a Title"*. By Federico García Lorca. New York: New Directions, 1983.

Belamich, André. *Lorca*. Paris: Éditions Gallimard, 1962.

Blume, Jaime. *Un prólogo y tres autores*. Santiago, Chile: Ediciones Aconcagua, 1977.

Bosch, Rafael. "El choque de imágenes como principio creador de García Lorca." *Revista Hispánica Moderna*, 30 Jan. 1964, 35-44.

Bowra, C.M. *The Heritage of Symbolism*. London: Macmillan, 1943.

Brenan, Gerald. *Historia de la literatura española*. Trans. Miguel de Amilibia. Buenos Aires: Editorial Losada, 1958.

Brooks, Cleanth and Heilman, Robert B. *Understanding Drama*. 3rd ed. New York: Holt, Rinehart and Winston, 1963.

___ and Warren, Robert Penn. *Understanding Poetry*. 3rd ed. New York: Holt, Rinehart and Winston, 1964.

Brower, Reuben Arthur. *The Fields of Light*. New York: Oxford Univ. Press, 1962.

Busette, Cedric. *Obra dramática de García Lorca*. Long Island City, N.Y.: Las Américas, 1971.

Byrd, Suzanne Wade. *García Lorca: "La Barraca" and the Spanish National Theater*. New York: Abra Ediciones, 1975.

Calderón de la Barca, Pedro. *El alcalde de Zalamea*. In *Obras completas*. Ed. Luis Astrana Marín, Madrid: Aguilar, 1951.

___. *El médico de su honra*. In *Obras completas*. Ed. Luis Astrana Marín. Madrid: Aguilar, 1951.

___. *La vida es sueño*, 8ª ed. Ed. Evangelina Rodríguez Cuadros. Colección Austral. Madrid: Espasa-Calpe, 1987.

___. *La vida es sueño: drama y auto sacramental*. Ed. José María Valverde. Barcelona: Editorial Planeta, S.A., 1981.

Campbell, Roy. *Lorca*. New York: Haskell House, 1970.

Cannon, Calvin. "The Imagery of Lorca's *Yerma*." *Modern Language Quarterly*, 21 (1960), 122-130.

___. "*Yerma* as Tragedy." *Symposium*, 16 Summer 1962, 85-93.

Cao, Antonio F. *Federico García Lorca y las vanguardias: hacia el teatro*. London: Tamesis, 1984.

Carrier, Warren, "Poetry in the Drama of Lorca." *Drama Survey*, 2, No. 3 Feb. 1963, 297-304.

Chapman, Hugh H., Jr. "Two Poetic Techniques: Lorca's *Romance de la luna, luna* and Goethe's *Erlkönig*." *Hispania*, No. 39 Dec. 1956, 450-455.

Chiari, Joseph. *Symbolisme from Poe to Mallarmé*. 2nd ed. New York: Gordian Press, 1970.

Chica-Salas, Susana. "Synge y García Lorca: aproximación de dos mundos poéticos." *Revista Hispánica Moderna*, 27, No. 2 abril de 1961, 128-137.

Cobb, Carl W. "Federico García Lorca and Juan Ramón Jiménez: The Question of Influences." *Tennessee Studies in Literature*, 15 (1970), 177-188.

Correa, Gustavo. "Honor, Blood, and Poetry in *Yerma*." Trans. Rupert C. Allen, Jr. *Tulane Drama Review*, 7, No. 2 Winter 1962, 96-110.

___. "El simbolismo de la luna en la poesía de Federico García Lorca." *Publications of the Modern Language Association*, 72, No. 5 Dec. 1957, 1060-84.

Darío, Rubén. In *Antología/Rubén Darío*. Ed. Carmen Ruiz Barrionuevo. Colección Austral (1987), Literatura. Madrid: Espasa-Calpe, 1992 (?).

___. In *Antología poética/Rubén Darío*. Ed. Arturo Torres Rioseco. Berkeley: Univ. Of California Press, 1949.

___. *Azul.../Cantos de vida y esperanza*. Ed. Álvaro Salvador. Colección Austral. Madrid: Espasa-Calpe, 1992.

____. "*Yerma*: estudios estilísticos." *Revista de las Indias*, 35, No. 109 (1949), 11-63.

De Long, Beverly J. "Sobre el desarrollo lorquiano del romance tradicional." *Hispanófila*, No. 35 Jan. 1969, 51-62.

Del Hoyo, Arturo, ed. *Obras completas*. By Federico García Lorca. 12th ed. Madrid: Aguilar, 1966.

Díaz-Plaja, Guillermo. *Federico García Lorca*. 4th ed. Mardid: Espasa-Calpe, 1968.

Disandro, Carlos A. *Tres poetas españoles*. La Plata, Argentina: Ediciones Hosteria Volante, 1967.

Durán, Manuel, ed. *Lorca: A Collection of Critical Essays*. Englewood Cliffs, N.J.: Prentice Hall, 1962.

Edwards, Gwynne. *Lorca, The Theater Beneath the Sand*. London: Marion Boyars, 1980.

Eich, Christoph. *Federico García Lorca: poeta de intensidad*. 2nd ed. Madrid: Editorial Gredos, 1970.

Engelberg, Edward, ed. *The Symbolist Poem*. New York: E.P. Dutton, 1967.

Entwistle, William J. *European Balladry*. Oxford: Clarendon Press, 1939.

Feal Deibe, Carlos. *Eros y Lorca*. 1st ed. Barcelona: Editora y Distribuidora Hispano Americana, 1973.

Fergusson, Francis. "*Don Perlimplín*: Lorca's Theater-Poetry." *Kenyon Review*, 17, No. 3 Summer 1955, 337-348.

____. *The Human Image in Dramatic Literature*. New York: Doubleday Anchor Books, 1957.

Ferreres, Rafael. *Verlaine y los modernistas españoles*. Madrid: Editorial Gredos, 1975.

Fogelquist, Doñald F. *Juan Ramón Jiménez*. Boston: Twayne, 1976.

Frazier, Brenda. *La mujer en el teatro de Federico García Lorca*. Madrid: Playor, 1973.

Fulbeck, John. "A Comparative Study of Poetic Elements in Selected Plays by John Millington Synge and by Federico García Lorca." *Disseration Abstract* 21 (1961), 1564-65.

García Lorca, Federico. *Amor de don Perlimplín con Belisa en su jardín.* In *Obras completas.* 12th ed. Ed. Arturo del Hoyo. Madrid: Aguilar, 1966.

___. *Bodas de sangre.* In *Obras completas.* 12th ed. Ed. Arturo del Hoyo. Madrid: Aguilar, 1966.

___. *La casa de Bernarda Alba.* In *Obras completas.* 12th ed. Ed. Arturo del Hoyo. Madrid: Aguilar, 1966.

___. "Charla sobre el teatro." In *Obras completas.* 12th ed. Ed. Arturo del Hoyo. Madrid: Aguilar, 1966.

___. *Deep Song and Other Prose.* Ed. and trans. Christopher Maurer. New York: New Directions, 1980.

___. *Doña Rosita la soltera o El lenguage de las flores.* In *Obras completas.* 12th ed. Ed. Arturo del Hoyo. Madrid: Aguilar, 1966.

___. "La imagen poética de don Luis de Góngora." In *Obras completas.* 12th ed. Ed. Arturo del Hoyo. Madrid: Aguilar, 1966.

___. "Imaginación, inspiración, evasión." In *Obras completas.* 12th ed. Ed. Arturo del Hoyo. Madrid: Aguilar, 1966.

___. In "Lorca Discusses His Plays." Trans. Rupert C. Allen, Jr., Ed. Barnard Hewitt. *Tulane Drama Review,* 7, No. 2 Winter 1962, 111-119.

___. *El maleficio de la mariposa.* In *Obras completas.* 12th ed. Ed. Arturo del Hoyo. Madrid: Aguilar, 1966.

___. *Mariana Pineda.* In *Obras completas.* 12th ed. Ed. Arturo del Hoyo. Madrid: Aguilar, 1966.

García Lorca, Francisco. Introduction to *Five Plays--Comedies and Tragicomedies.* By Federico García Lorca. Trans. James Graham-Lujan and Richard L. O'Connell. New York: New Directions, 1963.

___. *In the Green Morning: memories of Federico.* Trans. Christopher Maurer. New York: New Directions, 1986.

García-Posada, Miguel. *Federico García Lorca.* Madrid: Edaf, D.L., 1979.

___. *Lorca: interpretación de "Poeta en Nueva York".* Madrid: Akal Editor, 1981.

___. ed. *Teatro,* I. By Federico García Lorca. Madrid: Akal Editor, 1980.

Gaskell, Ronald. "Theme and Form: Lorca's *Blood Wedding*." *Modern Drama*, 5 (1963), 431-439.

Gassner, John. *Form and Idea in Modern Theater*. New York: The Dryden Press, 1956.

Gates, Eunice Joiner. "Góngora and Calderón." *Hispanic Review*, V (1937), 241-258.

___. "The Metaphors of Luis de Góngora." *Publications of Univ. of Penn.* 25 (1933), 1-190.

Gerstinger, Heinz. *Pedro Calderón de la Barca*. Trans. Diana Stone Peters. New York: Frederich Ungar, 1973.

Gheorghe, Ion. *Les images du Poète et de la Poésie dans l'oeuvre de Valéry*. Paris: Lettres Modernes, 1977.

Gil, Ildefonso-Manuel. *Federico García Lorca*. Madrid: Taurus Ediciones, 1973.

Giordano, Enrique. *La teatralización de la obra drámatica*. México, D.F.: Premia Editora, 1982.

Gomez Lance, Betty R. "Muerte y vida en el drama de Federico García Lorca." *Hispania*, 43 (1960), 376-377.

Góngora, Luis de. *Soledades*. In *Soledades de Góngora*. Ed. Dámaso Alonso. Madrid: Revista de Occidente, 1927.

___. *Sonetos completos*. Ed. Biruté Ciplijauskaité. Madrid: Editorial Castalia, 1969.

González del Valle, Luis. *La tragedia en el teatro de Unamuno, Valle-Inclán y García Lorca*. New York: Eliseo Torres and Sons, 1975.

Greenfield, Sumner M. "Poetry and Stagecraft in *La casa de Bernarda Alba*." *Hispania*, 38, No. 4 (1955), 456-461.

Gullon, Ricardo. "Motivos en la poesía de Lorca." *Insula*, a. IX, No. 103 1º de julio de 1954.

Higginbotham, Virginia. *The Comic Spirit of Federico García Lorca*. Austin: Univ. of Texas Press, 1976.

___. "Lorca's Soundtrack: Music in the Structure in His Poetry and Plays," in *"Cuando yo me muera...": Essays in Memory of Federico García Lorca*. Ed. C. Brian Morris. Lanham, Md.: University Press of America, 1988.

Honig, Edwin. *García Lorca*. Norfolk, Conn.: New Directions, 1944.

Houston, John Porter. *French Symbolism and the Modernist Movement.* Baton Rouge: Lousiana State Univ. Press, 1980.

Jiménez, Juan Ramón. In *Segunda antolojía poética (1898-1918).* Madrid: Espasa-Calpe, 1959.

Jones, R.O. *A Literary History of Spain: The Golden Age Prose and Poetry.* London: Ernest Benn, 1971.

___. ed. *Studies in Spanish Literature of the Golden Age Presented to Edward M. Wilson.* London: Tamesis, 1973.

Keats, John. In *Complete Poems/John Keats.* Ed. Jack Stillinger. Cambridge, Mass.: The Belknap Press of Harvard Univ. Press, 1982.

Kermode, Frank. *Romantic Image.* New York: Vintage Books (Knopf and Random House), 1957.

Klein, Dennis A. *"Blood Wedding," "Yerma," and "The House of Bernarda Alba:" García Lorca's Tragic Trilogy.* Boston: Twayne Publishers, 1991.

Knapp, Bettina. *Maurice Maeterlinck.* Boston: Twayne, 1975.

Knight, G. Wilson. *The Crown of Life.* New York: Barnes and Noble, 1964.

___. *Poets of Action.* London: Methuen, 1967.

___. *The Shakespearian Tempest.* 3rd ed. London: Methuen, 1960.

___. *The Wheel of Fire.* 4th ed. London: Methuen, 1965.

Laffranque, Marie. *Les idées esthétiques de Federico García Lorca.* Paris: Centre de recherches hispaniques: Institut d'études hispaniques, 1967.

Lara Pozuelo, Antonio. *El adjetivo en la lírica de Federico García Lorca.* Barcelona: Editorial Ariel, 1973.

Laurenti, Joseph and Siracusa, Joseph. *The World of Federico García Lorca: A General Bibliographic Survey.* Metuchen, N.J.: The Scarecrow Press, 1974.

Lawler, James R. *Form and Meaning In Valéry's "Le Cimetière marin".* Carlton: Melbourne Univ. Press, 1960.

Lázaro Carreter, Fernando. "Apuntes sobre el teatro de García Lorca." In *Federico Garica Lorca.* Ed. Ildefonso-Manuel Gil. Madrid: Taurus Ediciones, 1973.

Leighton, Charles H. "The Treatment of Time and Space in the *Romancero gitano.*" *Hispania* No. 43 Sept. 1960, 378-83.

Lima, Robert. *The Theater of García Lorca.* New York: Las Américas, 1963.

Londré, Felicia Hardison. *Federico García Lorca.* New York: Frederich Ungar, 1984.

McGarry, Francis de Salas, Sister. *The Allegorical and Metaphorical Language in the Autos Sacramentales of Calderón.* Wash., D.C.: The Catholic Univ. of America, 1937.

Machado, Antonio. *Poesías completas.* 3rd ed. Madrid: Espasa-Calpe, S.A., 1977.

Maeterlinck, Maurice. *The Blue Bird.* Trans. Alexander Teixeira de Mattos. New York: Dodd, Mead and Co., 1965.

___. *Pelléas et Mélisande.* Paris: Fasquelle Éditeurs, 1950.

Mallarmé, Stéphane. In *Selected Poems by Stéphane Mallarmé.* Trans. C.F. MacIntyre, Berkeley: Univ. of California Press, 1957.

Marquina, Eduardo. *La ermita, la fuente y el río.* In *En Flandes se ha puesto el sol/La ermita, la fuente y el río.* Ed. Beatriz Hernanz Angulo. Clásicos madrileños, 13 Madrid: Editorial Castalia: Comunidad de Madrid, 1996.

Martínez-Bonati, Félix. *Fictive Discourse and the Structures of Literature.* Trans. (with the author's collaboration) Philip W. Silver. Ithaca, N.Y.: Cornell Univ. Press, 1981.

Martínez Nadal, Rafael. *"El público". Amor, teatro y caballos en la obra de Federico García Lorca.* Oxford: Dolphin, 1970.

___. *"El público." Amor y muerte en la obra de Federico García Lorca.* 3ª ed., ampliada e ilustrada. Madrid: Hiperión, 1988.

Martínez Sierra, Gregorio. *Canción de cuna.* Ed. Aurelio M. Espinosa. Boston: D.C. Heath, 1921.

___. *The Cradle Song and Other Plays.* Trans. John Garrett Underhill. New York: E.P. Dutton, 1929.

___. *Teatro de ensueño.* Madrid: Renacimineto, S.A., 1911.

Menéndez Pidal, Ramón. *Flor nueva de romances viejos.* 16th ed. Buenos Aires: Espasa Calpe Argentina, 1967.

___. ed. *Flor nueva de romances que recogió de la tradición antigua y moderna R. Menéndez Pidal.* Madrid: Tip. de la "Revista de archivos, bibliotecas y museos," 1928.

Moore, John Rees. *Masks of Love and Death: Yeats as Dramatist.* Ithaca, N.Y.: Cornell Univ. Press, 1971.

Morris, C. Brian. *García Lorca: "La casa de Bernada Alba."* London: Grant & Cutler in association with Tamesis Books, 1990.

Nice, W.N. *The Poetic Theory of Paul Valéry.* 2nd ed. London: Leicester Univ. Press, 1970.

Nickel, Catherine. "The Function of Language in García Lorca's *Doña Rosita la soltera.*" *Hispania,* 66, No. 4 Dec., 1983, 522-531.

Nourissier, François. *F. García Lorca, dramaturge.* Paris: l'Arche, éditeur, 1955.

O'Connor, Patricia W. *Gregorio and María Martínez Sierra.* Boston: Twayne, 1977.

Oliver, William I. "The Trouble With Lorca." *Modern Drama,* 7, No. 1 May 1964, 2-15.

Onís, Federico de. *Antología de la poesía española e hispanoamericana.* New York: Las Americas, 1961.

Pabst, W. *La creación gongorina en los poemas "Polifemo" y "Soledades".* Trans. Nicolás Marín. Madrid: Imprenta Aguirre, 1966.

Palley, Julian. "Archetypal Symbols in *Bodas de sangre.*" *Hispania,* 50, No. 1 March 1967, 74-79.

Pattison, Walter T. *Representative Spanish Authors,* Vol. I. New York: Oxford Univ. Press, 1954.

Petersen, Fred. "La vida corta pero eterna de Antonio el Gitano." *Hispanófila,* 28 (1966), 39-47.

Pownall, David E. Vol. 3 of *Articles on Twentieth Century Literature: An Annotated Bibliography 1954-1970.* New York: Kraus-Thompson Organization, 1973.

Praz, Mario. *The Romantic Agony.* Trans. Angus Davidson. London: Oxford Univ. Press, 1933.

Ramos-Gil, Carlos. *Claves líricas de García Lorca.* Madrid: Aguilar, 1967.

___. *Ecos antiguos, estructuras nuevas, y mundo primario de la lírica de Lorca.* Bahia Blanca: Cuadernos del Sur (Univ. Nacional del Sur), 1967.

___. "Hacia una revisión del teatro lorquiano." *Revista de Literatura*, XLII, N°. 83 Enero-Junio de 1980.

Raymond, Marcel. *From Baudelaire to Surrealism.* Trans. G.M., New York: Wittenborn, Schultz, Inc., 1950.

Robertson, Sandra Cary. *Lorca, Alberti, and the Theater of Popular Poetry.* New York: P. Lang, 1991.

Rubia Barcia, J. "El realismo 'mágico' de *La casa de Bernarda Alba*." *Revista Hispánica*, 31 (1965), 385-398.

Ruiz Ramón, Francisco. Vol. 2 of *Historia del teatro español.* Madrid: Alianza Editorial, 1971.

Sage, J.W. *Lope de Vega: "El caballero de Olmedo".* London: Grant and Cutler, in association with Tamesis, 1974.

Scarpa, Roque Esteban. *El dramatismo en la poesía de Federico García Lorca.* Santiago de Chile: Editorial Universitaria, 1961.

Schevill, Rudolph. *The Dramatic Art of Lope de Vega.* Berkeley: Univ. of California Press, 1918; Revised, 1964, by Russell and Russell, New York.

Shakespeare, William. *Hamlet.* In Vol. II of *The Tragedies of Shakespeare.* New York: Random House, in The Modern Library, n.d.

___. *The Tempest.* Ed. Alfred Harbage. New York: Appleton-Century-Crofts, 1946.

Sharp, Thomas F. "The Mechanics of Lorca's Drama in *La casa de Bernarda Alba*." *Hispania*, 44 (1961), 230-233.

Silver, Philip W. *La casa de Anteo.* Versión española de Salustiano Masó. Madrid: Taurus Ediciones, 1985.

Skloot, Robert. "Theme and Image in Lorca's *Yerma*." *Drama Survey*, 5 Summer 1966, 151-161.

Symons, Arthur. *The Symbolist Movement in Literature.* Rev. ed. 1919. New York: E.P. Dutton, 1958.

Touster, Eva K. "Thematic Patterns in Lorca's *Blood Wedding*." *Modern Drama*, 7, No. 1 May 1964, 16-27.

Trend, J.B. *Lorca and the Spanish Poetic Tradition*. New York: Russell and Russell, 1971.

Valbuena Prat, Angel. Vol. II of *Historia de la literatura española*. 8th ed. Barcelona: Editorial Gustavo Gili, 1968.

Valéry, Paul. Vol. I of *Oeuvres*. Ed. Jean Hytier. Paris: Éditions Gallimard, 1957.

Vega, Lope de. *El caballero de Olmedo*. Ed. Francisco Rico. 6th ed. Madrid: Ediciones Cátedra, 1985.

___. *Peribáñez y el Comendador de Ocaña*. In Vol. II of *Comedias*. Ed. Luis Guarner. Barcelona: Editorial Iberia, 1955.

Verlaine, Paul. *Oeuvres poétiques complètes*. Ed. Jacques Borel. Paris: Éditions Gallimard, 1962.

Villegas, Juan. "El leitmotiv del caballo en *Bodas de sangre*." *Hispanófila*, No. 29 Jan. 1967, 21-36.

Wardropper, Bruce W. "Poetry and Drama in Calderón's *El médico de su honra*." *Romanic Review*, 49 (1958), 3-11.

___, ed. *Critical Essays on the Theater of Calderón*. New York: N.Y. Univ. Press, 1965.

Wheelwright, Philip. *Metaphor and Reality*. Bloomington: Indiana Univ. Press, 1962.

Williams, Oscar, ed. *Immortal Poems of the English Language*. New York: Washington Square Press, Inc., 1960.

Wilson, Edward M. "The Four Elements in the Imagery of Calderón." *Modern Language Review*, XXXI (1936), 34-47.

___. *Spanish and English Literature of the 16th and 17th Centuries*. Cambridge: Cambridge Univ. Press, 1980.

___, trans. *The Solitudes of Don Luis de Góngora*. Cambridge: The Minority Press, 1931.

Worth, Katherine. *The Irish Drama of Europe from Yeats to Beckett*. Atlantic Heights, N.J.: Humanities Press, 1978.

Xirau, Ramón. "La relación metal-muerte en los poemas de García Lorca." *Nueva Revista de Filología Hispánica*, 7 (1953), 364-371.

Yeats, W.B. *Ideas of Good and Evil*. New York: Russell& Russell, 1967.

___. *The Land of Heart's Desire*. In *The Collected Plays of W.B. Yeats*, Revised Edition. New York: Macmillan, 1953.

___. *The Shadowy Waters.* In *The Collected Plays of W.B. Yeats*, Revised Edition. New York: Macmillan, 1953.

Young, David. *The Heart's Forest.* New Haven: Yale Univ. Press, 1972.

Young, Howard T. *The Line in the Margin.* Madison, Wisconsin: The Univ. of Wisconsin Press, 1980.

Zardoya, Concha. "*Mariana Pineda*, romance trágico de la libertad." *Revista Hispánica Moderna*, 34 (1968), 471-497.

Zdenek, Joseph W., ed. *The World of Nature in the Works of Federico García Lorca.* n.p." Winthrop Studies on Major Modern Writers, 1980.

Ziomek, Henryk. "El simbolismo del blanco en *La casa de Bernarda Alba* y en *La dama del alba.*" *Symposium*, 24, No. 1 (1970), 81-85.

Index

"À Clymène" (Verlaine) 59-60
Abel, Lionel 83
El alcalde de Zalamea (Calderón) 134
Allen, Rupert C. 44-45
Alonso, Amado 9
Alonso, Dámaso xi, 7, 9
Amor de don Perlimplín con Belisa en su jardín (Lorca) vi, x, 11, 29, 110-125, 127, 134, 146, 154, 162, 166, 180, 205; imagery continuities in 110, 113, 116, 117, 121, 125; key images in: outer-inner, body-soul 112-114, 116-117, 118-119, 120, 121-122, 124-125, violence, 114-115, 120; metaphorical continuities in 112-113, 114, 117, 120, 121-122, 125; metaphorical language in 110, 112, 114, 115-116, 117, 120, 121, 122, 125; *romances* in 110, 124, 125, 127; songs in 29,118-122, 125; and traditional ballads 11, 28, 111, 123-124; and traditional songs 29, 110-111, 117-118, 119, 124-125, 127, 146; and traditional Spanish *romances* 110-111, 122, 127
Anderson, Andrew A. 127,128
Anderson, Reed xviin28
"El año lírico" (Darío) 72
"L'après-midi d'un faune" (Mallarmé) 168,202
"Ariettes oubliées" (Verlaine) 83,121
"Art poétique" (Verlaine) 23, 77-78
Así que pasen cinco años (Lorca) 127
"Autre Éventail" (Mallarmé) 90
"Autumnal" (Darío) 90
Babín, María Teresa xviin28, 49n6

ballads ix, xi, xii, xiv, 10, 11, 12, 13, 19, 20, 27, 28, 29, 80 ,94, 98-99, 111, 122, 124, 128, 146-147, 151, 171, 180; and Lorca ix, xi, xii, xiv, 10, 11, 12, 13, 18-19, 20, 27, 28, 29, 94, 98-99, 111, 128, 146-147, 151, 171, 180; traditional ballads and *Amor de don Perlimplín con Belisa en su jardín* 11, 28, 111, 123-124, and *Bodas de sangre* 12, 27-28, 146-147, 151, and *La casa de Bernarda Alba* ix-x, and *Doña Rosita la soltera* 10, 171, 173, 180, and *El maleficio de la mariposa* xii, 28, and *Mariana Pineda* xii, 10, 11, 29, 80-81, 94, 98-99, 124, 171, 173; *See also romances* and traditional Spanish *romances*

Barnes, Robert xiv

La Barraca xi, xiii, 14, 128, 147

Baudelaire, Charles 5, 9, 59, 72; "Car Lesbos" 59; "Correspondances" 72; *Fleurs du Mal* 78n9, 79n22

Belamich, André xviin27, 49n2, 185

"La Belle Dame sans Merci" (Keats) 52, 70

Benavente, Jacinto 6

Blake, William 22; "The Sick Rose" 22

The Blue Bird (Maeterlinck) 17, 18, 54, 57, 58, 59, 72, 76, 133; and *Bodas de sangre* 133; and *El maleficio de la mariposa* 17, 18, 54, 57, 58, 59, 72, 76; and *Mariana Pineda* 17

Bodas de sangre (Lorca) vi, vii, xiii, xiv, 4, 12, 13, 14, 18, 20, 24, 26, 27, 28, 30, 31, 33, 42, 43, 44, 45, 47, 48, 127-156, 159, 162, 166, 174, 180, 182, 198, 202, 205; imagery continuities in 34, 47, 128, 129, 133, 135, 140-141, 142, 143, 146, 153; key images in: blades 129-131, 135, 142, 153, 155, 156, blood 48, 136, 138-142, 149-150, 154-156, 198, flowers 131-132, 153, heat (and passion) 138, 141, 146, 149, horse 44-45, 47, 135, 143-146, 147, 151-152, light and darkness 33, 128, 132-133, 135; metaphorical continuities in 26, 28, 132, 150; metaphorical language in 127, 129, 132, 133, 138-139, 142, 144, 146, 147, 150, 151, 152, 153, 154, 182; moon in 132-134, 135, 150, 153, 198; *nana* in 13, 45, 47, 139, 140, 141, 143-145, 146, 147-148, 149, 150, 152, 153, 174; *romances* in 129, 143, 146, 151, 152, 154, 156; songs in xiii, 14, 128, 139, 143, 146-150, 155; and traditional ballads 12, 27-28, 146-147, 151; and traditional songs 13-14, 30, 128, 146, 147, 148, 150,156; and traditional Spanish *romances* 128, 146, 151-152, 156, 174

Bowra, C.M. 2

Brower, Reuben Arthur viii, ix, x, 33, 132, 146, 157n3, 160, 175, 178, 185, 191, 202

El burlador de Sevilla (Tirso de Molina) 147

El caballero de Olmedo (Lope de Vega) xiii, 13, 30, 96, 98, 111, 118, 147, 162, 176, 177-178

Calderón de la Barca, Pedro vi, xii, xiii-xiv, 1, 13, 14-16, 29, 31-34, 52, 112, 128, 132, 133, 134, 136, 137, 139, 141, 142, 156, 160, 161, 162, 164, 174, 182, 186, 198, 205, 206; *El alcalde de Zalamea* 134; *El mágico prodigioso* 52; *El médico de su honra* 15, 31, 136-137, 162, 174-175; *La vida es sueño* xiv, 14, 32, 164, 183n5; *La vida es sueño: auto sacramental* 14-15, 33, 133, 141, 142

"Canción de una gentil dama y un rústico pastor" (anon.) 122-123

Cannon, Calvin xv, 41-42

Cao, Antonio F. 46, 47

"Car Lesbos" (Baudelaire) 59

La casa de Bernarda Alba (Lorca) vi, vii, ix, x, xiii, 1, 2, 4, 14, 15, 20, 21, 30, 31, 42, 43, 46, 47, 48, 127, 159, 184-203, 204, 205, 206; imagery continuities in 48, 184, 185, 186, 187, 198, 203, 206; key images in: heat-relief 186, 187-193, 194, 196-198, 200, 203, imprisonment (stasis)-regeneration 186, 187, 193-196, 197, 200, silence-outburst 186, 187, 199-202, 203; metaphorical language in 184, 185, 186, 188, 189, 190, 191, 192, 193, 196, 199, 202, 203, 204, 205, 206; songs in xiii, 191-193, 195; and traditional ballads ix-x; and traditional songs ix-x, xiii, 14, 30, 186, 205; and traditional Spanish *romances* 186, 205

Cervantes Saavedra, Miguel de 13

"Chanson d'Automne" (Verlaine) 73

Chiari, Joseph 3, 6, 20

Le Cimetière marin" (Valéry) 23, 202

"Clair de Lune" (Verlaine) 68, 69, 132

Comedia sin título (Lorca) 127

Correa, Gustavo 49n6

"Correspondances" (Baudelaire) 72

"Crépuscule du soir mystique" (Verlaine) 89
Cuento de labios en flor (Martínez Sierra) 84, 132
Darío, Rubén 4, 6, 7, 67, 70, 72, 90, 134, 202; "El año lírico" 72; "Autumnal" 90; "Dice Mía" 70; "Divina Psiquis" 70; "Ite, missa est" 70; "Nocturno" 202; "Yo soy aquel . . ." 67
"Dice "Mía" (Darío) 70
Disandro, Carlos A. X
"Divina Psiquis" (Darío) 70
Doña Rosita la soltera (Lorca) vi, x, 10, 20, 21, 24, 25, 33, 42, 46, 159-182, 198, 205; imagery continuities in 163, 164; key images in: flowers 160,161, 162, 163-165, 166-170,171-174, 175-182, rose 159, 160-162, 163, 164, 165-168, 169, 170, 171, 173, 174, 176, 178, 179-180, 181, 198; metaphorical continuities in 33, 160, 173, 175, 180; metaphorical language in 20, 21, 33, 159, 160, 163, 165, 168, 171, 172, 173, 174, 175, 177, 178, 180, 182; romances in 21, 160, 170, 171, 172, 173, 174, 176, 179, 180; songs in 169, 176-177; and traditional ballads 10, 171, 173, 180; and traditional songs 160,176,177; and traditional Spanish romances 21, 170-171, 174, 180
el duende 6; duendes in Amor de don Perlimplín con Belisa en su jardín 116, 117
Edwards, Gwynne 15
Eich, Christoph 184
Engelberg, Edward 5
"En la muerte de tres hijas del Duque de Feria" (Góngora) 85-86
"En sourdine" (Verlaine) 54
Entwistle, William J. 11, 29
La ermita, la fuente y el río (Marquina) 4, 21, 84, 85, 97, 102, 111, 118, 121, 156
Espronceda, José de 52; El estudiante de Salamanca 52
El estudiante de Salamanca (Espronceda) 52
Fergusson, Francis 11, 111, 185, 204
Ferreres, Rafael 6
Fleurs de Mal (Baudelaire) 78n9, 79n22; "Car Lesbos" 59; "Correspondances" 72

Fuenteovejuna (Lope de Vega) 111, 118, 147

García Lorca, Federico: and *el duende* 6; and Golden Age vi, ix, xi, xii-xiii, xiv, 1, 12-13, 14, 15, 80, 125, 127, 128, 132, 143, 147, 148, 156, 160, 205, (*See also* Golden Age); and Góngora vi, ix, xi-xii, 1, 7-10, 12, 14, 15, 24-27, 51, 60, 85, 87, 154, 160, 186, 205, 206; (*See also* Góngora); and imagery (*See* imagery); and metaphorical language xii, xv, , 8, 12, 14, 15, 16, 31, 40, 44, 48, 65, 94, 99, 104, 125, 127, 129, 132, 138-139, 142, 146, 147, 151, 152, 154, 159, 160, 165, 170, 174, 175, 180, 182, 185, 188, 189, 191, 192, 193, 199, 202, 204, 205, 206; and *romances* 11, 30, 44, 94, 97, 98, 101, 102, 104, 105, 118, 129, 180, (*See also* traditional Spanish *romances* under *romances*); and traditional songs xiii, 12, 13, 14, 30, 97-98, 119; (*See also* songs); and Symbolism xi, 1, 2, 5, 6, 12, 20, 21, 22, 27, 73, 87, 90, 108, 111, 132, 136, 165, 168, 206, (*See also* Symbolism); and Symbolist imagery ix, 20, 22, 51, 58, 59, 68, 77, 83, 87, 89, 90, 110, 116, 119, 124, 132, 133, 134, 156, 159, 165, 182, (*See also* Symbolist imagery); and Symbolist poetry x, xiv, 1, 4, 6, 7, 10, 18, 20, 51, 54, 77, 111, 128, 132, 186, (*See also* Symbolist poetry); and Symbolist theater x, 1, 2, 4, 10, 18, 19, 21, 22, 42, 45, 51, 55, 60, 65, 77, 87, 97, 132, 156, 186, 205, (*See also* Symbolist theater); and Symbolist works 53, 58, 80, 84, (*See also* Symbolist works); and Symbolist writers 62, 70, (*See also* Symbolist writers); and Symbolists xi, 2, 4, 6, 19, 20, 22, 52, 64, 156, 205, (*See also* Symbolists); and traditional Spanish *romances* 80, 97, 106, 108, 122, 127, 151, 152, 156, 170, 180, 186, 205, 206, (*See also romances*); works (*For the following works, see individual titles*): *Amor de don Perlimplín con Belisa en su jardín, Bodas de sangre, La casa de Bernarda Alba, Comedia sin título, Doña Rosita la soltera*, "La imagen poética de don Luis de Góngora", *El maleficio de la mariposa, Mariana Pineda, Poeta en Nueva York, El público, Romancero gitano, Yerma*

García Lorca, Francisco 46

García-Posada, Miguel x, xviin27, 4, 10, 13, 14, 15, 21, 28, 44, 48, 136, 197

Gates, Eunice Joiner 9,15

Golden Age vi, ix, xi, xii-xiii, xiv, 1, 12-13, 14, 15, 80, 125, 127, 128, 132, 143, 147, 148, 156, 160, 205; and Lorca (*See* García Lorca, Federico)

Góngora, Luis de vi, ix, xi-xii, xiii, 1, 7-10, 12, 14, 15, 24-27, 51, 60, 61, 68, 85-86, 87, 92, 115, 154, 160, 186, 205, 206; "En la muerte de tres hijas del Duque de Feria" 85-86; and Lorca (*See* García Lorca, Federico); *Soledades* 9, 15, 25, 61, 115; "Soledad primera" 60, 61, 92; "Soledad segunda" 8; *See also* "La imagen poética de don Luis de Góngora"

González del Valle, Luis xviin28

Greenfield, Sumner M. xviin27

Guillén, Jorge 6

"Hacia un ocaso radiante" (A. Machado) 90

Hamlet (Shakespeare) 96

"Hérodiade" (Mallarmé) 71

"L'Heure du berger" (Verlaine) 92

Higginbotham, Virginia 46, 48

Honig, Edwin 15

Houston, John Porter 55

"La imagen poética de don Luis de Góngora" (Lorca) xi, 34n10, 7, 10, 35n29, 35n30, 36n45, 80, 85, 154, 167, 183n6, 186

imagery: continuities 31, 33, 34, 44, 47, 48, 51, 52, 53, 63, 65, 71-72, 81-83, 87, 89, 91, 93, 96, 98, 101, 110, 113, 117, 121, 125, 128, 129, 133, 135, 140-141, 142, 143, 146, 153, 163, 164, 174, 184, 185, 186, 187 198, 203, 204, 205, 206; in *Amor de don Perlimplín con Belisa en su jardín* 110, 113, 116, 117, 121, 125; in *Bodas de sangre* 34, 47, 128, 129, 133, 135, 140-141, 142, 143, 146, 153; in *La casa de Bernarda Alba* 48, 184, 185, 186, 187, 198, 203, 206; in *Doña Rosita la soletera* 163, 164; in *El maleficio de la mariposa* 51, 52, 53, 63, 65, 71-72; in *Mariana Pineda* 47, 81-83, 87, 89, 91, 93, 96, 98, 101; expanding images 7, 8-9, 25, 27, 32, 33, 51, 60-61, 85-86, 88, 116, 136-137, 188, 193, 198; key images in plays by Lorca (*See individual titles by Lorca*)

"Ite, missa est" (Darío) 70

"La Jeune Parque" (Valéry) 53, 132

Jiménez, Juan Ramón 6, 11, 22, 90, 202; "Tenebrae" 90

juglares See romances

"Kaleidoscope" (Verlaine) 168, 183n8

Keats, John 52, 70; "La Belle Dame sans Merci" 52, 70
Kermode, Frank xv, 3
Klein, Dennis A. 46, 47
Knight, G. Wilson vii-viii, xvin2, 146, 162, 170, 175, 201
Laffranque, Marie 49n6
The Land of Heart's Desire (Yeats) 22, 84
Lara Pozuelo, Antonio 26
Lázaro Carreter, Fernando 4, 21, 29, 32, 41, 42-43, 97, 184
Machado, Antonio 6, 80, 84, 90; *Soledades (1899-1907)* ("Hacia un ocaso radiante") 90; "La tierra de Alvargonzález" 84
Soledades (1899-1907) ("Hacia un ocaso radiante")
Machado, Manuel 6
Maeterlinck, Maurice x, 1, 2-3, 4, 5, 9, 10, 17-19, 51, 54, 57, 58, 60, 72, 76, 80, 82, 90-91, 105, 111, 128, 132, 133, 156, 159, 166, 170, 201, 202, 205, 206; *The Blue Bird* 17, 18, 54, 57, 58, 59, 72, 76, 133; *Pelléas et Mélisande* x, 2, 17, 18, 19, 22, 82, 83, 84, 87, 90, 93, 97, 111, 170, 201, 202, 206
El mágico prodigioso (Calderón) 52
El maleficio de la mariposa (Lorca) vi, vii, ix, x, xii, xv, , 3, 4, 6, 17, 18, 19, 20, 22, 23, 24, 26, 27, 28, 42, 43, 46, 51-78, 80, 81, 83, 89, 110, 112, 114, 116, 117-118, 121, 124, 127, 134, 150, 154, 159, 162, 166, 184, 186, 205; imagery continuities in 51, 52, 53, 63, 65, 71-72; key images in: dew 52, 59, 60, 63, 65, 66, 68-70, 74, 75, dreams 52, 64, 66, 76-77, flight 52, 56, 57, 58-59, 61, 64, 65, 70-71 (butterfly), 74, flowers 52, 65, 66, 67, 68, 70-71, light-darkness 52, 57, 59, 63, 65, 71-72, stars 52, 57, 59, 63, 64, 65-67, 68, 71; metaphorical language in xii, xv, 24, 43, 51, 52, 53, 57, 69, 75, 80, 83; and traditional ballads xii, 28; and traditional songs 117-118
Mallarmé, Stéphane 5, 7, 9, 22, 71, 89, 90, 168, 202; "L'après-midi d'un faune" 168, 202; "Autre Éventail" 90; "Hérodiade" 71
Mariana Pineda (Lorca) vi, x, xii, xiii, 2, 4, 6, 10, 14, 17, 18, 19, 20, 21, 22, 23, 26, 27, 29, 30, 42, 47, 80-108, 110, 111, 112, 114, 116, 118, 121, 124, 127, 134, 146, 154, 160, 162, 166, 171, 173, 180, 205; imagery continuities in 47, 81-83, 87, 89, 91, 93, 96, 98, 101; key images in: blood 81, 84-87, 88, 101, 103, 108, dreams 81,

93-96, 103, 108, light-darkness 81, 89-93, 96, 99, 101, 103, 107, 108, rain and tears 81, 82-84, 88, 103, sea (and water) 81, 88-89, 91, 96, 102-103, 105; metaphorical continuities in 95, 96, 97, 103; metaphorical language in 21, 80, 83, 88, 94, 96, 99, 100, 103, 104, 106; *romances* in 14, 21, 30, 80, 81, 94, 95, 96, 97, 98, 99, 100, 101, 102, 103, 104, 105, 108, 118, 127, 146, 160, 173, 180; songs in 14, 30, 103-104; and traditional ballads xii, 10, 11, 29, 80-81, 94, 98-99, 124, 171, 173; and traditional songs xiii, 14, 80-81, 97-98, 111, 127; and traditional Spanish *romances* 21, 30, 80-81, 97-98, 101, 102, 104, 106, 108, 111, 118, 124, 127, 180

Marquina, Eduardo x, 3, 4, 6, 10, 51, 80, 84, 85, 97, 98, 102, 111, 118, 121, 134, 156, 163, 166, 205, 206; *La ermita, la fuente y el río* 4, 21, 84, 85, 97, 102, 111, 118, 121, 156

Martínez, Nadal, Rafael 41, 44, 47

Martínez Sierra, Gregorio x, 2, 3, 10, 17, 51, 54, 58, 80, 84, 132, 168, 205, 206; *Cuento de labios en flor* 84, 132; *Pastoral* 17, 54, 58, 168; *Teatro de ensueño* 3

Martínez Sierra, María 3

El médico de su honra (Calderón) 15, 31, 136-137, 162, 174-175

Menéndez Pidal, Ramón 12

metaphor viii, xi, 8, 14, 15, 16, 27, 30, 31, 37n70, 44; extended (expanded) xiii, 15, 16, 27, 60, 80, 85, 87, 92, 103, 128, 132, 133, 134, 135, 143, 156, 160, 178, 181, 186, 196, 205

metaphorical: continuities viii, ix, 26, 33, 40, 97, 132, 150, 160, 180, 205; *See also* imagery continuities; in plays by Lorca (*See under individual titles*); language and Lorca (*See under* García Lorca, Federico); in plays by Lorca (*See under individual titles*); process xi, 7, 8, 9, 14, 15, 27, 202

Modernismo x, 4, 21, 42, 106, 111, 121

Modernista: imagery ix, 24, 134, 159, 182; poetry 111; theater x, 4, 10, 21, 85, 97, 125, 127, 163; tradition 58; works 80, 84, 90, 97, 102

Modernistas 6, 22, 51, 62, 70, 89, 205

Molina, Tirso de *El burlador de Sevilla* 147

"Mon Rêve familier" (Verlaine) 70, 77

Morris, C. Brian 46, 48

nanas 13, 192; in *Bodas de sangre* 13, 45, 47, 139, 140, 141, 143-145, 146, 147-148, 149, 150, 152, 153, 174; in *La casa de Bernarda Alba* 192

"Nocturno" (Darío) 202

Nourissier, François 49n2

O'Connor, Patricia W. 3

"Orphée" (Valéry) 60

Pabst, W. X

Pastoral (Martínez Sierra, G.) 17, 54, 58, 168

Pelléas et Mélisande (Maeterlinck) x, 2, 17, 18, 19, 22, 82, 83, 84, 87, 90, 93, 97, 111, 170, 201, 202, 206

Peribáñez y el Comendador de Ocaña (Lope de Vega) 111, 118, 119, 147, 148

Poeta en Nueva York (Lorca) 44

"Por el val de las Estacas . . ." Sexto romance del Cid 158n17

Praz, Mario 51

El público (Lorca) 44, 127

Ramos-Gil, Carlos 5, 9, 10, 26, 41, 43-44

Raymond, Marcel 5, 9, 27

la Residencia de Estudiantes 6

Rimbaud, Arthur 5, 9

Robertson, Sandra Cary 46-47

"Romance de don Tristán" (anon.) 28

"Romance de la conquista de Alhama" (anon.) 124

"Romance del conde Arnaldos" (anon.) 170

Romancero gitano (Lorca) xi, xii, 10, 171, 180

romances 11, 21, 30, 44, 94, 96, 97, 98, 101, 102, 104, 105, 118, 129, 143, 146, 154, 160, 171, 172, 173, 180; *juglares* xii, 1, 11, 28, 81, 95, 97, 101, 105, 106, 123, 125, 170, 171, 173, and *Amor de don Perlimplín con Belisa en su jardín* 123, 124-125, and *Bodas de sangre* 28, and *Doña Rosita la soltera* 171, 173, and *Mariana Pineda* 81, 95, 97, 101, 105, 106; and Lorca 11, 30, 44, 94, 97, 98, 101, 102, 104, 105, 118, 129, 180; in plays by Lorca (*See under individual titles*); traditional Spanish *romances* vi, xiii, 1, 11, 29,

80, 94, 97, 106, 108, 110, 122, 124, 125, 127, 128, 151, 152, 156, 170, 180, 186, 205, 206, and Lorca   80, 97, 106, 108, 122, 127, 151, 152, 156, 170, 180, 186, 205, 206, examples of: "Canción de una gentil dama y un rústico pastor"   122-123, "Por el val de las Estacas . . ." Sexto romance del Cid   158n17, "Romance de don Tristán"   28, "Romance de la conquista de Alhama"   124, "Romance del conde Arnaldos"   170, "Rosaflorida"   106, 107, "Ya se salen de Castilla . . ." Historia de los siete infantes de Lara   151, 157n16; and plays by Lorca (*See under individual titles*); *See also* ballads and songs

"Rosaflorida" (anon.)   106, 107

Rubia Barcia, J.   49n2

Ruiz Ramón, Francisco   184

The Shadowy Waters (Yeats)   x, 19, 55-56, 57, 58, 59, 76, 87, 111-112

Shakespeare, William   vii, viii, ix, x, 3, 53, 175, 201; *Hamlet*   96; *The Tempest*   vii-viii, ix, x, xvin2, 33, 162, 178, 191, 202

"The Sick Rose" (Blake)   22

Silver, Philip   83, 94

Soledades (Góngora)   9, 15, 25, 61, 115; "Soledad primera"   60, 61, 92; "Soledad segunda"   8

Soledades (1899-1907) ("Hacia un ocaso radiante") (A. Machado)   90

songs   in plays by Lorca (*See under individual titles*); traditional songs   xiii, 12, 13, 14, 29, 30, 80, 97-98, 148, and Lorca   xiii, 12, 13, 14, 30, 97-98, 119, and plays by Lorca (*See under individual titles*); *See also* ballads and *romances*

"Sur l'Herbe" (Verlaine)   67

surreal, surrealist, surrealistic: dialogue   18; images   73, 75, 88, 114, 133

Surrealists   5, 9

Symbolism   x, xi, 1, 2, 5, 6, 12, 20, 21, 22, 27, 59, 71, 73, 87, 90, 106, 108, 111, 121, 132, 136, 165, 168, 205, 206; and Lorca (*see under* García Lorca, Federico)

Symbolist: imagery   ix, 20, 22, 51, 58, 59, 68, 75, 77, 83, 87, 89, 90, 110, 116, 119, 124, 132, 133, 134, 156, 159, 165, 182, and Lorca (*See under* García Lorca, Federico); poetry   x, xiv, 1, 4, 6, 7, 10, 18, 20, 23-24, 51, 54, 77, 89, 111, 128, 132, 186, and Lorca (*See under* García Lorca, Federico); theater x, 1, 2, 4, 10, 18, 19, 21, 22, 23-24, 42, 45, 51, 55, 60, 65, 77, 87, 97, 105, 127, 128, 132, 156, 159, 186, 205, and Lorca (*See under* García Lorca, Federico); works 53, 58, 61, 80, 84, and Lorca (*See under* García Lorca, Federico); writers 62, 70, and Lorca (*See under* García Lorca, Federico)

Symbolists xi, 2, 4, 5, 6, 7, 9, 19, 20, 22, 51, 52, 61, 64, 68, 156, 205; and Lorca (*See under* García Lorca, Federico)

Teatro de ensueño (Martínez Sierra, G.) 3

The Tempest (Shakespeare) vii-viii, ix, x, xvin2, 33, 162, 178, 191, 202

"Tenebrae" (Jiménez) 90

"La tierra de Alvargonzález" (A. Machado) 84

Trend, J.B. xii

Underhill, John Garrett 3

Valbuena Prat, Angel xiii

Valéry, Paul 6, 7, 23, 53, 60, 132, 202; "Le Cimetière marin" 23, 202; "La Jeune Parque" 53, 132; "Orphée" 60

Vega, Lope de vi, xii, xiii, 1, 12, 13, 14, 29, 30, 80, 96, 98, 111, 118, 119, 128, 147, 148, 150, 156, 161, 162, 178, 182, 186, 205, 206; *El caballero de Olmedo* xiii, 13, 30, 96, 98, 111, 118, 147, 162, 176, 177-178; *Fuenteovejuna* 111, 118, 147; *Peribáñez y el Comendador de Ocaña* 111, 118, 119, 147, 148

Verlaine, Paul x, 5, 6, 23, 51, 54, 59, 67, 68, 70, 73, 76, 77, 80, 83, 89, 92, 121, 132, 134, 166, 168, 205, 206; "À Clymène" 59-60; "Ariettes oubliées" 83, 121; "Art poétique" 23, 77-78; "Chanson d'Automne" 73; "Clair de Lune" 68, 69, 132; "Crépuscule du soir mystique" 89; "En sourdine" 54; "L'Heure du berger" 92; "Kaleidoscope" 168, 183n8; "Mon Rêve familier" 70, 77; "Sur l'Herbe" 67

La vida es sueño (Calderón) xiv, 14, 32, 164, 183n5

La vida es sueño: auto sacramental (Calderón) 14-15, 33, 133, 141, 142

Villegas, Juan 45-46, 143

Wardropper, Bruce W. xiii, 15

Wheelwright, Philip 9

Wilson, Edward M. xii, 11, 13, 15-16, 198
Worth, Katherine 94, 97
"Ya se salen de Castilla . . ." Historia de los siete infantes de Lara 151, 157n16
Yeats, William Butler x, 1, 3, 10, 19, 51, 53, 54, 55, 56, 57, 58, 59, 60, 76, 80, 84, 94, 111, 128, 205, 206; *The Land of Heart's Desire* 22, 84; *The Shadowy Waters* x, 19, 55-56, 57, 58, 59, 76, 87, 111-112
Yerma (Lorca) xv, 9, 41-42, 43, 49n6
"Yo soy aquel . . ." (Darío) 67
Young, Howard T. 22
Zardoya, Concha 21